When Roles Reverse will help you identify issues in your family that need attention and develop an action plan to deal with them. It will give you the tools to tackle the most important job you face: honest, ongoing, consistent communication.

- How can you tell when your parents really need assistance or intervention? (Page 176)

- How can you keep a sense of humor while dealing with hospitals, insurance companies, and wheelchairs? (Pages 66–68)

- How do you deal with a parent who keeps repeating the same question or story over and over? (Page 42)

- How do you tell a parent that it's time to stop driving? (Pages 50–52)

- What are the most important legal forms you need to have in place? (Pages 229–32)

- How do you protect your parents' assets? (Pages 221–24, 273–75)

- If your parents have few assets and may need nursing care, how do you qualify them for Medicaid? (Pages 221–22, 273–78)

- How can you tell a good facility from a beautifully decorated but poorly run one? (Pages 181–82, 194–95, 208)

- If your parents are sixty-five or older, is it too late to get long-term-care insurance for them? (Pages 240–41, 245)

- How do you find a good elder law attorney? (Pages 219–20)

- How do you know when to draw boundaries and tell your parents "No"? (Pages 85–86)

- How do you talk to Mom and Dad about burial plots and funerals? (Pages 98–100, 249)

This is overwhelming! Where do you begin? Start by answering the Fifty Questions That Will Save You Time, Money, and Tears on pages 145–53.

When Roles Reverse

A GUIDE TO PARENTING YOUR PARENTS

Jim Comer

HAMPTON ROADS

PUBLISHING COMPANY, INC.

Cover concept by Andy Choquette
Cover design by Steve Amarillo.
Cover art provided by Jim Comer.

Hampton Roads Publishing Company, Inc.
1125 Stoney Ridge Road
Charlottesville, VA 22902

434-296-2772
fax: 434-296-5096
e-mail: hrpc@hrpub.com
www.hrpub.com

If you are unable to order this book from your local
bookseller, you may order directly from the publisher.
Call 1-800-766-8009, toll free.

Library of Congress Cataloging-in-Publication Data

Comer, Jim, 1944-
  When roles reverse : a guide to parenting your parents / Jim Comer.
    p. cm.
  Summary: "Detailing Comer's experiences after his parents suffered major illnesses, When
Roles Reverse merges Comer's story with practical advice to create a guide for anyone faced
with caring for aging parents. When Roles Reverse helps the reader make sound decisions
regarding Medicaid, Medicare, nursing homes, assisted-living facilities, hospice, and much
more, and it provides a state-by-state resource list"--Provided by publisher.
  Includes index.
  ISBN 978-1-57174-500-2 (6 x 9 tp : alk. paper)
  1. Aging parents--Care. 2. Adult children of aging parents--Family relationships. 3. Aging
parents--Family relationships. I. Title.
  HQ1063.6.C68 2006
  649.8084'60973--dc22
                                        2006016361

                          ISBN 978-1-57174-500-2

                          10 9 8 7 6 5 4 3 2
                Printed on acid-free paper in Canada

For my parents

Anne Haynie Comer and John Smith Comer
With love, respect, and gratitude

Mother and Jim, 1945

Contents

Part Two: A Guide to Parenting Your Parents

Foreword

By Liz Carpenter, former press secretary to Lady Bird Johnson

This is the book you will keep between your Bible and your dictionary so it will be handy when you need it. You will find not only valuable information but also laughs, tears, insights, and moments that will touch your heart.

Jim Comer worked as an actor in New York in his twenties, but the role of his life came at the age of fifty-one, when his father suffered a stroke while caring for his mother, who has Alzheimer's disease. With no siblings to help him, Jim quit his job as a speechwriter in Los Angeles and moved back to Texas. That was ten years ago and he's still "on the job."

The challenge of parenting your parents is a growing issue for millions of American families. I know this firsthand because I'm an eighty-six-year-old widow living in Austin while my children live in Manhattan and Seattle with busy lives of their own.

So I sent them each a copy of Jim's book!

This is not a goody-two-shoes story. Jim takes us by the hand and shares his own mistakes and what he's learned from caring for his parents. He doesn't sugarcoat the challenges, but rather lets readers know that they can live through them and find growth and joy in the process.

The book is both a personal memoir and a helpful how-to manual. Jim has excellent advice on coming to terms with Alzheimer's and running the gauntlet of health care bureaucracies. He discusses how to find assistance from public and private agencies in your communities and provides a state-by-state list of the key resources you'll need. Each chapter ends with Comer's Commandments, a succinct summary of key points to remember.

Jim has become a sought-after speaker and consultant for those dealing with the issues of aging. He speaks to conventions, health care agencies, associations, churches, and corporations. Whether you are a baby boomer or a great-grandmother, Jim's message rings true: "Communicate early and often."

This book is going to be a best seller. Remember that you heard it from an aging writer who wishes that Jim Comer would take her in hand. He is a good-natured guide who offers important tips on how to take on the challenge of parental care while enjoying the process.

Introduction
You *Can* Do This!

If you're like I was when I began my journey, you are overwhelmed at the prospect of caring for your parents. Your life is already filled with responsibilities: you may have a demanding career, children in college, or a high-maintenance spouse. You may live hundreds of miles from your parents or not enjoy the best relationship with them. On the other hand, you may get along beautifully with your parents and feel eager to help, but can't get them to talk about their plans, finances, or health.

Whatever your situation, the experience of parenting your parents will stretch your comfort zone, test your patience, and strain your diplomatic skills. Whether you are dealing with a nine-month-old or a ninety-year-old, parenting is not a science but an art form. What works for one family might be disastrous for another. There is no one-size-fits-all approach. Emeril Lagasse can't give you a foolproof recipe. You must play the hand you've been dealt. I hope to demonstrate that even the least likely of us can rise to the occasion.

Some of you may not be able or willing to assume the responsibility of caring for your parents. That's perfectly fine. Being clear about what you can't do is as important as knowing what role you can play. Even if you will not be the primary caregiver, the more you know and the sooner you know it, the better prepared your family will be.

My goals are to help you make informed decisions, avoid disasters, and recover quickly from the occasional error in judgment. I encourage you to face facts rather than flee from them. There are actions you can take now that will make life much easier in the future. I won't downplay it. Some of what's ahead of you may be logistically difficult, physically exhausting, and emotionally draining. The same is true about building a career, sustaining a marriage, or raising children. The negatives are only a part of the story. In parenting your parents, you may also experience personal growth, a new level of intimacy, and unexpected joy.

Part 1 is my family's story from the first crisis phone call in 1996 until today, in early 2006. It chronicles ups, downs, mistakes made, and lessons learned. I invite you to profit from my steep learning curve; there is no reason to repeat my mistakes. No doubt you'll make some of your own. That's okay. If you do nothing wrong, you're probably not doing much.

Part 2 provides practical information to help you make sound decisions for your family. My parenting experience is limited. As an only child, I don't know what it's like to deal with siblings or argue over money and who gets the grandfather clock. My parents never moved into my house and I didn't move into theirs. I have not had to balance child rearing and parental care.

To give readers a wider perspective, I've interviewed administrators and owners of retirement homes, assisted-living residences, and nursing homes, as well as scores of frontline employees. I've talked to elder law attorneys, social workers, long-term-care insurance agents, funeral directors, experts on veterans' affairs, and a hospital chaplain. They all have worked with thousands of families from every background, income level, ethnicity, and religion. I've presented their views verbatim when possible, and their words are frank, helpful, often funny, and unencumbered by jargon.

The most important section of the book is "Fifty Questions That Will Save You Time, Money, and Tears." These are the questions that you need to ask your parents and siblings *now*, not after a stroke or broken hip. This pre-crisis planning is what I failed to do and I highly recommend it. If you skip the entire book and only answer the questions on pages 145–53 you'll miss some very good stories, but you'll get your money's worth. My friend Kay Christopher tells me that the answers to those questions could be worth $100,000 or more. I want her to tell that to Oprah.

The last chapter of the book, "Local Resources: State Insurance Departments and Agencies on Aging," provides you with a state-by-state list of resources including the departments of insurance, state health insurance assistance programs, and state agencies on aging. Their addresses, phone and fax numbers, and websites were updated in January 2006.

Parenting your parents does not require an advanced degree, saintliness, or a perfect parent/child relationship. What you will need is energy, flexibility, and patience—lots of patience. No one was less prepared for this under-taking than I. Despite a less-than-stellar caregiving resume, I was chosen anyway. Much to my surprise, it's been the most rewarding job of my life.

Parenting my parents has helped me grow in ways I could not have imag-ined. I would not trade the experience for all the Oscars I never won. If I can do this, anyone can. Even you.

PART ONE

When Roles Reverse

Mother and Dad in 1980

1

The Day Everything Changed

At the age of fifty-one I became a parent for the first time. Mine was not a planned parenthood. At the time I lived in Los Angeles, worked in public relations for a large corporation, and enjoyed a single man's life. On February 20, 1996, everything changed. I was awakened at seven in the morning by a phone call from my parents' next-door neighbor. In the thirty years she had lived by my parents, Lisa Huff had never called me. I braced myself for bad news.

She told me that my father was walking back and forth in front of his house in a daze. Her sidewalk diagnosis: he was having a stroke. Caring for Mother, who was dealing with early Alzheimer's, had taken its toll. By the end of the day, Dad was in intensive care, I was on a plane to Dallas, and our world had shifted forever.

When I arrived at the hospital I immediately became the designated decision maker. As the only child, everyone looked to me for answers; I wasn't even sure of the questions. I didn't know the names of my parents' doctors or accountant. I had never seen their wills. The only time Dad and I talked about money was when I needed a loan. Like many fathers and sons, our conversations focused on football, politics, and the relatives.

I knew nothing about their insurance, but over the next few days I learned. Once the hospital knew that Dad was not going to die, they wanted to know our exit strategy. Three days after his stroke, the hospital administrators were pushing me to choose a rehabilitation hospital for Dad.

There are excellent stroke centers in Dallas, but we had no relatives there. My aunts, uncle, and cousins lived near Austin, some two hundred miles south. When disaster strikes, friends and neighbors are a blessing but family is a necessity. I needed their support and I got it. My cousins Randy and Donna Stump were at the hospital when I arrived. Donna stayed with us for the next nine days.

Four days after Dad's stroke, I flew to Austin in a rainstorm to check out rehab centers. Another cousin, Bill Stump, met me at the airport and we visited four hospitals in six hours. I felt like I was holding auditions. I chose St. David's Rehabilitation Center because it was clean and two of the nurses smiled at me. I needed smiles badly that day. Like Americans electing a president, my decision was not an exercise in logic.

Once I selected a hospital, the question was what to do with Mother. She couldn't stay alone in Dallas, and I couldn't take her back to California with me because she needed constant supervision. For five years, my father had sheltered her from the reality of her disease. Mom needed watching, but didn't know she needed it. Dad spent much of his time keeping her in sight and out of trouble. Every time I mentioned moving to Austin she asked, "Why can't we stay in Dallas?" I told her we needed to be close to the family. She didn't buy it. Mother could not comprehend the enormity of the changes she faced. Instead she focused on being a good hostess to my cousins. One night she walked into their room at 4:00 A.M. to make sure they had enough blankets. Her grasp on reality was shaky, but her social skills were deeply rooted. On the other hand, Dad could not speak or walk, yet he understood all too well what had happened to him. He communicated his frustration through silent glares and by ripping out his catheter.

I went from no involvement in running my parents' lives to complete control. There were scores of decisions to be made. That first week I was dizzy with anxiety and overwhelmed by the number of things I didn't know. I came to appreciate the meaning of "comfort food." Texans love cafeterias and, despite three decades of living out of state, so do I. Luckily, the largest cafeteria in Dallas was located a block from the hospital. We ate lunch there every day, and I stuffed myself with turkey and dressing, brown gravy, sweet potatoes, carrot-raisin salad, and pecan pie. Those were the best ten pounds I ever gained.

I was running out of time to make a decision about Mother. As she would say, I was "fresh out of ideas." My cousins and their wives came to the rescue. They convinced me to let Mom stay with them in Georgetown, an all-American town of fifty thousand that is now a suburb north of Austin. Bill is an engineer and his wife, Bonnie, is a physician. Randy and Donna are lawyers. Between them, the two families had four jobs, five kids, and a number of elderly parents. Tending an eighty-three-year-old with Alzheimer's was not a small addition to their lives. I accepted their kind offer because I didn't know what else to do.

Nine days after Dad entered the hospital, we moved him to St. David's. Mother worried how we would pay for the ambulance. I reassured her that Medicare would cover the costs. With genuine concern she asked, "Can they afford it?"

While Mom read *The Dallas Morning News*, Donna and I went through her closet, packed her belongings as best we could, and got her into the car by telling a therapeutic lie. I said we were going for ice cream. Mother never turns down ice cream, not even at nine in the morning. We drove away from her home of thirty-four years as if going on an errand. She never saw Dallas again.

True to my word, I stopped at the first Dairy Queen and bought Mother a chocolate sundae. However, by the time we got to Waco, about one hundred miles south, it was clear we weren't just going for a sundae. Luckily, Mother's fragile short-term memory did not grasp the dimensions of my deception. She stayed in good spirits, humming Methodist hymns between comments on the colors of passing cars.

After the longest ride of my life, at 2:00 P.M. we pulled up to St. David's and met Dad's care team: doctors, nurses, therapists, and a social worker. They seemed relentlessly optimistic. Of course, they had yet to deal with my father. The staff said they'd keep me posted daily, which turned out to be more of a threat than a promise. I hugged Mother goodbye, left her in my cousins' care, and caught the five o'clock flight to Los Angeles.

Back in California, I faced a pile of work and the loving concern of co-workers. I didn't realize it yet, but I now had two careers. There was the full-time paying position as a corporate writer for a large HMO in California and my unpaid assignment a thousand miles away. I was painfully unprepared for the new role. I did not have the remotest idea of how to care for my parents, much less from a distance. Instant parenting allows little ramp-up time. I had to maintain a cordial telephone relationship with the staff at the rehab center, monitor Dad's recovery, and keep tabs on Mother while living four states away. At the same time, I had to look ahead and plan the next step in what would become more than a decade of care.

All I could see were obstacles. I had to figure out their finances, learn about insurance, and educate myself about Medicare. I needed to know about retirement homes, assisted living, and nursing homes. What should we do with their house, furniture, and fifty-five years of mementos? I crammed for conversations with doctors, therapists, and social workers as I once did for biology finals. If I didn't stay on top of things, my father risked more than a bad grade. And then there was the question of what to do about my own future. This was not how I'd planned to spend my fifty-second year.

What Got Me Through the First Ten Days: Comer's Intensive Care Gratitude List

- A boss who cut me some slack
- Relatives who showed up without being asked
- Neighbors who got Dad to the hospital by telling him they were taking him out for Mexican food
- Doctors who used one-syllable words
- Nurses who realized that a sense of humor is as important as a catheter
- Despite all the paperwork, Medicare
- Those who brought casseroles and cherry pies, and those who helped eat them
- Credit cards
- Friends who said nothing when there was nothing to say

2

Starting Over at Fifty-One

Parenting is a relentless calling. There is no time off, sick leave, retirement package, or vacation pay. My new career had no discernible job description. That first trip to Texas was not a cameo appearance, but the beginning of a long-running role to which I never aspired. Phone calls brought the hospital home to me each day. I heard from administrators, relatives, and insurance agents. The government required forms. And everyone expected me to know what to do.

Two weeks after the first trip, I was back in Austin for the first of many extended weekends. I took a cab to the rehab center and found Dad alone in his room. This man had flown seventy-six combat missions in World War II, supervised a sales force in thirteen states, repaired cars, knew about world religion and baseball, lectured at a junior college, and taught Sunday school. He also watched *Saturday Night Live* and argued existential philosophy. Dad is brilliant, cantankerous, and fiercely independent.

Now he was lying in a hospital bed unable to walk, speak clearly, or control his bodily functions. When he saw me come into the room, he knew exactly what he wanted. After a few awkward moments, he gathered his strength and forced out three words: "Get me pills." He took a long breath and repeated the phrase in case I'd missed the point.

I knew exactly what he meant. He wanted me to get pills so he could kill himself. In his mind, the thought of being dependent on others was worse than death. He was eighty-six and had lived a full life. If this was his future, he wanted out now. After a long pause, I said that I couldn't do that because it was against the law.

"Dad, I'll go to jail."

"You'll go to hell?"

"Not hell. Well, maybe hell, too. I can't do it."

Dad's look expressed unprintable volumes about my decision. I lied as forcefully as possible. "You're going to get well. You're going to walk again." I didn't believe a word of it. Neither did he.

My father is not an easy patient in the best of times. After the stroke, he was demanding, depressed, and unwilling to do the exercises that might allow him to recover. The big issue—one so humiliating he could not see beyond it—was incontinence. He felt a constant need to relieve himself and demanded instant attention from the nurses. He did not care that he was one of thirty stroke patients on the floor. If the staff did not respond quickly enough to suit him, they heard him yell all the way down the hall. He used words not included in his Sunday school lessons.

After three days in Texas, I flew back to California. Though I'd already used up my vacation days for the year, my manager told me to do what I had to do and kept paying me. Many caregivers are not so lucky.

For the first time, I received a "parent-teacher" call. I'd never had one of those uncomfortable conversations. The focus was not on a first-grader but on an octogenarian. We weren't talking about why Johnny can't read, but why John Comer raised so much hell. My father's caseworker bemoaned his negativity and lack of cooperation. She complained that he would not do his exercises, often screamed at the staff, and showed no signs of wanting to recover. She told me that his attitude was a serious problem and, if it didn't change soon, he would not be allowed to stay in rehab. I couldn't picture my Dad flunking out of a hospital.

"What are you going to say to him?" she wanted to know.

Not wanting to irritate the frustrated professional at the other end of the line, I vowed that I would talk to him immediately and straighten things out. That was another blatant lie. My dad was hard of hearing before the stroke and almost totally deaf after it. He could understand nothing on the phone. Even if he could have heard me, I had as much power to change his attitude as to restore his hearing.

Dad had been sound challenged for years. Under pressure from Mother and me, he had bought hearing aids five years earlier and had worn them three times. He claimed they were defective. The truth was that he hated their tinny, unnatural sound. Forced to choose between conversation with constant background noise or silence, he opted for silence.

Over the years Dad had adjusted gradually to his hearing loss. I had not.

If he watched TV, he turned up the volume all the way. When he wanted conversation, he talked. If you wanted to talk to him, you yelled. Either it was worth shouting or not worth saying at all. My friends knew when I'd spent time with Dad because I stood in their personal space and tripled my volume.

After the stroke Dad comprehended nothing I said on the phone and little when I was there in person. If I wanted to make sure he understood, I wrote notes. His lack of hearing, however, worried me less than his suicidal depression. On my next trip, Dad's doctor suggested a possible solution. If we could get him to agree to a simple prostate procedure, he might regain control of his bodily functions and become motivated to recover. The doctor wanted to operate immediately. Most stroke patients make their greatest gains within the first three months, and Dad had already used up six weeks. Time was running out.

Using a yellow legal pad, I wrote a detailed explanation of what the doctor wanted to do. Knowing Dad's analytical mind, I made a logical case for the surgery. To my surprise, he put up no argument and signed the medical release. When I saw Mother later that day, she wanted to know when they were going back to Dallas. I said something soothing and untrue, and then caught a peanuts-only flight to L.A. I was getting good at lying to those I loved.

The prostate operation was a complete success. Within a few days Dad was able to urinate unassisted. That's when he decided that he wanted to live. But he had a long way to go. He was not walking, talked only in short phrases, and was unable to get out of bed by himself. However, his attitude underwent a radical transformation after the prostate operation. For the first time since the stroke he was focused on recovery.

My relief was short lived. The next week St. David's informed us that Dad would have to leave because he did not meet their guidelines for "patient progress." We had one week to find another skilled nursing facility. I argued in vain for more time. I begged. My long-distance pleas proved ineffectual when pitted against the entrenched forces of medical bureaucracy.

I flew back the next weekend to check out care facilities. I had three days to find a place where Dad could receive intensive therapy and Mother could stay in assisted living. I could not foist her off on my cousins any longer. I visited nursing homes that ranged from decent to rip-your-heart-out depressing. Then I went to The Summit, aptly located on a hill with a view of the Austin skyline and surrounded by acres of trees and upscale landscaping. It offered apartments, assisted living, skilled nursing, and an Alzheimer's unit.

At The Summit, life was in session. The food was excellent, the waiters friendly, the napkins linen, and the rooms spacious. The atmosphere seemed more Ritz-Carlton than Motel 6. The residents looked genuinely happy, and there was no institutional odor when I walked in the front door. Of course, amenities are expensive, although Medicare would pay for Dad as long as he qualified for rehab. I asked the admissions director if they had openings in skilled nursing and assisted living on the following Monday. She looked at me as if I'd lost my mind but checked the bed count anyway. Suddenly her face brightened and she announced, "There are two rooms available on Monday! Your mom and dad will be only two floors apart!" She told me three times how lucky we were and acted as if we had won the lottery. Maybe we had.

That weekend, Randy and I drove two hundred miles to Dallas to get Mother's bedroom furniture. The staff said she would feel more comfortable if she was surrounded by her own things. It was a brisk early-April weekend, and we spent Friday night in my parents' home with no power or hot water. The lack of central heating was not an issue. I missed more essential warmth. Except for the lack of utilities, nothing had changed. The house was like a crime scene without the yellow tape. My father's swordfish still hung in the den. His hundreds of books still lined the walls. Mother's kitchen table, coffee cup, and newspaper were a still life waiting to be painted. There was only one difference: 9641 Spring Branch Drive was no longer their home.

We rented a U-Haul and loaded the truck with Mother's bed, chest of drawers, end table, and lamp. I gathered a few of her favorite paintings and family pictures. By late afternoon we were back in Austin, and Mother's new room was filled with the familiar.

On Monday morning, while Dad rode across town in yet another ambulance, I took Mother to Dillard's to buy her a new comforter. She was "scandalized" by the prices, remembering only what things cost in her Depression-era youth. Her protests did not stop me from using her Visa card. Unlike mine, it had rarely seen an interest charge.

When we got to her new lodgings, I took Mom to see Dad on the third floor, then went back to prepare her room. Our friend Peg Furr, a slim, stylish seventy-something from Oklahoma City, was there to help me hang pictures. Unfortunately we had no hammer. Peg didn't let that hold her back. She took off a shoe and pounded nails into the wall with her high heel. By the time Mother arrived, framed photos perched on her dresser, new bedding was in place, and fresh yellow roses smiled from a vase.

For the next few months I continued to fly back and forth between L.A.

and Austin every other weekend. Each trip cost me $400–500, including flight, food, parking, and taxis. Two trips a month added up to a thousand unbudgeted dollars. Randy was executor of Dad's estate and I told him I'd have to get reimbursed or I'd soon be hitchhiking to Austin. He said to charge it to Dad's credit card, and I did.

I wondered what happens to those who can't leave their jobs and jump on a plane. How do low-income families or single parents deal with family crises? What happens to minimum-wage workers? Many of them are forced to choose between their parents and jobs. Even with a supportive employer and a relatively affluent family, I was barely able to cope. What if my boss had been inflexible or I'd had no credit card? Each time I began to feel sorry for myself, I trotted out my blessings. Sometimes that helped.

As April moved into May and his bodily functions were restored, Dad underwent a miraculous turnaround and became an icon of rehabilitation. He was cooperative, eager, and determined to walk. His speech returned completely and, amazingly, he sounded just like he did before the stroke. Unfortunately his hearing did not stage a similar comeback and deafness was no longer a subject of debate. Finally, he agreed to get new hearing aids.

Walking was his top priority and Dad was making measurable progress. He took more steps every day and even began to take care of Mother again. One day he called the administrator to make sure she was getting enough to eat. I knew he had rounded a corner the day he asked me about the Dallas Cowboys' starting lineup for the fall.

It took Mother a few weeks to adjust to her surroundings. She had been married for almost fifty-six years and did not care for living alone. She knew Dad was nearby and she spent much of her time looking for him. One day they found her outside, two buildings away, searching for my father in the ninety-five-degree heat.

Sometimes Mother forgot to bathe. When an aide attempted to get her into a shower, she was outraged and put up a spirited resistance. To be honest, it was more than spirited; Mother socked her. Other than a few tense moments in the bathroom, Mom got along well. She spoke to everyone and charmed the staff—except for those carrying soap. When they held an open house, Mother assumed she'd given the party and joined the staff to receive her guests.

While things were clearly improving, I knew we were only in the first hundred yards of a marathon. The news from Texas was optimistic, but there was no certainty that Dad would recover fully. He might have another stroke. There was no guarantee that he would walk normally again. Most sixty-year-old stroke patients don't have a complete recovery. Very few eighty-six-year-olds do.

Then there was Mother's Alzheimer's. It's called a progressive disease, which is a cruel contradiction in terms. It "progresses" to complete helplessness and the inability to speak or walk, and there's no predictable timetable. Mother might stay sweet and charming for years or she might become angry, combative, and bed-ridden. There was no way to know how quickly or severely her condition would worsen.

As my long-distance bill approached the size of a car payment, it was time to make some hard decisions. I faced a menu of mutually exclusive choices:

1. Move my parents to California where they knew no one and the cost of living was much higher;

2. Put my folks in a care facility near my relatives while I remained in California, visited when I could, and went on with my life;

3. Quit my job, move to Austin, and become an active participant in my parents' lives.

I chose the third option because I couldn't do what needed to be done from a distance. If I was going to be there for my parents, I needed to be available not for a weekend, but for good.

It was a dicey decision. I would have to leave a well-paid position, move halfway across the country, and begin a new life. Fortunately, I'm an optimist. I figured that if I could move to Manhattan at twenty-three with $100 and no job, I could probably survive in Austin, Texas, at fifty-one.

In June, four months after Dad's stroke, I told my boss that I was moving to Texas when I finished writing the company's annual report. As I shared the news with coworkers, they were supportive and understanding, although some had that "Have you lost your mind?" look in their eyes. More than once I saw the expression people wear when a friend tells them he has cancer. Just below genuine sympathy lies real horror and a voice that says, "Please, God, don't let that happen to me."

For once I was ahead of the curve. Six weeks after I announced my impending departure, my employer, FHP Health Care, was acquired by its archrival, PacifiCare. In the next eight months, most of my coworkers lost their jobs. I lost mine, too, but there was a difference: I chose to leave.

As a parting gesture, the public relations department gave me a generous four-month contract until the acquisition was complete. Ironically, at the same time I landed a six-week freelance assignment with a nursing home chain. I didn't feel jobless, even though I was.

Since I was not sure where I would be living, I sold most of my furniture and gave truckloads of belongings to Goodwill. On moving day I was certain I'd pared my possessions down to a precious few. Such was not the case. I had fifty-one boxes, enough clothes to outfit an orphanage, and mountains of junk. I filled every available inch of a medium-sized U-Haul and my parents' 1990 Buick, which I'd bought from them over the summer. Unable to squeeze one more novel into the trailer, I left two chairs and probably a hundred books in the parking lot.

My friend Chris Jacobs assured his eventual sainthood by volunteering to ride with me to Texas. He told me we couldn't go more than fifty-five miles per hour while towing a trailer, but I didn't believe him and began driving at my usual speed. As we headed down a long hill at seventy, the trailer began shaking violently and we almost deposited my remaining possessions on Interstate 10.

Around dusk, we crossed the Los Angeles County line. After thirty years of living in Manhattan and Southern California, I was moving back to the state of my birth. Not everyone gets to start over in his sixth decade.

Comer's Commandments

Some may quibble with the word "commandments." If that conjures up an image of Charlton Heston descending a mountain with stone tablets, substitute the word "suggestions." Either way, pay attention to them.

- Remember that parenting is a relentless calling. There are no days off, sick leave, or vacation pay.

- When you start to feel sorry for yourself, put things in perspective. You are not in North Korea.

- Never forget that doctors are human, hospitals make mistakes, and nurses' aides are underpaid. If something seems wrong, question it.

- Try not to tackle everything at once. Don't have a garage sale while a parent is in intensive care.

- If you move into your parents' home to care for them and find yourself considering double murder, make other living arrangements.

Just Show Up

Woody Allen said, "Eighty percent of success is showing up." He's right, but it helps if you bring along a good book. Since 1996, my parents and I have spent hundreds of hours in doctors' offices. Now I know how waiting rooms got their name.

Since Dad's stroke, my parents have required eight hospitalizations and five operations. My father has bought and resisted using two pairs of $4,000 hearing aids. We have made at least twenty-five trips to the "ear doctor." There have been a number of three-doctor days, with appointments slated at two-hour intervals. My parents have seen ophthalmologists, internists, general practitioners, dentists, orthopedists, surgeons, plastic surgeons, and physical therapists. We are not strangers to emergency rooms.

By the time I moved to Austin, Dad was at about 75 percent of his pre-stroke capacity. Although his emotional equilibrium was shaky and his patience easily taxed, he was walking unassisted, without even a cane. Considering his age, the extent of his recovery was incredible. He was doing so well by mid-August that Medicare would no longer pay for his rehabilitation. He had to move for the fourth time in seven months.

He chose the Wesleyan Retirement Home in Georgetown, where I'd always hoped my parents would retire. My aunt and uncle lived one block away and my cousins' law office was within easy walking distance. I got an apartment in Austin, twenty-five minutes away.

There was only one problem: Mother. The Wesleyan is not a care facility.

Residents must be able to look after themselves and meet their own needs. While Dad met these qualifications, Mother was a borderline case. Her Alzheimer's was in an early stage, but she needed constant supervision. Someone had to make sure she got to meals and didn't wander away. That would have to be my father. I was beginning a freelance career and could not be there every day.

Mother would never have been admitted to the Wesleyan except for the quality of Dad's lobbying. He had spent twenty-five years as a sales manager for Sherwin-Williams Paints and he used his formidable powers of persuasion to convince the administrators that Mother would pose no problem. In an unwritten agreement, they agreed to admit her on a trial basis. It would be up to Dad, six months out of intensive care, to look after her.

There was no two-room apartment available, so my parents chose rooms next to each other on the fourth floor. When a double became available, they intended to move into it. Fortunately, no such vacancy occurred because their separation turned out to be a walled blessing. With their own rooms, they had privacy. The "temporary" arrangement worked beautifully. The phone was in Dad's room, but Mother could hear it ring. She could take my messages and write them down. He could read them and respond. As they had for more than fifty years, they made a good team and we communicated successfully.

There were some close calls in the first few months. Mother wandered away twice. The first time, a cousin saw her ambling unaware two blocks from the retirement home. The second time she was standing at a busy intersection, frightened and confused. A passing motorist noticed the worried look on her face and instinctively brought her to the Wesleyan. A third strike and she might have been kicked out. Fortunately, she never walked away again.

Once she got used to the routine, Mother was pleased with her accommodations. She quickly adjusted to the daily maid service. There was good food that she did not have to cook, group singing twice a week, a full schedule of activities, entertainment from local churches, a beauty shop on the premises, and a lovely garden. Best of all, there were friendly people to greet each day. Although Mother could not remember their names, she didn't let that hold her back. She visited with everyone and bantered with ease. While her short-term memory was gone, her social skills remained impeccable. Like a good politician on the stump, she had effortless charm and a ready sense of humor.

Apart from her lack of recall, Mother's health was excellent. While Mom heard everything and remembered little, Dad heard little and remembered everything. Together they formed a potent duo. Mother's vision was acute. She noticed birds invisible to me, pointed out trees half a block away, and picked up microscopic litter from the carpet. No discarded tissue was too small to escape her trash-trained eye. Whether it was a chewing gum wrapper that needed picking up or a bush that needed pruning, she missed nothing.

She busied herself watering plants, both real and artificial, and loved to sweep the elevator. She dazzled me with her wit. When I told her that a ninety-two-year-old gentleman had been praising her charms, she said, "Honey, that's the kind I attract!"

She loved to make me laugh and was famous for her one-liners. When she had me bent over in laughter, her face glowed with joy like that of a young comic who just scored big on *The Tonight Show*. One day I showed up with scuffed loafers and she announced, "Jim, you have got to buy some new shoes! Those are a scandal to the jaybirds!" I replied, "Mother, I'll buy some new shoes when I'm rich." With genuine concern, she said, "Oh, honey, don't wait that long."

Our conversations had a definite symmetry. They always included the same vital questions. She wanted to know if I was working, because she remembered the times when I wasn't. During my years as a struggling actor in New York, she sent me banana bread, inspirational clippings, and $20 bills.

One of her main concerns was the level of my gas tank. "Jim, tell your mother the truth. How are you fixed for gas?" The only acceptable answer was "Full tank." Once that high-octane subject crossed her mind, she was loath to leave it. She might question my car's fuel status five times during one visit. There was an upside to this prodding: I have not run out of gas since moving to Texas.

Inevitably Mother asked what time I had gone to bed the night before. She never believed me when I said, "Early." She could not recall who was president, but her long-term memory was still intact. She recalled how I resisted bedtime as a child and knew I didn't get enough sleep. Of course, she was right.

Like Queen Elizabeth, Mother carried a purse wherever she went. In it were her room key, reading glasses, and many wads of Kleenex. I once asked her why she needed her purse in the dining room. She looked at me with genuine shock and said, "A lady never goes anywhere without her purse."

For the first few months, my father's enjoyment of the retirement home was mitigated by his responsibility for Mother. He was terrified that she'd wander away and be banished from the home. He was emotional and easily excitable as he struggled with his own recovery while keeping track of his wife. Newly arrived on the scene, I thought I should do something to relieve him of the pressure.

I was concerned that he had too little time for himself and needed to get away from Mother for a few hours a week. I remembered how impressed he'd been with the efficiency of The Caring Place, Georgetown's version of Goodwill. When we cleared out my parents' storage unit, Dad had donated two truckloads of furniture to them. I thought it would be a perfect place for him to volunteer.

We toured their facility, which was only a mile from the retirement home. The staff welcomed Dad warmly and I knew he would fit in perfectly, make friends, and enjoy a break from supervising Mother. We arranged for him to volunteer there two days a week and I could already see him being named Volunteer of the Year. I congratulated myself on my accomplishment. I'd been back just one month and had already made an impact. Sure I had. The night before Dad was to report for his first day as a volunteer, he called me.

"Jim, this is your father."

He always started our telephone conversations with that formal announcement.

"I've decided not to work at The Caring Place."

"Why? It's all set."

"I don't think it's a good idea."

"What's the problem?"

"There's no problem. I just don't want to do it."

That was that. He never gave me a reason. Most likely he was afraid to leave Mother alone even for a few hours. Or, maybe he didn't believe he had enough to offer in his post-stroke condition. I'll never know because he wasn't talking.

Dad was not famous for his patience, and the stroke did not help matters. If anything, he became even more high-strung. He did not like to be kept waiting and was hyperpunctual. Unfortunately, I did not inherit this trait. To me, punctuality meant getting there within ten minutes of the appointed hour. Dad believed that on-time arrival was borderline tardiness. He liked to be at least fifteen minutes early and have plenty of time to become agitated at the possibility of others' lateness.

If I did not show up on the dot, he pointed out the precise number of minutes by which I had missed the mark. If I was supposed to arrive for dinner at 5:00 P.M., Dad got to the lobby at 4:45 and began pacing. By 4:50 he was looking at his watch with deep concern. At 4:55 he was irritated. By 5:00 he was upset. At 5:05 he was certain I was not coming. And at 5:10 he would say, "To hell with him" and go to the dining room "before my food gets cold."

When we stopped at a red light, if the signal did not turn green within five seconds, Dad would begin to squirm. "This is the slowest damn light I've ever seen. Is it ever going to change?"

I marveled at his octogenarian urgency and wanted to ask, "What's the rush? Are you late for a merger or an acquisition? We're going to the drugstore." It required superhuman restraint to resist such comments. I managed to keep my mouth shut forty-nine times out of every fifty.

I knew that Dad liked the Wesleyan even though he insisted on calling it "the hotel." To my knowledge he has never used the words "retirement home." For three years, he had an Air Force buddy who lived on the second floor, and they loved to get together and refight the war. While they were shellacking the Germans, they drank a little scotch. Sometimes they drank a lot of scotch. Twice Dad did not make it back to his room after these military reenactments. He eased himself down to the plush hallway carpet, passed out, and was later found there by horrified fellow residents. Certain that he'd had another stroke, they called 911 and an ambulance arrived in minutes. Twice in one year, Dad was rushed to the emergency room of Georgetown Hospital. Diagnosis? Bombed.

I got another parent-teacher call from his doctor. "Jim, what are you going to do about your Dad's drinking?"

What do you say to a man nearing ninety about drinking too much? "It's going to stunt your growth?"

I said very little.

Comer's Commandments

- Do not expect to change your parents. Altering the habits of a lifetime is a daunting task. It's like talking abstinence to eighteen-year-olds.

- Despite our certainty and best intentions, we do not always know what is best for our parents.

- Pick your battles carefully and refrain from micromanaging. Wallpaper replacement is not life threatening.

- Your parents will appreciate your ideas on how they should run their lives as much as you enjoy their thoughts on how you should run yours.

- Practice the "wear them down" principle. When one of your suggestions is rejected, don't take it personally. Bring up the subject again. And again.

- When faced with a choice between being "right" and being kind, opt for kind.

4

Dealing with Denial

If you want to know how bad things really are, ask a friend who enjoys telling painful truths.

To parent our parents successfully, we must first realize that they need our help. That understanding does not always come quickly or easily. Mother and Dad had been healthy for so long that I didn't consider what might happen when things changed. On both sides of the family, genes were in their favor. Three of my grandparents lived past ninety.

My parents had a loving marriage, close friends, caring neighbors, a paid-for house, and a wide range of interests. In addition, they were emotionally self-sufficient. Their happiness did not depend on mine. That was a good thing because my personal and professional life had endured more ups and downs than a thrill ride at Six Flags. I'd been the recipient of parental aid more often than its provider. It was difficult to imagine that the situation might suddenly reverse.

Even though we had always been close, I'd lived out of state most of my adult life. I moved to Manhattan in 1968 and then to Southern California in 1982. Most of our communication took place in letters and on the phone. I called every Sunday night. One parent got on the black rotary phone in the kitchen while the other talked simultaneously on the bedroom extension.

Although I visited Texas two or three times a year and was almost always there at Christmas, my visits were "prime time." We saw friends, went to parties, and traveled "the relative route" to see family in central Texas. I sang solos at their church, went to Cowboys games with Dad, and took Mother to lunch at Neiman's. While we had a good time, it was heightened reality. When they visited me in New York or Los Angeles, we had a similarly full schedule. Our visits were to life what Sweeps Weeks are to normal television programming. Everyone was determined to make the most of our time together. Best feet were put forward.

Like so many of my contemporaries, I wanted my parents to remain forever as they were, somehow frozen in time. That was not to be. In the early 1990s I saw that Mother was slipping, but I told myself it was only natural. So what if she got confused or repeated herself? She had earned the right. Living in California, it was easy for me to ignore the symptoms I would have had to confront if I'd been around regularly. I realize now that I was in denial, though mine was a mild case. Dad's was full-blown.

Mother's Alzheimer's moved in silently and began to shut down her short-term memory cell by cell. By 1992, her symptoms were difficult to ignore. They showed up most clearly in the kitchen. She had been a cook whose rolls were prized in twelve states. Her homemade peach ice cream was so good I volunteered to turn the crank on her 1937 ice cream maker. Mom's culinary skills suffered dramatically as her mind eroded. Meals began to take hours to assemble.

Her memory lapses became more flagrant. When I came to Dallas, she no longer remembered to make my favorite 1950s congealed salad: lime Jell-O, crushed pineapple, cream cheese, and pecans. I still prefer it to caviar. When she went to the supermarket, Mother no longer bought the items on her list. Instead she came home with an increasingly odd assortment of groceries. Dad began shopping with her in self-defense. He had stayed happily out of the kitchen for his entire life, and then was forced to discover Safeway in his eighties.

Mother began spending much of her time looking for misplaced purses or disappearing glasses. Since she would not leave the house without these necessities, if Dad wanted her to go somewhere, he had to join the search party. Even more alarming was her failure to turn off the stove. Dad added checking the oven and turning off burners to his growing to-do list.

One day Mother went to the beauty shop where she'd been a customer for three decades and could not find her way home. She had to stop at a pay phone and call Dad to come get her. She was less than a mile from their front door. That was the day she gave up driving, a doubly unfortunate turn of events, since she was a better driver than Dad. Mother had the eyes and ears of a thirty-year-old, but Dad remembered how to get home.

Family and friends were deeply concerned. When I came to Texas, they took me aside to talk about Mother. They said she was acting strangely. She wasn't herself. She wrote them the same letter three times. No one wanted to say the "A" word out loud, so their voices fell to an ominous whisper.

"You don't think it could be . . . Alzheimer's?"

That was the last thing I wanted to consider. Their friends weren't trying to upset me, but they thought I should know how bad things had gotten. I knew. There was no escaping that fact unless you were my father. He refused to acknowledge what was happening. In media parlance, he declined to comment. I wanted Mother to be tested by a neurologist in hopes that the problem would turn out to be a vitamin deficiency or chemical imbalance. I prayed there was a medication to reverse her memory loss. When I broached the subject, Dad cut me off in mid-sentence. He would not discuss Mother's health because there was no problem in his eyes. She didn't need any tests. She was fine. Dad and I had the same non-conversation five times in two years.

Each time I came to Texas, Mother was more confused. Each time I attempted to raise the issue, Dad turned an abrupt conversational corner. He dug a trench of denial and would not give an inch. Mother's mental state was off limits, a conversational no-man's-land. Dad did not consciously ignore the situation; he refused to see it. If Mother had fractured her leg, he would have rushed her to the emergency room. Unfortunately, a shattered memory can't be put in a cast. I tried to understand how difficult Mother's condition must have been for my father. They had been married since 1940 and their relationship was the centerpiece of his life. His own security was tied to the maintenance of their shared status quo. If Mother was not okay, how could he be? How would their marital fortress hold?

I wish I'd challenged his denial sooner, but at the time I lacked the courage for a confrontation. I didn't want to rock the boat or cause an argument. Our family was always guarded about feelings. We debated politics and religion with ease, but avoided stepping on emotional land mines. We talked about my brother, Chris, but never in a way that revealed the devastation of our loss from his death in a traffic accident at the age of twenty-three. We discussed the plight of urban ghettos more easily than our own inner cities.

Chris, Mother, and Jim, 1969

Instead of seeking medical advice that might tell him what he didn't want to know, Dad hunkered down and held the fort. Since he couldn't change Mother's behavior, he altered his own. He did what many couples do: one by one, he assumed his spouse's roles. He took over bill paying and check writing, chores that Mother had handled since they married in 1940.

When he realized that she no longer remembered phone conversations, Dad began monitoring their calendar. He responded to invitations and began turning down many of them. Increasingly, Mother did not feel like socializing. Large groups and strange settings made her nervous. When confronted with attending a party, she would come down with a headache that disappeared as soon as Dad told her they didn't have to go.

I realized that her condition had reached a new low in 1994, the year Mother resigned from Christmas. She had always loved the holidays. Soon after Thanksgiving she would get out the candied cherries and pineapple and become serious about making fruitcakes. A dozen fortunate friends would receive these baked works of art sprinkled with hand-shelled pecans from my grandmother's front yard.

Before alcohol became acceptable at our house, unwritten family rules were temporarily relaxed during this annual ritual. After all, Mother needed a little brandy flavoring for her cakes. As a teenager, when I questioned this blatant bending of the rule, Mother rationalized brilliantly: "It's for cooking, not drinking. You can't get drunk from a cake." Her brandy bottle, hidden under the sink from December to December, lasted several years. When her creations were complete, she wrapped them in brown paper and mailed them to friends across the country.

Writing Christmas cards consumed weeks. Once on her list, you were there for life. She was a devoted correspondent who wrote notes on the back of each card. I'm not talking about your generic Christmas letter. She added a lengthy personal message on each card. She wrote *to* her friends, not *at* them. Recipients included long-unseen neighbors from five states, college friends, and girlhood tree-climbing pals.

When Mother declared she was not doing fruitcakes or Christmas cards, I felt as if Santa had canceled his flight. She had entered a new phase that saddened and frightened me. Rather than talk about this radical change, Dad stepped into the breach. He had never addressed a Christmas card in his life; however, he knew it would look bad if no holiday missive arrived from the Comers. He gritted his teeth and got to work. If he could shoot down German fighters, he could send holiday cards.

Unwisely assuming he would find an alphabetized list of readable names and addresses, Dad went through Mother's beat-up black address book. It had more scratched-out entries than current ones. There were seven addresses for me alone. Mother had been promising to recopy this historic document since the sixties. After several grim days working his way through four boxes of silver angels, Dad mailed out a hundred of them. He wrote no notes, of course, but the Comers' cards arrived two weeks early.

That Christmas I realized it was time to confront Dad about Mother's condition. We had to get her to a neurologist for an evaluation, and I vowed that I would do whatever it took to make it happen. The previous summer Dad had left the room when I brought up the subject. This time I had a foolproof plan.

Mother at her writing desk

I chose a venue for our conversation that would not allow him to walk out on me.

It was a family custom for both parents to meet me at the Dallas airport; however, Dad always drove me back to the airport alone. I assumed this was because my departure made Mother too sad to join us. Now I understand it was her way to promote "quality time" between Dad and me. During our ride to the airport I could count on thirty minutes alone with him. Not this year. As I carried my bags to the car, Mother began putting on her coat.

"Where are you going?"

"To the airport with you. I don't want Pappy to get lost."

In twenty years she had never gone with us. My plans for a candid conversation suddenly evaporated. I had to cut to the chase.

"Dad, I need to talk with you privately. Let's go out on the front porch."

He looked at me as if I'd lost my mind. A bone-rattling norther had blown in from the prairies of Oklahoma and the temperature was twenty-three degrees. We stepped outside. I had thirty seconds to make my case.

"If you don't take Mother to a specialist for a complete medical evaluation in the next two weeks, I'm going to fly back and take her to the doctor myself. We have to find out what's going on. Will you do it?"

"Okay."

"Good."

That was the full extent of our conversation. We hadn't even raised our voices. I wanted to believe this meant that things were going to change. I told myself that Dad had given an inch, but I should have known better. His agreement was merely part of a deeply conservative nature. The thought of me spending $400 to fly back to Dallas was too much for him. He figured it was worth a trip to the doctor to keep me from squandering money on an airline ticket.

As promised, he made an appointment with a specialist and kept it. The results were inconclusive. Unfortunately, the doctor did not say the dreaded word, "Alzheimer's," thus enabling Dad to maintain the fiction that Mother was fine. Nevertheless, our front-porch exchange began to melt the iceberg of his denial.

Dad at his seventy-fifth birthday party, March 1985

My father was staring down age on several fronts. He had a three-bedroom home on a large corner lot to maintain. Since 1962, he had mowed his lawn every Saturday and saw no reason to stop. Neighbors half his age watched in amazement as he cut the grass with the agility of a twenty-five-year-old. Not content to walk behind his mower, Dad trotted. His rows were razor-straight, and he allowed himself no breaks. He had a job to do and did it the only way he knew how—all out.

Even in Texas heat and humidity he never missed a week. Finally, in the summer of his eighty-third year, he hired a local teenager to mow the yard. It was a rare semi-surrender to the reality of age: Three months later he was up on the roof removing limbs after a windstorm.

Although Dad knew it was time to think about selling the house, it was another subject he did not wish to discuss. Every time I mentioned putting it on the market, he would say, "I'll think about it next summer." I realized that their home was a refuge against an encroaching world, a last bastion of independence. Mother's kitchen had been her command post; Dad's garage his holy of holies. He owned more tools than most hardware stores, and the thought of leaving his workshop was devastating.

Despite excellent health, high energy, and a positive attitude Dad had far too much on his plate. Keeping up with Mother took more and more of his time. As he approached his eighty-sixth birthday, I wondered how long he could keep all the balls in the air. On February 20, 1996, his body answered that question definitively with a major stroke. Denial was over.

Comer's Commandments

- To parent our parents successfully, we must first realize that they need our help.

- While denial is natural, there are times we need to take the initiative and risk causing raised voices and tears.

- It's better to cause a scene than to ignore the truth.

- Never minimize the effects of aging and loss. Understand how painful it is for one parent to watch the other lose health or memory.

The house where Mother was born, Smithville, Texas

5

Role Models Are Forever

During my acting days in New York, I turned down a lucrative corporate job to work in summer stock as "Snoopy" in *You're a Good Man, Charlie Brown*. The pay was $80 a week. Foolishly, I mentioned this strategic business decision in a letter home. Mother was so upset that she destroyed the offending page so that my father would not drop dead while reading it. He never noticed the obvious deletion.

Nineteen years later, I accepted a full-time job with a two-billion-dollar-a-year HMO in Southern California. My parents actually screamed out loud when I told them. I had a secretary, three weeks' vacation, and full health benefits. For twenty-five years, they had dreamed of my getting and keeping a secure position. From their point of view, I was finally where God intended me.

Given the absence of parental prodding, why did I pull up stakes and move back to a state where the humidity is higher than the IQs of many legislators? My relocation was not a sign of innate goodness. Prolonged commitment had always gone against my grain. I admired unselfishness but had achieved it only in small doses. The greatest influence on my decision was my parents' example. It was not what they said, but how they lived their values. When it came to coming through, nobody did it better.

Doing your duty gets a bad rap these days. We live in an era that glorifies self-gratification. Americans pump up, slim down, and replace body parts as if they were stereo components. We can get so caught up in the search for our inner, thinner selves that we lose sight of who we really are.

From the time we moved to Dallas in 1962 until her last sister died in 1990, Mother made a monthly five-hundred-mile round-trip to Smithville, the small central Texas town where she was raised. Her loving supervision and frequent visits allowed my grandmother and aunt to remain in their family home. Each time she arrived, Mother had a full schedule. She cleaned, did laundry, looked after banking, paid bills, and took them to the beauty parlor or for checkups at the doctor's office. She treated them to hamburgers, celebrated birthdays, and helped fix Thanksgiving and Christmas dinners. Once he retired, Dad often came with her and helped maintain the hundred-year-old house.

Mema and five-month-old Jim, 1945

Mother never complained about shouldering this responsibility. To my recurring amazement, she seemed to shed ten years each time we drove up to the house where she was born. Her face relaxed because she knew she was where she was supposed to be.

My grandmother—whom I called Mema—had to drop out of school in the sixth grade when her mother died of diphtheria and left her with several small brothers and sisters to care for. Despite the absence of a high school diploma, she possessed a keen mind and an eclectic skill set. She had a home remedy for every ailment, knew the Methodist hymnal by heart, and could wring the neck of a chicken and fry it for dinner. Mema picked pecans on a ladder from her favorite tree until she was eighty-five. She didn't have to slow down because the pace of her life was steady and sure. She never lived in a care facility, spent the night in a hospital, or used a walker. In 1973, she died on her front porch at the age of ninety-one.

Mother's attention then shifted to her two unmarried sisters, whom she called "unclaimed treasures." Estelle was what southerners refer to as "slow" instead of the politically correct term "challenged." She lived at home her entire life and was childlike in outlook and behavior. When I was eight, she was my favorite relative because we spoke a common language. The only money Estelle earned came from babysitting, for which she charged fifty cents an hour. Her services were a bargain if you didn't count what she ate. She had no compunctions about helping herself to whatever was in a client's refrigerator.

Mother's other sister, Mattye Mae, was a school teacher who had moved four hundred miles north to carve out a life in the "big city" of Wichita Falls. She taught art at the high school, sponsored an award-winning year-book, and was active in the Democratic Party. She returned to Smithville in her seventies when she began to feel the need of a safer haven. With Mattye Mae back home, Estelle felt that her territory had been invaded. The two sisters had apartments in the same house, but lived separate lives. Mother got along well with both of them and served as a peacekeeping force without UN charter.

Mother and Estelle with Mema, 1914

Though Mom's example was inspiring, I watched the years of responsibility wear her down. The long round-trips were physically exhausting, and she made them every three or four weeks no matter what. When she was not in Smithville, she worried about how her sisters were doing. A self-proclaimed calamity howler, she spent part of each day imagining catastrophes. She called them frequently, expecting to hear that their house had been reduced to ashes.

For years I urged my parents to hire someone in Smithville to drop by once or twice a week to check on my aunts, take care of the yard, and see that the laundry was done. Many locals would have jumped at the chance for low-stress income. Money was not the issue. My parents could afford to hire help, but their personal sense of duty precluded that possibility. Every time I brought up the subject, Mother said, "There's no one in Smithville who would do that." Of course, they never looked for local assistance and spurned my suggestion to run an ad in the local paper. Asking for help didn't fit their picture of responsibility. You didn't pay someone to take care of your family. You did it yourself or died trying. On one visit I pressed the issue forcefully during dinner and did not stop when given the usual excuses. "Why are you risking your own health when you don't have to? Why won't you look for help?"

Mother's eyes filled with tears, and her emotion was too much for my father.

"Can't you see that you are upsetting your mother?"

I thought tears were less dangerous than a nervous breakdown or a car wreck. When I attempted to continue the conversation, Dad rose from the table.

"Dinner is over."

Mother cleared the dishes. Dad took out a book. There was no more discussion. Unfortunately, I let the subject drop. I wish I'd acted instead of argued. If I had gone to Smithville and hired someone to do the job, Mother could not have claimed such a person didn't exist. Action was called for, but it never occurred to me to take the initiative.

In 1987 Aunt Mattye broke her hip and had to go to a nursing home thirty miles from Smithville, in Flatonia. She stayed there three years. A few months after being named queen of the home at their Valentine's party, she died in her sleep.

Estelle remained alone in the house where she had been born. Two hundred miles away, Mother fretted about her sister. What if she got sick? How would anyone know? One freezing February day in 1988, Estelle slipped in the bathroom and could not lift her two-hundred-pound frame from the floor. She lay there for four days until a neighbor stopped by and found her. She died of pneumonia three days later. Mother's worst nightmare had come true.

I flew to Smithville to give the eulogy at Estelle's funeral, and then returned to my life. I made a silent vow that I would never allow myself to be sidetracked by family obligations the way my parents had been for twenty-five years. I would do my part, but would never put family first. Not me. I was not going to sacrifice for anyone. Fortunately I've had to eat those words.

The power of my parents' example must have been subterranean. Today I find myself attempting to emulate behavior I once judged so harshly. I surprised myself by moving to and staying in Austin. That first summer, when the temperature hovered around one hundred degrees for ten weeks, the thought of leaving never occurred to me. As the thermometer plunged back to the mid-eighties, I joined the natives in saying how nice it was to have a "cool spell."

When my California friends asked how long I planned to stay in Texas, they made it sound as if I was serving time. They believed I had given up something. In truth, I'd found what I was looking for all along.

Comer's Commandments

• You don't have to be naturally unselfish in order to act unselfishly.

• Don't expect your parents to ask for help. Be creative in finding inconspicuous ways to provide assistance.

• Whenever possible, allow your parents to save face.

• Take initiative. If your parents aren't dealing with a situation, handle it yourself.

• Follow your hunches. If you think something is wrong, it probably is. (For example, you should be concerned about the substitution of Fritos for fresh fruit.)

Mother at the Wesleyan, May 2003

6

It's Okay to Talk about the Hard Stuff

Good parenting is not about avoiding issues. It's about facing them. Postponing difficult conversations only makes them more painful or sometimes impossible. We tell ourselves we'll have a long talk with our parents eventually. Too often "eventually" is a euphemism for "not until I have to." It's my father promising to put the house on the market "next summer."

There is no ideal time to tackle hard stuff. Just as we don't schedule a stomach virus for next Tuesday, there will never be a perfect day to ask a parent to hand over the car keys. At some point we must put the taboo on the table. For example, intensive care is not the place to discover that Dad doesn't have a will. There are no meaningful discussions with someone on a respirator. *We need to communicate early and often.*

What keeps families from having these necessary conversations? Why do we remain stuck talking sports and weather for decades? The culprit is the original four-letter word: fear. It can immobilize us like a deer caught in the headlights and cause entire families to enter a conspiracy of silence. We'd rather play it safe than risk confrontations and upsetting conversations. Hard stuff may include:

- Answering the fifty questions in the center of this book and discussing them with your parents

- Making an appointment for a parent with a gerontologist or neurologist, and getting your parent to keep it

- Hosting next year's Christmas or Thanksgiving dinner so your mother doesn't spend a week in bed following the holiday

- Finding someone to help with house or yard work—even if that means paying for it as well

- Arranging for someone to do your parents' shopping and to deliver groceries to them

- Having a friend visit your parents regularly to make sure everything is okay

- Taking your parents for a tour of a local retirement home or to visit a friend who enjoys living in one

- Finding out if your parents have long-term-care insurance and possibly buying a policy for them

- Having a candid discussion about their driving before it has become dangerous

- Telling your parents that you love them and will be there for them no matter what

My family placed a high premium on being pleasant. We wanted our time together to be "nice" and paid a heavy price for our mutual lack of candor. Authenticity entails necessary risks. If we discussed my debts, Dad's scotch, or Mother's memory loss, it could lead to awkward silences or painful outbursts. I've learned since that honesty is worth the risk.

In twelve-step programs they refer to "the elephant in the living room." The pachyderm can refer to any subject that we don't want to discuss: alcohol, drugs, overeating, gambling, or the *realities of aging.* Instead of dealing with the problem openly, many families choose to pretend it isn't there. They refuse to acknowledge the obvious. Spouses and children may spend years tiptoeing around an ever-worsening situation hoping it will disappear. It will not. Elephants ignored are only elephants enabled.

Too many families confuse proximity with closeness. If they travel hundreds of miles to see each other and gather in the same room, they assume that they've connected. That is not necessarily true. Intimacy is not a contact sport. It requires candor and open-ended conversation.

For decades, each time I flew to Dallas I vowed to talk with my parents about what was really going on in my life. Within half an hour of landing, my resolve vanished and I slid back into familiar patterns of safe, surface, careful conversation. In my mid-forties I had a problem that could not be ignored. I called ahead from California to say I was coming back to talk about something painful and difficult. I'll never forget Mother's response. She said, "Whatever it is, we'll handle it." And we did. When I finally told them about my struggle with substance abuse, they were supportive and nonjudgmental, and that made a positive difference in my recovery.

The greatest compliment we can pay our parents is to be honest with them. By sharing our authentic selves, we invite the possibility of closeness. Many families expend tremendous effort in not saying "the wrong thing." What is the wrong thing? It's the right thing no one has the guts to bring up. I do not take the risks of candor lightly. I am a people-pleasing, smooth-the-water, keep-things-light kind of guy. I hate to offend, much less cause anyone to be upset or angry. I want the entire planet to be happy and healthy, a trait that often leaves me in tears during *The News Hour with Jim Lehrer*. I've learned that if I want to save the world, the best place to start is with my own family.

No matter our age or achievements, we remain forever our parents' children. The flip-flop of caregiving responsibilities is difficult on parents and children. Ten years into this journey I still find it tough to balance an inner child with an outer adult. Making decisions for our parents can be uncomfortable because it's not a role for which we have rehearsed. There are still days when I forget that I'm in charge. I was a natural at being a kid. It has taken me fifty years to become a card-carrying grown-up.

Helping our parents make necessary decisions and consider changes they may strongly resist is like walking an emotional tightrope. We find ourselves balancing the past and the present, while fretting about the future. Often our fears are unreasonable and untrue. We need to stay focused on the present. Mother, who now lives only in the moment, is an excellent role model for me.

No Guarantees

While I believe strongly in open communication, I must offer a disclaimer. There are no guarantees that honesty and candor will be successful. Just because we gird our loins, deal with denial, and face facts does not mean our parents will agree with us and cheerfully accept our suggestions. They may fight us every step of the way, refuse our help, cut us out of the will, and throw fits or furniture. They may spurn our suggestions and ignore the most well-intentioned advice. That is their right. When I'm eighty-five and someone suggests I move into a motel-sized room, I may raise hell, too.

Although being self-sufficient is a noble goal, there may come a time when our parents think they are doing wonderfully and we think otherwise.

There are fine lines between self-respect and stubbornness, dignity and delusion. Sometimes we have to make hard calls without the benefit of instant replay. How do we know whether we are responding to fears or facts? Sometimes we don't. We must hope, pray, and, ultimately, act.

I know an eighty-five-year-old who is trapped in his home caring for a wife who has suffered several strokes. His devotion is admirable, but his zealous sense of duty may kill him and leave her without his love or assistance. He hires nurses and therapists to help him, and then doesn't like the way they do things and fires them. His children are in a quandary. They know it's time to move their mother to a nursing home, but their dad won't consider it. They rationalize that when their mother gets a little worse, he'll see the light and move her to a care facility. Are they being respectful or kidding themselves?

A doctor who specializes in Alzheimer's told me that he found his ninety-four-year-old aunt in her front yard, holding a flashlight and watering her plants at midnight. He asked why she didn't do her yard work during the day and she replied, "My son fusses if he sees me working in the yard, so I do it when he's not around." This same aunt goes to the nursing home every week to visit the "old people."

The most basic rule for physicians is "Do no harm." This rule applies to children as well. We must consistently advocate for what we believe is right and hope our views will prevail. If our parents don't agree or refuse to see the problem, we may need to step back and allow them to live their lives. On the other hand, there are times when we need to intervene no matter what our parents say. The gut-wrenching difficulty is deciding between what is harmful and what is helpful. The border between the two is as blurred as the vision of some ninety-year-olds. I never said this would be easy.

Comer's Commandments

- Good parenting is not about avoiding issues but about facing them.

- We must accept the fact that, no matter our age or achievements, we will remain forever our parents' children.

- Do not ignore the elephant in the living room. Steer the conversation away from "safe" subjects and talk about what's really happening.

- If you want to make the streets safe, start at home. It takes real courage to tell an eighty-seven-year-old parent to stop driving.

7

Go into Her World

The first few years of my parenting career were an improvisation. Day after day, descending the empty stairwell from the fourth floor to the lobby of the retirement home, I yelled at the walls,

"I don't know how to do this!"

Some days screaming in the stairwell was the best I could do. It was part release, part reaction. I needed gentle feedback from a wise manager, but none was available. I had no supervisor. There was no evaluation committee or report card. Caregivers get no orientation, no mentoring or CliffsNotes. There is no "right" way to do the job. You do the best you can, and hope that's good enough. After ten years, I worry less about doing things perfectly and more about doing them with love.

The most valuable advice I ever received about Mother's Alzheimer's came from a client. I'd been hired to write a series of training videos for a chain of nursing homes and interviewed staff members as part of my research. One of them was an Alzheimer's expert, and I told her about my difficulty in dealing with some of Mother's behaviors. She said, "You can't control her disease. You have to accept it."

"But she wants to go see her dead sister."

"So?"

"She thinks most of the dresses in her closet belong to other people and will only wear four of them."

"That's okay. She can only wear one at a time."

Her smile told me that she'd heard this before. Then she gave me a slice of wisdom I have tattooed to my frontal lobe.

"Don't try to keep her in your world. Go into her world."

The moment I heard those words, I knew she was right. I could not hold Mother hostage in a reality she no longer inhabited. She could enter my world only as a visitor, not a full-time resident. I had to accept her and love her as she was. Logic was not going to change her mind. Reason would not prevail. Instead of obsessing about what she ought to remember, I had to deal with what she recalled. The next time Mom wanted to go to Smithville to see the deceased Estelle I said, "We'll go next week." She smiled at the prospect of a visit with her sister and forgot about it within ten seconds. Next week never came.

Once I made myself at home in her world, both of our lives became easier. We no longer debated her clothing choices. If she didn't want to wear her elegant blue dress because its owner might accuse her of theft, I acquiesced. I stopped being an unsought wardrobe consultant and focused on making sure the clothes she wore were clean. Mother had moved beyond fashion.

I adopted the attitude of a woman in an Alzheimer's support group. She came home one afternoon to find her husband mowing the lawn in his underwear. She had to make a choice. Would she worry about what the neighbors might say, or see that he was happily occupied and that the lawn was getting mowed? She decided to let him enjoy his work.

Despite Dad's devotion and my best efforts, we watched Mother's universe slowly shrink. She stopped writing letters in her perfect penmanship. She no longer made phone calls. She repeated the same questions over and over. Sometimes it seemed like she was disappearing one inch at a time.

Miraculously, Mother kept her social skills and held on to her unique brand of humor. She still has a comeback for every comment. Instead of bemoaning what has been lost, I try to celebrate what remains.

One day I was in the elevator heading for my parents' rooms on the fourth floor. We stopped on the second floor, and I saw Mother sitting in a chair with a puzzled look on her face. I got off and asked, "What are you doing here?"

"I don't rightly know, but it's sure good to see you." She had no more to say on the subject, so I took her home to the fourth floor.

One of the touchiest issues in keeping Mother in the retirement home was personal hygiene. She did not always remember to shower. Eventually the administrator told me there had been some pointed comments from other residents about her lack of bathing. He told me he knew I'd find a way to handle the situation. I did not share his optimism.

Overseeing Mother's toilette was not in my repertoire. As she does not take kindly to personal-care suggestions, the matter had to be treated with the delicacy of Palestinian peace talks. I had no choice but to bring in the big gun: I reported the problem to Dad. He said he would handle it, and he did. I have no idea how he achieved this feat, but water soon began flowing in Room 407. Complaints ceased and the administrators never mentioned the subject again.

My father's communication techniques remain a mystery to me. In 1990, when I wanted to give a luncheon for their fiftieth wedding anniversary, Mother demurred. She "didn't want us to make a fuss." I was determined to make a sit-down fuss and needed her active participation to host one hundred guests. Finally, I appealed to my father for help. He said, "I'll talk to her."

The next day she announced, "Since you and your father are determined to have this party, I'll endure it." Of course, she had the time of her life.

Mother has coping strategies I don't understand but am forced to admire. One morning I arrived at her room earlier than usual and was surprised when it took her several minutes to open her door. Once she appeared, everything seemed fine. I asked, "What took you so long?" She replied, as if explaining to a dull child, "I had to move the furniture." That was how I found out about her nightly barricade.

I checked with the fourth-floor maid who knows everything about everybody and needs little incentive to talk. She said matter-of-factly, "Your mother piles her chairs by the door every night and removes them in the morning. Didn't you know that?" I did not. My father was covering for her once again.

Recalling my childhood, I understood why Mother piled up furniture. It was her time-tested method of burglary prevention. When we lived in Atlanta in the fifties, Dad traveled three to five days a week and Mother stayed home with my brother and me. She never seemed frightened about being alone in a house with two little boys. When Dad was away, the three of us slept in my brother's room. Mother and Chris were in a big double bed while I was tucked into a rollaway nearby. Before turning off the light, Mother locked the bedroom door and pushed Chris's bookcase in front of it. Separating us from harm were three shelves of Golden books, a plywood door, and a laughable lock. It worked for me.

Fifty years later, faced with a more subtle menace, Mother fell back on proven experience. Stacking the furniture had worked once and might work again. Her method might not make the fire department happy, but it allowed her to feel safe. I understood her logic and never mentioned it again.

In parenting of any kind, it is essential to know which battles are worth fighting. I have friends with teenagers who go along with green hair and body piercing, but stand firm on doing homework and making good grades. While nose rings come and go, a good education is ineradicable.

Comer's Commandments

- If a parent has dementia, don't expect her to stay in your world. Get a passport to hers.

- Never remind an Alzheimer's patient that he has asked you the same question before. Answer it the third time or the sixtieth.

- You can't control the progress of a disease, only your progress in responding to it with kindness and restraint.

- Instead of obsessing about what your parents have forgotten, enjoy what they remember.

- The old Kenny Rogers song says, "You've got to know when to hold 'em, know when to fold 'em." There are times to back off and let go. There are also times to stand fast.

I didn't have all the answers in 1951, and I don't have them today.

8

You Don't Have to Be an Expert

When I first began parenting my parents, I thought I had to do everything perfectly. I believed that people were looking over my shoulder, judging how I handled things. I assumed that one wrong decision would be disastrous, one false move unalterable. Such was not the case. My perfectionism was merely one symptom of a Comer-centric world view. Dealing with my parents' aging has helped me realize that I do not reside at the center of the universe.

Parenting is a slowly acquired art. Unlike studying for an exam, there is no way to pull an all-nighter on patience or cram for the kindness quiz. Responses can't be memorized; they must be refined slowly. No caregiver gets it right all the time. When we take a false step, we adjust our behavior and move on.

I've made lots of mistakes—so far none of them fatal. One sweltering August Sunday, I took my folks for a ride in the local park. As we crossed the low-water bridge of the San Gabriel River, I turned my attention momentarily from the road. While pointing out a gaggle of geese, I drove into an abutment and blew a tire mid-bridge. A hubcap hurtled toward a surprised goose that squawked loudly and gave us a dirty look. Fixing that flat was a picnic compared to watching the pained look on my father's face as he began a ten-minute monologue on safe driving.

Like traditional parents, I have found myself in places I never planned to be. Most moms and dads do not plan to become chauffeurs. They have no inborn yearning to attend soccer games at eight on Saturday mornings. Their idea of a swell sleepover is not a group activity. They do not relish making peanut butter and jelly sandwiches. They would rather give blood than go to McDonald's. Nevertheless they learn to chauffeur, cheer, trim crust, and pay for Happy Meals with a smile.

Likewise I have mixed feelings about some of the activities on my parenting schedule. For five years I attended the father-son picnic at the retirement home. The event was always scheduled for mid-June when the daytime temperature does not budge from the mid-nineties. One year I had to come directly from the airport in a coat and tie. I got there just in time to bat flies from the barbecue and sweat through my white dress shirt. Despite the heat the ribs were succulent, the music was lively, and Dad beamed at having me there. Mother looked on with the other women from the air-conditioned dining room and occasionally sneaked outside to grab a slice of watermelon on the sly.

At the retirement home, my constant personal challenge was to keep the conversation going at the dinner table. Mother has no access to her past, but connects well to the current sentence. Dad couldn't hear the current sentence, but would gladly do a monologue on quantum physics or reconstruct air battles over Germany. Left to ourselves, the possibilities for repartee were limited. Fortunately, we weren't left to ourselves.

For three years we enjoyed delightful companions at my parents' table. I never found out how their table partners were selected, but we lucked out. There was Lily Mae, a stylish widow who dressed beautifully and loved gossip and soap operas. My favorites were Mr. and Mrs. Davis, a couple in their early nineties who'd been married sixty-seven years at the time and were devoted to each other.

Mrs. Davis had a droll sense of humor. In the 1920s, she taught English in a small country school. One year she was told by the superintendent of schools that she would also have to teach auto mechanics, a course that involved taking apart an engine. Mrs. Davis knew nothing about cars, but she needed to keep her job. She and her class dutifully disassembled the engine of a fellow teacher's car and put it back together as best they could. Unfortunately, when they finished there were a number of excess parts that no one could identify. Unfazed, Mrs. Davis put them in her desk drawer and returned the car to its owner, who drove it for years and never knew the difference. That's the kind of spunk she brought to our table.

We enjoyed lively discussions on current events, sports, scandals, old times, and new fashions. Some days we laughed so hard that we caused heads to turn at more sedate tables. I looked forward to our lunches and dinners, and was deeply disappointed when the cast of characters changed. One day Lily Mae collapsed in her room and died of a heart attack. A few months later, Mr. Davis's legs would no longer support his body weight, so he and his wife moved to a private room at the nursing home a mile away.

Soon my parents inherited a less talkative couple who looked as if they had posed for Grant Wood's classic painting *American Gothic*. The only thing missing was a pitchfork. In the six months they sat with us, they never smiled. He was a master of complaint and his servile wife waited on him hand and foot, worn down by fifty years of submission. She had the pursed lips of a domestic martyr and, I fantasized, the repressed soul of Lorena Bobbitt.

I made it my mission in life to get them to lighten up. I tried every conversational gambit in my repertoire and failed. Once resigned to their sullen company, I felt guilty when the husband's breathing got as bad as his disposition and he had to move to the nursing home. It may have been my imagination, but I could swear his wife looked relieved. After two weeks of freedom, she had a hint of happiness on her face.

As I became a retirement-home regular, I got to know staff and residents on a first-name basis. Over the next few years, I gained skills I never expected to acquire, several of which have helped to keep me sane.

Patience

This quality has never been my strong point: I chafe at taking time to match arrows on childproof aspirin bottles. After a decade of practice, I can calmly maneuver into my Toyota Camry three ninety-year-olds, twelve Christmas presents, two wheelchairs, and a walker.

Treating older people with respect, no matter what the situation, often requires me to shift gears and slow down. I have learned that life does not have to be lived in an endless sprint. I am a little less harried and hurried than in my former life. I do not scream during freeway traffic jams. I can sit at red lights without complaining. I honk rarely and have not extended a finger to another driver in years. Well, months.

Humility

For years I confused humility with humiliation. Humiliation is what happens when I attempt to program a VCR. Humility is a realistic sense of our place in the scheme of things. I experience it every time I attempt to talk with

Dad. His deafness is not a character defect, but it brings out mine. The most difficult times are shouted conversations about private subjects in public places.

"Yes, Dad, I picked up your laxative."

"What?"

"I said I picked up your laxative."

Bellowing about bodily functions in the dining room embarrassed me for a while, but I've adjusted. Genuine humility is not caring how things look to people who aren't thinking about you anyway.

Dad is not the only one who keeps me humble. Mother still questions me openly about the basics.

"Jim, when did you go to bed last night?"

"Around eleven."

"That means you stayed up too late."

"Probably."

"There's no probably about it. Honey, you are going to become an old man before your time."

That comment never fails to send me to the nearest mirror where my fluorescent-lit visage affirms her dire prediction. Warming to her subject, Mother may do a variation on the "when did you go to bed last night" question five or six times in the next half hour. If I manage to answer each question without judgment, I consider myself somewhere in the vicinity of humility.

Boundaries

What is a boundary, you ask? If you have to ask, you probably don't have any. Boundaries are walls of self-protection that are essential for caregivers.

When parenting your parents, it's easy to overdo it and wear yourself out in the process. That's when setting boundaries can make a tremendous difference. For years, I saw my mother push herself to the limit in caring for her mother and sisters. Sometimes I catch myself doing the same thing with her and Dad.

Let's say that you're staying with your mother after she's had an operation. She is doing fine, but it's been ten days since you had a night to yourself so you buy tickets for a touring company of *Rent*, and your brother promises to stay with her. At four on Saturday afternoon he calls to say he can't do it.

What is your immediate response? Anger? Stunned silence? If you have good boundaries you will say, "Since you can't stay with her yourself, what arrangements have you made for her care?" There may be a long silence. He who breaks it first loses. Primary caregivers must know when to stand up for themselves and ask siblings to do their part.

Boundaries work for parents of all ages. I have a friend in California whose son went off to college a thousand miles from home. During freshman orientation, the university sponsored a parent-only event. They told the assembled mothers and fathers that sometime during the freshman year they would likely receive "the dump call." It might come at any time for any reason, but come it would. One day their child would phone home and announce that he or she was miserable and lonely and hated school. The parents were told to take a deep breath and state firmly, "That sounds like a real problem. What are you going to do about it?"

When my friend got "the dump call" the following April, she used the response they'd taught her and placed the problem back in her son's hands. He stayed in school, got over what was bothering him, and graduated with honors. My friend is now a tuition-free woman.

Like freshmen, aging parents may give their caregivers the dump call in person or on the phone. They may demand to stay at home when that is impossible. Or they may complain bitterly about a perfectly acceptable care facility. Like the parents of college students, children need to be prepared for these confrontations and not take them personally.

A Healthy Sense of the Absurd

What do I mean by absurd? One day I arrived to find Mother asleep at the dining table and could not interest her in conversation. She spoke to me but would not open her eyes. Finally, I played my ace:

"Mom, you can't see me with your eyes closed."

"I've seen you."

"That was funny."

"I thought so. Now leave me be."

Like children, the elderly often tell it like it is. My parents' unvarnished bluntness provides a stream-of-consciousness commentary on everything they see. Their inner censors disappeared long ago. For instance, Dad points out every overhanging stomach or ample derrière he encounters. Since Texas is the fried-food capital of the world, he sees a lot of them.

"Look at the rear end on that woman."

"Dad, not so loud. She'll hear you."

He makes a face and shrugs his shoulders. "I don't care if she does hear me. It might do her some good. That weight could kill her."

Mother chimes in. "See the lady over there? She's sound asleep and her mouth is wide open. She's liable to catch a fly."

There was one long-time retirement home resident whose mealtime coughing and wheezing attacks assaulted Mother's ears in the dining room. Each time he emoted, she was offended anew. She screwed up her face, rolled her eyes, nodded in his direction, and said loudly, "How would you like to listen to that morning, noon, and night?"

I whispered, "Mother, don't say anything. He'll hear you."

"Somebody needs to say something."

"It doesn't have to be you."

"He needs someone to teach him some manners," she announced, with a strong implication that it should be me.

In such situations, I try to change the subject or leave the table to get another helping of dessert. I've learned it's best to let Mother have the last word.

While I will never earn a Ph.D. in parenting, such a degree is not required. Patience is. Although I've made progress in overcoming a few cherished character flaws, some days my fuse is short and my buttons get pushed. When I'm at my wit's end, I remind myself to focus on doing "the next right thing." Often that means keeping my mouth shut and taking deep breaths. My respiratory system has never been better.

Comer's Commandments

- Do not expect parenting skills to come quickly. Like yoga or gardening, caregiving is a slowly acquired art.

- Unlike studying for a final, there is no way to pull an all-nighter on patience or cram for the kindness exam. You have to work at it every day.

- Parenting will provide many opportunities to learn humility. They include not caring how things look to people who aren't thinking about you anyway.

- When all else fails, remember to breathe.

9

Opportunities for Spiritual Growth I Could Have Done Without

Nietzsche claims that, "What does not destroy me, makes me stronger." He never spent five days in a tin-roofed storage unit with my father. Seven months after his stroke, Dad and I walked into the humid, dusty bin where we had moved everything from their house in Dallas. And I mean everything. There were 112 large, sealed boxes along with furniture, artwork, mementos, clothes, and junk. Fifty-six years of family life confronted us, awaiting a thumbs-up, thumbs-down verdict. I felt like Nero at a gladiatorial contest. We had to decide what my parents would keep in their rooms, what I would take to my apartment, what went to The Caring Place, and what was beyond charity.

There was the sailfish Dad caught in West Palm Beach in 1955, his first and only deep-sea trophy. Much to Mother's dismay, he had it mounted. She could not believe my cost-conscious father would spend a hundred dollars on taxidermy. That was a month's rent! It was one of their few in-front-of-the-children fights, and Dad won it. For forty-one years that fish had eyed us placidly. Now the tattered trophy was showing its age. What would Dad do with this over-the-hill wall ornament? Sentiment lost out to lack of space. The fish went in the dumpster.

I winced at a painfully bad painting of French fishermen perpetrated by my late Aunt Mattye Mae, a work I had loathed for years. Even Mother knew it was hideous, but it was her sister's creation and therefore not subject to the usual laws of good taste. For thirty years it hung in my parents' bedroom. Dad and I ditched it with relish.

I came across the embarrassment of my own first art purchase, a bull-fighter that I bought as a college freshman in the French Quarter of New Orleans. A mean-spirited classmate had informed me that black velvet was frowned on in the art world. Embarrassed at my gaffe, I wanted to pitch the painting in 1964, but Mother would not allow "art" to be thrown away. The bullfighter stayed in my closet for decades, a silent reminder that we are not born with finely tuned critical faculties.

If They Have Hearing Aids in Heaven, I'd Rather Go to Hell

While Dad's deafness does not seem to bother him, it drives me crazy. I have fought a long, losing battle to get him to use his hearing aids. In six years, he has spent $8,000 on computerized earpieces. He still won't wear them.

No matter what adjustments we make, the hearing aids don't work to my father's satisfaction. Batteries fail, the case cracks, or he drops them in his soup. When they do work, they screech and buzz obnoxiously. We've had them programmed, cleaned, and sent back to the factory for repairs at least eight times. What needs adjusting is Dad's attitude about wearing them. Most of the time they remain locked in a drawer at the nurses' station.

Every time I visit I face an immediate, critical choice. Do I spend ten minutes finding a nurse to unlock the drawer so I can put in new batteries, and then struggle to fit the hearing aids into Dad's ears? Or do I bow to his wishes and yell our conversation, never sure of what he has heard? If I go the route of least resistance, my head is pounding within minutes as I scream into his ears. Dad has grown accustomed to the sound of very little, and I suspect he likes it that way. He doesn't have to bother responding to sentences he doesn't hear.

When I prevail on him to wear the hearing aids, he is always surprised by the world of sound. He forgets that moving tires make noise, horns honk, children cry, doors slam, and life is a constant cacophony. He'll say in amazement, "What is that racket?"

"That's life, Dad."

Car Troubles

During the three years I owned my parents' 1989 Buick, every time I visited Mother asked how "her" car was running. Dad noticed missing hubcaps before I did and found scratches and nicks that escaped my detection.

Driving with Dad is a patience stretcher. Incapable of being a passenger, he insists on serving as copilot. He gives directions loudly from the passenger side and announces each approaching stop sign as if it were invisible to me. If I go beyond twenty-five miles an hour, he demands loudly that I slow down. He reminds me regularly that I tailgate and exhibit a lethal over-dependence on brakes. At major intersections he rears back in his seat as if preparing for a collision. He gets that "I'm about to meet St. Peter" expression on his face and stomps his foot to the floorboard. Subtlety is not his strong suit.

For most Americans, no right is more fundamental than driving. Many of our parents first got behind the wheel in their early teens and never planned to stop driving. A car represents independence and power. It is an integral part of their emotional terrain. One of the most difficult parent-child discussions concerns whether Mom or Dad should stop driving. On this subject, I cannot speak from experience. My parents stopped voluntarily. Mother quit because she got lost in her own neighborhood, and Dad had to stop after his stroke.

All of us are affected by elderly drivers whose skills are impaired. I once stood in line at a Motor Vehicle Department office in California and observed an older couple renewing their licenses. They must have been in their late eighties and had obvious difficulty negotiating the long line. Both were frail, and my heart went out to them.

One hour later they left proudly clasping licenses granting them five more years as legal drivers. That's when I realized I should have saved some of my sympathy for the thousands of unsuspecting drivers who will face them on the road. I'll bet no California Highway Patrol officer volunteered to give them a driving test.

The most dangerous drivers are not necessarily teenagers. I have a friend whose father is ninety-four and still drives a big Cadillac sedan. He says, "I may have to stop in a year or two" but today remains an unguided missile. His children can't bring themselves to tell him to stop because they are afraid it will break his spirit. They ought to fear more tangible breakage.

Another friend's mother promised to stop driving when she was ninety, but that day came and went, and she remained behind the wheel. When her family reminded her of the pledge to stop driving, she said sweetly that they were mistaken. She had promised to quit at *ninety-five*, not ninety. And they let her get by with that. She makes regular 360-mile round-trips from Houston to Austin. On one of her recent sojourns, she knocked down three mailboxes while passing through a small town. This good Christian woman stopped the car, wrote down the addresses, and sent each family $100 and a letter of apology that ended with, "God loves you."

My friend King Cole (that's his real name) told me how his father handled the driving situation. He told King to tell him when it was time for him to stop driving and he would hand over the keys that day. When his dad turned eighty-five, King said he thought the time had come. His Dad gave him the keys by dusk. Now that took courage and clarity—and it's extremely rare.

I spoke on "parenting your parents" at a local Rotary club and when I got to the section of my speech about driving, a member in his late eighties shouted from the back of the room, "Jim, you done quit preaching and gone to meddling!" While he got a big laugh, he meant it.

Sadly, the danger of diminished driving ability is no laughing matter. In July 2003, an elderly driver lost control of his car and killed ten people in an outdoor shopping mall in Santa Monica, California, briefly focusing national attention on the issue. I have a friend in Los Angeles who goes to church with the driver and described him as a kind and gentle person. Unfortunately, no one in his family had told him he needed to stop driving. Now his legacy will be that of needless negligence and manslaughter.

Families have a responsibility to do everything possible to get parents who have become dangerous drivers off the road. If children don't speak up, we become part of the problem. Parents interpret our silence as assent. There may come a time when caregivers have to cause a scene, confiscate the keys or disable the engine, and get Dad a charge account with Yellow Cab.

Temperance

While I did not have to deal with the driving dilemma, I did have to confront Dad about alcohol. My father drank scotch regularly for sixty-five years—give or take a decade. It was not a problem until his eighties, when his metabolism no longer kept up with his consumption. At holiday dinners, when my cousins asked if anyone would like a glass of wine, Dad liked four. He was the only one in the family who came back for more. As a result of his imbibing, he nodded off before the dinner was served. After several years of seeing him slumped over the turkey, my cousins stopped serving wine.

On occasion, Dad would fortify himself for an evening out by having a couple of pre-event shots in his room. By the time we went to dinner, his balance was long gone. One Saturday night at an upscale restaurant, the hostess led us to a table across a crowded dining room. Dad could barely walk, but did not view that as a problem. He used the shoulders of seated diners to balance himself as he unsteadily made his way to our table. I followed this progress with horror, but could see from the looks on their faces that our fellow patrons understood. Someday the tottering figure might be their dad, or them.

For several years I debated about whether to talk with Dad about his drinking. Eventually I went to two retirement home administrators, one of whom was a Methodist minister, and asked if I should do something about the situation. I was surprised at their response. They said, "Leave your father alone. He does a great job with your mother, and if he drinks a little scotch, that's okay. We'll let you know if it gets to be a problem." I followed their advice.

Soon after his ninetieth birthday, Dad fell in his room and injured his back. He was unable to walk for several weeks. When he became ambulatory again, he had to use a walker and was much more unsteady on his feet. One night I showed up after he'd had a few drinks, and he couldn't get out of his armchair.

Clearly it was time to do something about his alcohol consumption. I checked the closet where he kept his liquor, expecting to find one medium-sized bottle. Instead I discovered three gallons of scotch placed neatly in a corner behind his shoes. He was nothing if not well stocked. While Dad watched a football game on TV, I quietly removed the bottles and took them to a friend who was having a party that night. She was stunned by my 100 proof generosity.

The next day I asked the staff to help me find his supplier. They already knew the name of the culprit. He was a former resident who visited Dad regularly. I gave him a call and asked him not to bring any more liquor. He was embarrassed at being fingered and agreed to stop delivering the Dewar's. Dad never mentioned the missing booze, and neither did I. I told you that we Comers hate confrontation.

You Want Me to Do What?

One Sunday I joined my folks for lunch at the retirement home and had no sooner started on my roast beef than Dad announced that he wanted me to give him an enema after the meal. There went my appetite. I wanted to say, "You're kidding," but knew he wasn't. I didn't remember signing up for enema giving. My pathetic efforts gave new meaning to the term "unskilled nursing." Dad complained loudly during the procedure and was so disappointed by my lack of dexterity that he never requested such assistance again.

Several years later, when Dad was in the hospital, one of his nurses started to change his soiled underwear, and instinctively I moved to the hallway. She knew I was working on this book and said, "Jim, this is part of parenting your parents, too." Slowly I slinked back into the room.

Comer's Commandments

- If your parents' driving is a danger to themselves or others, ignoring the situation is not a good option. Find a way to take away the keys and get them an account with a local taxi company.

- In dealing with difficult issues such as substance abuse, saying nothing is interpreted as approval. Do not become a silent accomplice.

- If your parent would rather not wear a hearing aid and miss your sparkling conversation, that is a legitimate choice.

- Don't expect to solve every problem. Sometimes the best you can do is damage control.

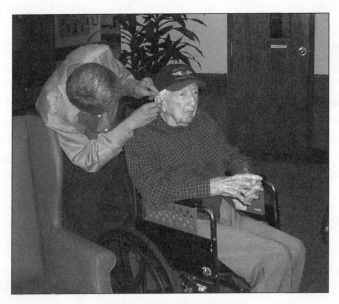

The ritual of the hearing aids

10

I'm Great in a Tornado, but Save Me from the Daily Grind

There is much to say for rising to the occasion. I know because I've risen. Crisis often brings out the best in us. I can deal with ambulances, hospital beds, and worried looks. I can talk to doctors in hushed tones and navigate my way around beeping monitors. It's not disasters that test me, but the deadening sameness of routine visits and predictable conversations. I'm sure every parent deals with this dilemma. There are decades of grunt work between the maternity ward and college graduation.

Giving birth has become a home-video event to treasure and play for unsuspecting guests. No one records the making of the three-thousand-and-third tuna sandwich. Parents make a big fuss over a son or daughter who lives far away and swoops in once or twice a year with presents and pronouncements. They may show little appreciation—or downright hostility—to a child who shows up two or three times a week, fifty-two weeks a year to bring groceries or take them to church. Until I moved back to Texas, I thought doing my family duty meant jetting in for the occasional weekend. For thirty years, my visits were more like personal appearances than real life. I was a hit-and-run son. Now I understand that genuine caring is not a week-long performance but an ongoing exercise.

Visiting your parents once or twice a year can be like a long-distance love affair. If you see each other only occasionally, your hours together tend to be heightened reality. You go to restaurants, see friends, and attempt to stay on your best behavior. Most of us can manage that for three to five days. Living in the same town, or the same house, is a different proposition altogether. There is no way to sustain illusion on a full-time basis. Authenticity will soon raise its ugly, all-too-real head and you'll discover each other on a non-holiday basis. You'll get to share bad moods as well as good ones, and go through Monday mornings as well as Saturday nights.

There is no way to escape conversational bogs and long silences. I'm a good listener and genuinely interested in a variety of subjects. I don't mind hearing a good story twice or, as with Dad's Air Force tales, for the eighty-seventh time. However, finding subjects to discuss with an Alzheimer's patient and a deaf man would be a challenge for Barbara Walters.

Mom no longer has a context for conversation. She does her best to make up for that deficit through charm, wit, and repartee. She can improvise with genius and is rarely at a loss for words. At the onset of her disease, when she realized something was wrong, she would say, "Your mother is really slipping." She knew that her mental agility was ebbing and felt self-conscious at its desertion. Eventually her embarrassment disappeared because she didn't remember that she forgot.

One day at the retirement home we walked back to her room after lunch. From her purse she pulled a jagged piece of metal and tried to insert it in the lock on her door. She was holding a Dentu-Cream tin. When I pointed out that it was not the key, Mom remained unruffled. She said, "I wonder where that rascal could be." She put the can back in her purse and soon came up with the key.

Although Mother's concern for others has not altered, her ability to follow through is gone. No one got more joy out of keeping up with friends and relations than she did. Her chest of drawers was stuffed with greeting cards, sometimes even mildly risqué ones. Hallmark stock suffered when Mother's card-sending days ended.

Even today when I tell her someone is sick or has a birthday coming up, she responds by saying, "I'll drop them a note this afternoon." And she would if the thought stayed with her. Mother remains especially sympathetic with the elderly. When I inform her that an acquaintance has moved to a nursing home, she always says, "Bless her heart. That poor thing."

Dad never excelled in note writing or sending birthday greetings. That was his wife's department. Other than Mom's Christmas and birthday presents, he rarely bought gifts and cared little for shopping. He had to change those habits in his mid-eighties. To my amazement, he made a rapid transition.

For the four years they lived in the retirement home, Dad and I did the family Christmas shopping together. One year he wanted to buy Mother a necklace from Wal-Mart's jewelry department. I was sure we could get better quality at a small store. After visiting three jewelers that did not have the necklace he wanted, we headed to the largest parking lot in town. Much to my surprise, Sam Walton's store had exactly what Dad had in mind, and the salesperson was kind and helpful. Once again, my best thinking proved incorrect. Dad emerged from the store in triumph, necklace in hand.

We had been gone for less than two hours, but had not gotten three feet inside the lobby when a resident told us that Mom was upset. She had been looking for Dad and could not find him. We walked another few feet and a second resident said the same thing. By the time we arrived at the elevator, three people let us know that Mother was terribly worried about her missing husband. When the door opened on the fourth floor, she was standing by the elevator door, only a few feet away, with a terror-stricken look on her face.

"Where have you been? I've been looking for you everywhere."

We told her we'd been buying her Christmas present, but that did not assuage her fears. For two hours she felt totally abandoned. Even though Dad told her he was going shopping and left her a note, that information had not been processed. In her mind he was not there and she didn't know where he was. Her lost look has stayed with me ever since. It gave me a new appreciation for the relentless pressure Dad faced daily. At ninety he was monitoring Mother and fending for himself. I do my best to remember that when he tells me for the seven hundredth time not to drive so close to the car in front of me.

When I see other adult children with their aging parents in stores, restaurants, or churches I feel a deep sense of kinship. We share a look of clenched patience. I understand their frustration as they struggle to stay calm and serene. I want to hug them as they help their parents into waiting rooms or steer them safely to the table at Chili's. It is not easy duty.

Dad and I had a midweek ritual of going to his bank. Until he hit ninety, he was actively involved in managing his own finances. Dealing with Union State Bank took much of his time because he insisted on doing all his business in person. In 1980, when I first suggested he get an ATM card, he looked at me as if I'd recommended dancing in the nude. He said, "Handling all that money in broad daylight is an invitation to every criminal within a hundred miles."

While he still preferred going to the bank in person, time had softened his attitude toward cash machines. He told me that he was willing to forgo the obvious danger of armed robbery so it "would be easier on you." I ordered a card from his bank and spent the next two years trying to teach him how to use it.

I wrote out the steps, and we went over them again and again. He understood the concept in theory, but had difficulty putting it into practice. When it came to mechanical devices, he had once been a man of great skill and patience, but that quality deserted him in the post-stroke world. His inability to follow a digital pathway was frustrating to a man who had fixed moving parts on a B-17 in the middle of air raids over Germany.

Our Sunday afternoon visits always concluded with the ATM conversation.

"Is there anything you need, Dad?"

"I think I could use a little money."

He would take out his billfold and count every dollar. No matter what the total, he always felt he could use a little more "just in case." He never said in case of what. I never asked.

We drove four blocks to the nearest bank and parked in the handicapped zone. I lifted Dad's walker from the back seat, opened the passenger door, helped him up, and put the walker in front of him. Slowly he negotiated the fifty feet to the teller machine.

"What's your number, Dad?"

He never hesitated in reeling it off. Dad knew his secret code better than I recall my checking account number, although that's faint praise indeed. I pushed the appropriate buttons, bells and whistles sounded, and money and receipt arrived. I handed the cash to Dad, who was looking over his shoulder for masked men. He folded the bills and slipped them into his wallet, and we headed back to my car. Each week, as we slowly made our way down the ramp, I gained new appreciation for the Americans with Disabilities Act.

Knowing I was opening a can of worms, I said, "Do you need anything from the store?"

"Not really."

He paused and I held my breath.

"Well, if you have the time . . ."

"I have the time."

I knew what was coming next.

"It might be a good idea to stop by Albertson's."

I prefer the outer rings of Hades to visiting a football-field-sized supermarket on a Sunday afternoon.

"What do you want?"

"Oh . . . several things."

His calculated lack of specificity meant he wanted to purchase the chocolate-flavored laxative his doctor had expressly forbidden but to which he had strong brand attachment.

"What about the laxative your doctor recommended? You have a whole bottle in your medicine cabinet."

"Doesn't do a thing for me."

It's hard to argue with firsthand experience. On this subject he was the expert. The opinion of a baby-faced doctor fifty-five years his junior meant little when compared to proven success.

Today I look back on those shopping trips as the good old days. My parents lived happily in adjacent rooms at the retirement home from September 1996 until December 24, 2000. They had almost four and a half good years there, a gift of time I appreciate more fully in retrospect.

On Christmas Eve, the day of our traditional family dinner, Mother fell in her room and broke her hip. Someone heard her scream and alerted the front desk. They called the ambulance and then me. I was told to get to the emergency room at once. As I headed toward Georgetown, I knew that this Christmas would not be merry.

Comer's Commandments

• If you live far from your folks, regularly show appreciation to the caregivers who live nearby.

• Give yourself credit where credit is due. Grocery shopping on a Sunday afternoon with an elderly parent places you on the short list for the Nobel Peace Prize.

• Realize that IQ, life experience, and mechanical ability do not guarantee that a parent will learn how to use an ATM.

• Remember that real heroes are those who do dull daily duties with humility and a smile.

Jim and Mother at the nursing home, 2003

11

Oh, God, Not a Nursing Home!

As Christmas 2000 approached, my biggest worry was the sorry state of my finances. Freelancing had hit a wall. Austin's high-tech economy was shifting into recession, and I had been living on the edge for six months. Fortunately I could not see past the edge. I did not realize how good my parents and I had it before Mom's fall. Her broken hip would alter our lives as drastically as Dad's stroke had five years earlier.

Christmas Eve was cold and gray. Georgetown Hospital had a skeleton crew holding down the fort, but one surgeon was on duty. He said he would operate on Mother at noon if I agreed, and I did so gratefully. When she went into the operating room, my father and I were left standing in the hospital hallway. There was nothing to do but proceed with the day. Our family dinner and gift exchange were scheduled for one o'clock.

Going from surgery to celebration was a drastic disconnect. The tree was lit, my younger cousins were hyper, and the smell of rolls and sweet potatoes filled the air. I had no appetite. At four o'clock we went back to the hospital to see how Mother was doing. The doctor told us she got through the operation just fine and would sleep until the next day. We returned to my cousins' house in time to open gifts. Mother's presents remained untouched under the tree.

The next morning, Christmas Day, Dad and I arrived at the hospital early. The effect of the anesthesia on Mother was dramatic. She was deeply disoriented and agitated. When she tried to get out of bed, she was hit with a terrible pain in her hip and let out a scream that reverberated throughout the fourth floor.

She didn't understand where she was or what had happened. Between Alzheimer's and postoperative confusion, she was completely lost. There were tubes running in every direction, monitors flashing, and strange faces staring at her. She flailed about, yelling for help. Mother didn't know how to use a call button, but she got the nurses' attention.

The staff asked permission to tie her down so she wouldn't pull out her catheter. I agreed reluctantly, though visions of Olivia de Havilland in *The Snake Pit* ran through my mind. (If you are younger than fifty and have never heard of Miss de Havilland, rent *Gone with the Wind* or ask an AARP member.)

Mother's understandable confusion upset my father, and he became visibly agitated. He wanted to do something to help when there was nothing we could do. He wouldn't leave the room, and demanded a chair so he could sit by her bed. He planted himself there, determined to stay for what Mom would call "the duration."

There is no place lonelier than a hospital at Christmas. The staff had decorated the nurses' stations and there were carols playing in the elevators, but it was still a hospital. When my relatives came to see Mother that morning, she was incoherent. After two hours of watching her struggle with the restraints, I was relieved when the nurse gave her a shot to calm her down.

I had been invited to a Christmas dinner in Austin and was eager to go. For a few hours I wanted to be around people not wearing white. I asked Dad if he wanted to go back to the retirement home, but he declined. He planned to stay at the hospital, even though Mom had fallen asleep.

I told him that I'd be back in the afternoon to give him a ride home. Then I drove to Austin and stopped at my apartment to change clothes. The moment I got inside the door, the phone rang and I made the mistake of answering it. It was the head nurse, and she was furious. She said they had walked into Mother's room and found Dad messing with her IV tubes. They wanted me there immediately to get him out of the hospital. He was no longer allowed to visit Mom without supervision.

I knew there must be some misunderstanding. I told her that Dad was deaf and probably couldn't hear her. The nurse said he was a danger to Mother and if I did not remove him within the hour she'd call security and have them do it. She slammed down the phone. I called my friends and told them I wouldn't be coming to lunch, and then headed back to Georgetown in a downpour.

When I got to the hospital and asked what happened, Dad said he didn't know what they were talking about. He hadn't tried to pull out any tubes. Like a parent trying to assess responsibility after a fight in the kids' room, with one child bleeding and another in tears, I had no way to reconstruct the scene. I told Dad that the nurses were upset and we had to leave for the day. I explained that from now on he would have to wear his hearing aids when he visited Mother. He greeted this news with a scowl and a grunt.

For once I understood why my father didn't want his hearing amplified electronically. The hospital offered an array of unpleasant noises: buzzers, beepers, loudspeakers, elevator chimes, and the chatter of staff and visitors. Even worse were the cries of those in pain, including my mother. For Dad silence might be a refuge, but it was no longer an option.

After taking him back to the retirement home, I headed to Austin for the second time in four hours. I drove slowly on the slick highway because I had no place to go. This was the most depressing Christmas of my life. What would I do for the rest of the day? Then I recalled that another group of friends was having a dinner for those who had no family in town. When I first heard about this gathering, I thought, "How sad to have nowhere to go on Christmas." Now I couldn't get there fast enough. I walked into their apartment feeling like a lost child and was welcomed with warmth and affection. After a few hours of good food and laughter, my spirits and perspective were restored.

When I returned to the hospital on December 26, the head nurse casually mentioned that Mother's upper dentures were missing. We looked for them. God knows we looked. We searched her room, alerted Lost and Found, and scoured the kitchen. The staff went through all of the dumpsters to no avail. Her uppers were gone. Most likely they had been placed on her dinner tray and scraped into the garbage, not an uncommon occurrence in hospitals.

If you have your own teeth, you may think this is no big deal. You'd be wrong. Half a set of false teeth is no teeth at all. Uppers and lowers don't work independently. Replacing them is a long and tedious ordeal, especially if you are eighty-eight and have been wearing the same set of dentures for decades. In seventy-two hours, Mother had lost the ability to walk and to chew.

Four days after her operation, deeply confused, minus teeth and still sporting several tubes, Mother was sent to the rehab center. I didn't think she was ready to move, but the staff was eager for our family unit to depart. Fortunately rehab was only fifty yards away, on a new wing of the same floor. Compared to the rest of the hospital, the rehab center was luxurious. There were antiques in the lobby, shined wood floors, tasteful paintings, soft lights, and a large staff. Everything looked good except the patients.

For someone sixty-five or older, Medicare will pay for up to five weeks of rehabilitation. However, the patient must meet stringent federal guidelines. To be reimbursed by the government, the facility must document patient progress daily—and they document with a vengeance. Because of her Alzheimer's, Mother was not a good candidate for rehab. They told me up front that her chances of staying were iffy at best. In reality, it wasn't even a close call. She lasted six days, banished before the end of her first week. There would be no second chance.

The staff informed me she'd have to move across the street to the nursing home, the same facility where Dad's mother had spent her last six years. They gave us twenty-four hours to make arrangements. When I heard the words "nursing home," I realized Mother had received a life sentence from which there would be no parole.

Comer's Commandments

- Never say, "Things can't get any worse." They can. Your mother can break a hip on Christmas Eve.

- If a parent is in the hospital, guard those dentures with your life. Teeth matter.

- Don't confuse hospitals with "safe places." Medical centers are busy, crowded, noisy buildings where things can go wrong in a heartbeat. Question everything.

- Remember that hospitals are full of dangerous drugs, needles, and large knives. Don't let any of them be used on your parent by mistake.

12

Get Over It!

I'd been to nursing homes scores of times in the previous thirty years. During the Christmas holidays of 1979 I sang at seven facilities in three towns. While these mini-concerts were not officially sanctioned, our aging friends and relatives seemed to enjoy them. It never occurred to me then that most visitors don't belt out show tunes. I sang because it beat trying to make conversation. I never questioned my role as a performing seal on the bedpan circuit.

Based on occasional visits, I thought I knew what nursing homes were all about. Having my own mother in one altered my perspective rapidly. The hardest part about parenting your parents is that the story line keeps changing. As soon as we learn our lines, we have to improvise new ones. Duties expand and new skills are required. I had mastered folding a walker in seven seconds. Now there was a fifty-pound wheelchair to tackle.

There are few private rooms at the Wesleyan, so I assumed Mother would have a roommate. I did not realize that she would have three of them. With only a day's notice, we took what we could get. There was one bed available in the entire facility, and I signed up Mother for it gratefully. Well, maybe not gratefully, but I signed.

Her bed was by a window with a view of the hospital she'd just left and a school playground. It was a big sunlit room, only a few seconds' walk from the nurses' station. Mother had a bed, a chest of drawers, a small closet, and a privacy curtain. Her world had grown much smaller, but she didn't seem to notice.

That first day, there was far too much for me to process. A retirement home is like a library: dignified, genteel, and quiet. A nursing home is an elementary school cafeteria: full of noise, powerful smells, and controlled chaos. The halls at the retirement home were newly carpeted. The nursing home had linoleum floors and lots of wheelchair traffic.

From before six in the morning until well after six at night, there was a constant hum of activity. Irritating buzzers signaled overworked nurses, alarms sounded, announcements blared over the intercom, and there was a constant parade of aides, housekeepers, and visitors. Even more disturbing were the plaintive sounds of residents calling for help, talking to themselves, trying to make sense of their situation.

The woman in the bed next to Mother's had been in a coma for a year, staring at the ceiling unblinking and inert. Across the room, a tiny lady caressed a doll. Another resident wailed at the wall. In the dining room, I saw dribblers and droolers. Many residents were not only feeble, but terribly ill. Some were living in another world. Mother was too tired to notice.

I was horrified, depressed, and in shock. I couldn't believe she was going to live here for the rest of her life *and I was going to have to visit her*. I'd like to say that I handled this transition with style and grace, but I don't want to lie in print. No one was more surprised by my reaction than I was. I thought I had the caregiving routine down pat. I had done a video for the retirement home and spoken about our family's experience to a number of civic groups and churches. I thought I was ready for whatever happened next. I was not.

People in retirement homes may have health problems, but they can care for themselves and walk to meals. They "ambulate" even if they need a walker to do so. In a good retirement home there is no sense of impending doom. Residents are as fully engaged in life as they want to be.

In a nursing home, physical handicaps, chronic conditions, and dementia are the norm. Except for the relatively few undergoing intense rehabilitation, most nursing home residents never go home. This is the last stop on the line. Resignation hovers like a layer of smog over Southern California. Angels wait in the wings. At least that's how it seemed to me on that first day.

Over the next few weeks Mother adjusted beautifully, and Dad continued to live in the retirement home and visit her daily. I, on the other hand, experienced a regression and was catapulted back to the time Dad suffered his stroke. Had I learned nothing in the previous five years? Every time I walked through the door, my spirits sank. It was all I could do to plaster a fake smile on my face.

Here's the good news: I got over it. It took several months, many visits, and letting go of stereotypes, but gradually I learned to accept and appreciate the realities of nursing home life. Week by week, as I got to know the staff and the residents, and their families, they became more human and so did I. Once I jettisoned fear and judgments, the environment became less disturbing and the residents less intimidating. Despite my initial fears, I soon became a part of the community.

I had a conversation with one of Mother's roommates and discovered that she had been head nurse at an army hospital in World War II. I'd seen her only as helpless, not the helper she had once been. Slowly, as I grew past my own limitations, I viewed A-Wing not as a scene of institutionalized suffering but as Mother's new home.

When she first arrived from the hospital, our biggest concern was Mother's weight loss. She had dropped ten pounds in the hospital and looked terrible. Her lack of appetite and pallor convinced me she was dying. I told the staff how worried I was and they responded by creating a personal nutritional plan. They put Mother on dietary supplements and had an aide sit with her at each meal to make sure she ate.

Within a few days she began gaining weight, and in two weeks she was out of danger. Her condition stabilized, and within three months she was back at her normal weight. After three years at the nursing home, she'd gained ten pounds.

There was still the question of what to do about replacing Mother's dentures. I couldn't wait for her to have teeth again. She never mentioned the subject. I called a local dentist who sounded eager to help and was willing to come to the nursing home. When he walked into Mother's room I thought he was a high school student. I didn't know you could be a dentist before you got your driver's license.

He said he was there to make an impression and he made a quick one on me when he called Mother "Honey," which she liked and I didn't. After the exam he told me it would take six weeks and two more visits to make the $2,000 dentures. Even then, he could not guarantee that Mother would be able to wear them due to her advanced age and bone loss. He warned me that getting used to new dentures might be too painful for her. I responded, "Let's get started."

Even before her impressions could be sent to the lab, Mother's lower dentures disappeared. I was furious, but I didn't know where to aim my anger. She probably took them out herself, but I wanted to blame it on the nursing home. This new loss meant we would have to start the process all over again. I was upset but not defeated. My mother was going to have teeth.

A few days later, the dentist called me at home and said he thought it was a mistake to replace the dentures. He believed the adjustment to new ones would be too difficult and doubted Mother would be able to wear them. He told me that he hated to see us waste our money. Since the check would have gone to him, I was impressed by his honesty.

The nurses and administrators agreed. Even if Mother got used to new dentures, they thought her Alzheimer's would make it impossible for her and the staff to keep track of them. They showed me a drawer filled with false teeth found on floors, in the laundry, and even in potted plants. There was no way to identify their owners, so the dentures remained locked away, a yellowing city of teeth.

It was a hard call. The missing teeth altered her appearance dramatically and made me uncomfortable. I had to ask myself who was I doing this for, Mother or me? Me, of course! Mother didn't know her teeth were gone; she never once mentioned them. Reluctantly, I followed the dentist's advice and sentenced Mother to a blenderized life of liquid meat and gooey vegetables.

As a result of residual guilt, I bring her more ice cream than is recommended by the American Dental Association. Dairy Queen is an equal-opportunity, no-teeth-required delicacy. Mother loves Dad, me, and ice cream without reservation, but not particularly in that order. When I show up with a sundae, she doesn't care about the flavor, brand, or if there's a cherry on top. Her reaction is always the same:

"Jim, you shouldn't have given me so much."

Then she eats all of it, no matter the amount. The staff never questions her consumption. They are glad there is something non-chewable that gives her such profound pleasure. So am I.

Comer's Commandments

- If your parent moves to a nursing home, don't expect to adjust overnight. It will take time for each of you to get comfortable.

- Focus your concern on the quality of the food, the attitude of the staff, and the cleanliness of the home.

- Don't confuse your priorities with those of your parents. Before complaining about anything, ask yourself if it's really important. Safety matters. Consistent kindness trumps almost everything else.

- Try to see nursing home residents not only as they are now, but as they were in their prime.

- Become part of the solution. Speak to residents who look lonely. Smile at everyone. Make jokes with the staff members because they need a laugh.

- When you see family members of a new resident, go out of your way to introduce yourself, welcome them, and let them know that you like the facility. If you don't like it, your parent ought not to be there.

13

Life Behind the Polyester Curtain

In the first sentence of *The Road Less Traveled*, Scott Peck states, "Life is difficult." Caring for the elderly makes it even more so. As those we love age, it's painful to deal with the slow, silent accumulation of surrenders. There are so many things to let go of along the way: houses, cars, home-cooked meals, and shared anecdotes no longer remembered.

I miss letters from Mother written in her elegant 1920s penmanship. I long for those articles she sent me from *Reader's Digest*. I would give anything to find a loaf of her banana bread in my mailbox. I remember the mom who took twelve third-graders on a streetcar to a Saturday matinee in New Orleans when I turned eight. I still feel eight some days.

There are many times when I long to turn back the clock. I no longer get to argue politics with Dad or hear him bemoan another Dallas coaching error on Sunday afternoons. I'd give anything to talk to him once more at a normal decibel level. I am exhausted at screaming my way through our conversations. I hate it that Mother and Dad can no longer remember my birthday, and am guilt-stricken for feeling that way.

At Christmas I buy, wrap, and distribute everyone's presents—including my own. I'll admit that it takes the surprise out of opening gifts; however, there is a positive side. One year Dad asked me what kind of shirt I wanted, and I told him I wanted "a cell phone." For once his lack of hearing was a plus. Dad said, "Fine," and I joined wireless America. Of course, I would gladly trade that Sprint phone for a J.C. Penney shirt he picked out himself.

My friend Tommy Callan likes to say, "It's better to be looked over than overlooked." That is especially true of aging parents. They welcome whatever attention we give them. I know my dad appreciates my visits because I can read his feelings in his smile. Mother never fails to say, "Come see us again. I love you . . . don't drive too fast!"

I have learned that the quality of a visit has little to do with its length. In my rookie year of parenting I thought I had to stay at the retirement home a certain length of time to get credit with the good son angel. That was my expectation, not that of my parents. Mother no longer has a standard concept of time. She doesn't know how long I stay or when I've seen her last. For her there is no yesterday or tomorrow, no workdays or holidays. Every day might be Christmas.

On the other hand, while Dad is eager for me to come, he doesn't want me to stay too long. Though happy to see me, he has his own agenda and I'm not always the most important item on the list. After I've been there half an hour, he may look at his watch and say, "Do we have anything else we need to take care of?" Translated, that means "It's time for you to get back to making money." If I don't make a move to leave, he'll ask what I'm doing the rest of the day. If I tell him I have an appointment in Austin, he'll furrow his brow and announce that I'm going to be late.

"Hadn't you better get going, Jim? You don't want to keep those people waiting."

I know an exit line when I hear one.

Mother does not know where she is living, though she is generally happy to be there. She can't recall the day, month, or year, but she enjoys amazingly acute social skills. She never passes anyone without speaking, smiling, or nodding. When people greet her, she responds with genuine warmth and enthusiasm—unless they are trying to give her a shower or make her swallow foul-tasting medicine.

She does not know the name of the president, but she recognizes really important people like me. She grins when she sees my dad and calls out, "How you doing, Pappy?" For the hundreds who do not register on her shrinking database, she has a quick, toothless smile, snappy greeting, and a verbal retort for all seasons. Mother makes everyone feel that she's delighted to see them. Given the choice, I'll take a good disposition over a good memory any day.

I admire her effortless charm. When I bring friends to visit her, she flashes a big smile, gives them a hug, and says how happy she is to meet them. She may add, "How do you know this varmint?" That would be me. She listens with what appears to be great interest. Thirty seconds later she may ask the same question and listen just as intently the second time around. Somewhere between the onset of Alzheimer's and her arrival at the nursing home, she learned to improvise with style. If she had not chosen to teach third grade in 1932, Mother might have been an actress of Meryl Streep's caliber.

Even more than sweets, Mother loves babies. One Sunday afternoon we were sitting in the lobby as a young couple showed their new daughter to her great-grandmother. When Mom saw the infant, she exclaimed, "Look at that precious thing! Have you ever seen a cuter little boy?" She wheeled over uninvited to join the family circle. I raced after her, trying to restrain her enthusiasm. The handsome parents took in the situation and graciously allowed Mother to hold the baby.

"What is your name, young man?" Mother said to the infant.

"Jill," said the mother.

I piped in, "It's a girl, Mom."

"He looks like a boy to me."

I gently returned the baby to her parents. For the next fifteen minutes Mother rediscovered that child six times and enjoyed an identical response with each sighting. Again and again, I had to hold on to her wheelchair to keep her from breaking into the family gathering. In desperation, I wheeled Mom to the garden so they could visit uninterrupted.

Mother has a hidden reservoir of strength that she can summon in the midnight hours. Although she never walks unassisted during the day, several times she has awakened at two in the morning with an urgent need to go to the bathroom. Because she doesn't remember there is a call button by her bed, she doesn't ring for assistance. If she is unable to get anyone's attention, she has been known to take matters into her own hands.

Although she wears a monitor to alert the staff if she tries to get out of bed, Mother has learned to disengage the device. On more than one occasion, she has scooted to the end of her bed and edged her way down to the floor. Without a walker or any assistance, she has ambled across a large room and walked forty feet to the nurses' station. With a smile, she informed the night nurse that she needed to use the bathroom.

One winter's night, Mother felt cold, got out of bed, and crawled in with one of her roommates. The alarm sounded, but when the staff came, they could not find her anywhere. The doors leading outside were secure. She wasn't in the halls or the public rooms. Finally, after frantic minutes of searching, they discovered her happily sharing a neighbor's bed. When she was asked to get back in her own bed, Mother was indignant.

"I'm sleeping with my husband. Leave me alone."

When a child learns how to get out of his crib, the world becomes a more interesting and dangerous place. Mother had proved her ingenuity and athletic ability. The question was what to do about it? The last thing anyone wanted was another fall. That left us with several mutually exclusive options. A nurse could strap her down to the bed each night. That would keep her from climbing out but would make sleeping more difficult. Besides, Mother hated being tied down. Another choice was to put a higher gate on her bed. That sounded like a simple solution, but it had a down side. If Mother was determined to get out, a taller gate might not hold her back. If she climbed over an even higher barrier, there could be a longer, more dangerous fall.

The other choice was to leave things as they were. We opted for the status quo. So far, it's been the right choice. It's been more than two years since her last midnight ramble. Of course, that's no certainty she won't do it again. As with many caregiving decisions, there are no guaranteed solutions, only choices.

Mother is a favorite of the staff because she always has something to say. Her responses are unpredictable, saucy, and frequently funny. When she gets a laugh, and she gets many, Mother lights up. She may not realize why she has the staff in stitches, but that's beside the point. When she elicits a response and connects with people, she is delighted.

Since she's been at the nursing home, at least forty staff members have told me how much they love "Mrs. Comer." She couldn't tell you their names, but basks in their attention. They give her unsolicited hugs that warm her heart and mine. I have a dear friend whose father lived in a nursing home in Oklahoma. When she came to visit him, she often saw a lipstick mark on his forehead, which meant he'd received a kiss from his favorite nurse. That kind of care can't be marketed because it comes from the heart.

I remember showing up one weeknight around eight-thirty. The residents of A-Wing were asleep, except for Mother. She was in the dining room entertaining three nurses' aides. She had them laughing out loud. As I gave her a hug, she was beaming with the joy of being appreciated. I sat down to join in the fun. Then I noticed that Mother was wearing some zebra-striped house slippers.

I said, "Whose shoes are those?"

"If you don't like 'em, look the other way."

"Mother, it's not that I don't like them; it's just that I've never seen them before."

"You haven't seen everything."

She had no idea whose shoes she was wearing or where they came from. One of the aides intervened.

"We let her wear those because her shoes were . . . well, to be honest, they didn't smell so good."

"You're kidding!"

"Yeah, they stunk pretty bad."

"Stunk? I'll get her some new ones tomorrow."

I appreciated the no-holds-barred feedback. Administrators are unlikely to send you a letter saying that your mother's shoes stink. A good nurses' aide will let you know in a New York minute.

I also get information through more traditional channels. There are regular Care Team meetings for each of my parents, and I go to most of them. The team includes the medical director, the head nurse on the wing, a social worker, the activities director, and a dietary director.

The staff gives an update on my parents' medical conditions, current medications, and any new problems or unusual events. I have a chance to ask questions, express concerns, or make suggestions. The most important information often comes not from the charts but in candid conversation. Staff members were the ones who pointed out that I should not leave Mother's jewelry, pearls, watches, or other valuables at the nursing home. Anything small and valuable is likely to disappear. That doesn't mean most staff members are dishonest, just that many are underpaid and subject to temptation. At even the best homes, the turnover rate is high and a disgruntled employee may soon be gone, along with a diamond ring.

Lois Brown-Mosley, head nurse on A-Wing, told me, "Your mother is almost always pleasant and friendly except when we try to give her a shower. She has a strong sense of privacy. Bathing her is a tricky proposition. A lot depends on who is giving her the shower and it better be someone she likes, preferably female. Otherwise they could get hit."

"Mother hits people?"

"Absolutely. She has whacked me a couple of times."

Vanessa Grall, the affable social worker, jumped to Mother's defense. "Of course, if she didn't have Alzheimer's she'd handle it differently, but she is confused so sometimes she socks people."

Lois has an office not far from Mother's door. "Your mother is very social. She almost never stays in her room. She wheels herself all over the place and she is fast. One day we heard an alarm go off and somehow she had gotten out the back door and rolled down the sidewalk."

"Sometimes your father comes over to see how she's doing. I wave at him and say, 'Mr. Comer, everything's okay. I'm going to take care of Anne for you.' Sometimes he tries to get her to come eat with him and pushes her wheelchair, which aggravates her. One time after he'd gone, she said, 'He thinks he's all that!' I couldn't believe that expression came from your mother."

"What does it mean?"

"It means he thinks he's cool."

"I can't believe my mother is using hip phrases I've never even heard."

"That's because she spends a lot of time with nurses' aides who are in their early twenties. It's a good thing that your parents live on different wings. Otherwise they would drive each other nuts. Your father would be trying to control her and she'd resent it. Besides, they don't have the same hours. He goes to bed soon after seven and she's a night owl."

The Care Team meetings are an easy way to connect with the staff and stay up-to-date on your parent's appetite, medications, temperament, and other issues. Because of what I've learned at these meetings, we have tried new medications, ended other prescriptions, and reached decisions about walkers and exercise. Attending Care Team meetings allows me to be an integral part of the process, not an outside observer.

From the aides, I learned about Mother's floral preferences. Despite the six growing plants on tables near her bed, her favorites are the plastic flowers at the nurses' station. She thinks they come from her mother's yard in Smithville. I do my best to share her enthusiasm; once I asked her why she didn't keep them in her own room.

"Because I like to share and so should you."

Mother believes it's never too late to be instructive.

From my apartment in Austin, it's a seventy-mile round-trip to the nursing home. From four to seven on weekday afternoons, Austin traffic rivals that of Southern California. There are times when I am stuck on I-35, squeezed between a pick-up truck and an eighteen-wheeler, diesel fumes darkening the air. To my right is a billboard for a topless gentleman's club. To my left sprouts a forest of towering fast-food signs. I surrender to feeling sorry for myself. Stuck in self-pity, I ask, "Why me, God?" The answer is always the same: "Why not?"

When I get to the nursing home, I sometimes grab a quick nap on Mom's bed. She is rarely in her room unless sleeping, so I can plop down for fifteen minutes. The first time I tried this, I was afraid they might admit me. An aide came in during one of my siestas and threatened to give me a shower. I told her to go right ahead as I was sure I could use one. That shut her up.

I never knew what would confront me when I entered the nursing home. Three buzzers would go off simultaneously and jangle my nerves. A resident gave me a dirty look. Another started clapping as I walked into the dining room. There were tears at one table, screams at another, and high-pitched laughter at a third. Dad complained about dinner being served late. Mom was wearing a garish frock that did not belong to her.

"Mother, I've never seen that dress before."

"Do you like it?"

"It's colorful."

"Good, I think I'll keep it."

After she'd eaten, I wheeled Mom to B-Wing, where Dad, by then a resident as well, waved a greeting from thirty yards away. Trying not to envy his eyesight, I found a comfortable chair and put one wheelchair on either side of me, within yelling distance of Dad. Once, I turned to talk to a nurse and when I looked back, my father was gone. I said to Mother, "Where's Dad?" Without batting an eye she said, "He's trying to make his escape."

I can relate to that. There are some days when I want to disappear and leave all responsibility behind. I acknowledge those moments and pray they will pass. They always do.

Comer's Commandments

• If you want to know what's going on with your parents, show up for Care Team meetings. If you can't be there in person, set up a conference call.

• If the facility doesn't have regular conferences between staff and family, tell them you want monthly meetings.

• Don't obsess about your parent's lack of recall. A good disposition beats a good memory any day.

• When stuck in self-pity, remember that the feeling is temporary, like everything else.

Vanessa Grall and Lois Brown-Mosely with Mother

14

Make Friends with the Staff

Those who spend the most time with your parents are not doctors and nurses, but a diverse group of overworked caregivers. It's important to get to know them as friends and allies. Although their jobs are physically and emotionally exhausting, if you have chosen a good facility, the staff members genuinely care about your parents.

The Wesleyan is more than forty years old and showing its age. The roof has been known to leak on occasion. It has won no interior design awards. What matters to me, however, is the commitment of the staff and the quality of care they provide. Everything else is window dressing. Expensive wallpaper, plush carpet, and flowing fountains are marketing tools. Rugs can be replaced and roofs repaired. A caring staff is a gift from God.

Administrators set the tone, make the rules—and bend them on occasion. However, they do not spend much time with residents on a day-to-day basis. Nurses are responsible for overseeing care and delivering medication. Nurses' aides, dining room staff, housekeepers, and laundry aides do almost everything else. They feed, dress, and shower the residents; get them up in the morning and to bed at night; and take them to the bathroom and change their diapers. Equally important are their emotional connections. For many residents the staff members are family. I've witnessed hundreds of hugs and smiles, and countless kindnesses that do not come from an employee rulebook.

On top of all the work they do, staff members are an invaluable source of information. They combine the best qualities of the FBI, an Internet chat room, and *The National Enquirer*. If you want to know what's going on, ask them. They provide up-to-the-minute information that won't be found on your parents' charts. Whenever I come to visit, I ask someone at the nurses' station how my folks are doing.

Recently one of the nurses asked Mother, "Mrs. Comer, how long have you been married?"

"Too long."

While Mother can't remember her wedding date, she knows how to deflect questions that test her lapsed memory. Her recall may be in retirement, but her wit is going strong. She doesn't care much for birthdays but she likes the candles, cards, and cake that accompany them. Recently we talked about her impressive longevity.

"Mother, do you know that your birthday is coming up?"

"It is?"

"Do you remember the date?"

"Not offhand."

"Come on, what is your birthday?"

"If you're so smart, you tell me."

"September 15, 1912. You're going to be ninety-four years old."

"I most certainly am not! Why are you trying to make your mama so old?"

Mother in 1915

"I'm only telling the truth."

"Your version of the truth."

"Okay, let's do a little subtraction. 1912 from 2006 equals . . ."

"Have it your way. I'll be as old as you want me to be."

I've come to understand the truth of the saying, "It's easier to ask for forgiveness than permission." There is a good beauty salon at the nursing home only one minute from Mother's room by wheelchair. Soon after she moved into the home, I asked the beautician to do her hair every two weeks. Over the next month I noticed Mom's hair getting longer and wilder. I went to the beauty shop and asked why she hadn't worked on Mother. She said, "Every time I go to get her, Mrs. Comer says that her hair is just fine. She never wants to come, and I can't force her."

"I give you blanket permission to do her hair every two weeks."

"But we aren't supposed to take them if they don't want to come."

"Think of President Clinton and gays in the military: don't ask, don't tell. Just do her hair. When you come to get Mother, give her a big smile and say, 'How are you today?' She'll say, 'Mighty fine. How about you?' Ask no questions. Just wheel her down to the salon while you are chatting and she'll be in your chair in no time."

There is a time for asking and a time for doing. Mother will never want a shower or a shampoo, but she must have them. My goal is to help her get what she needs with as little hullabaloo as possible.

❦

Nurses' aides never fail to fill me in on the realities of my parents' lives.

"What's Mama been up to today?"

"She watered the plastic plants again."

❦

"You know how many cups of ice cream Mr. Comer ate today?"

"Three?"

"Thirteen! He got a cup from everyone on the first shift, and then started all over again. He set the all-time record!"

❦

"Your mama won't take her heart medicine. She spit it out three times today. So I put it in some chocolate pudding and she ate the whole dish and asked for seconds."

❦

"Umm, your daddy got into it today!"

"Got into what?"

"He had a fistfight with a one-legged man in the front hallway. They were bouncing their wheelchairs off each other and yelling ugly words."

"What happened?"

"Who knows? We wheeled 'em off in different directions."

The staff not only shares good news and gossip, but calls me when Mom has a bruise or Dad tries to get from his wheelchair to the toilet and ends up on the floor. What I appreciate most is the knowledge that they enjoy my parents and have fun with them. They joke with Mother and give Dad an audience for his war stories. They appreciate the fullness of my parents' past, not just the fragility of their present.

While the overwhelming majority of staff members are caring, it is important that administrators remain alert for those who are not. Six months after Mother moved to the nursing home, I got a call from the administrator. I could tell by his tone of voice that he was upset. He had learned that a nurses' aide was seen pushing my mother and speaking roughly to her. Although Mother was not hurt, another staff member was concerned enough to report what had happened. The A-Wing supervisor confronted the aide, who denied the accusation. But the aide had a well-known habit of talking crudely to her own family on the phone. After weighing the facts, the administrator believed that the report was likely true and fired the aide.

I was glad to know that a staff member had reported the incident and that I had been informed promptly. That level of honest communication would not have happened at every nursing home. The administrator's handling of the matter did not shake my faith in the facility; instead, his candor and concern substantiated it.

Comer's Commandments

- Your parents' caregivers can be your best allies. Let them know regularly how much you appreciate what they do.

- If you don't think your parents are getting the care they need, don't complain to friends and siblings. Tell the director of nursing or administrator. Gripe where it will do some good.

- A caring nurses' aide who works with your parents every day may be more important to their well-being than all the administrators combined.

15

A Force of Nature Called Dad

On July 4, 2001, six and a half months after Mother's fall, Dad slipped in his bathroom and broke a hip. It was like seeing a rerun of a bad movie. He was taken for surgery to the same hospital where Mother had gone, stayed on the same floor, and was transferred to the same rehab unit. He managed to stay in rehab for two weeks before the staff decided he wasn't making sufficient progress to satisfy Medicare's watchdogs. Like Mother, he was sent across the street to the nursing home.

Even though he was ninety-one, Dad considered himself to be a temporary resident at the nursing home. For three months we paid rent on his room at the retirement home, hoping that he would be able to move back. I knew his chances of returning were slim, but Dad had faced longer odds and beaten them.

The nursing home therapists worked with him every day and he plunged into the routine with enthusiasm. They did their best to help him regain his strength and balance. To become self-sufficient, he

Dad at five years old

had to master walking, dressing, and self-care. When I asked how he was doing, his response was always upbeat. He'd say, "I'm making excellent progress." I did not hear the same report from the staff. He could walk one lap around B-Wing if an aide accompanied him, but he made little headway in dressing himself. He was unable to put on his pants or shoes unassisted, and needed help getting on or off the toilet.

After six weeks, his therapists told me that he was no longer making progress and would need to stay at the nursing home. His mind and spirit were willing, but his body was not cooperating. Dad took this news hard and so did I. Once he realized he was a nursing home lifer, he became understandably depressed.

Dad stopped reading books or newspapers because he said the print was too small. I took him to the ophthalmologist and got a new prescription for reading glasses, but he no longer showed interest in the World War II histories I brought him. I got him large-print versions, but to no avail. He said, "I'll read them next week when I'm not so busy."

He no longer watched television because, even at an ear-splitting volume, he could not hear what was being said. When I asked how the Cowboys were doing in pre-season play, he shrugged his shoulders. When Dad lost interest in football, I knew we were in big trouble.

I brought up his attitude at the Care Team meeting and they agreed he was deeply depressed. After living fully for so long, he faced a major adjustment in adapting to life in a wheelchair and the constricted routine of a nursing home. The doctor recommended Prozac and I said, "Bring it on." Antidepressants may not be a panacea, but they worked wonders for Dad. What Viagra did for Bob Dole's sex life, Prozac did for my father's depression. Within a month he began to be his old self and accept life as it was.

Dad had been so focused on walking that, for once, he had not worried about Mother. He knew she was nearby and saw her regularly, but felt no need to manage her life. She was happily settled in A-Wing when Dad arrived, and I did not think it a good idea to move her. He was in B-Wing, one minute away.

Mother took her meals in a small dining room near the A-Wing nurses' station where she could be observed easily by the staff. Dad ate in the main dining room, where the healthier residents took their meals. When I discovered that Mr. and Mrs. Davis, the lively couple who had once shared their table at the retirement home, were now living in B-Wing, I was overjoyed. I thought it would be wonderful for the four of them to be reunited and take their meals together again. In my great wisdom, I suggested that the staff arrange this. I did more than suggest; I pushed. Making a table change is not an easy task, but the social workers bent over backward to go along with my request.

The big day arrived and they wheeled in Mother from A-Wing, pried Dad from his table, and moved Mr. and Mrs. Davis from theirs. All four of them took one look at each other and loudly demanded a return to their regular tables. Mother missed her usual companions. My father abhorred change of any kind, especially one in which he had no say. The Davises said that they had never seen my parents before in their entire lives. No one ate a bite of lunch or spoke to each other. My social engineering was an unmitigated disaster. Why? For one thing, I had failed to consult with the principals. My best-laid plans were in tatters. By the next meal, everyone was back at their former tables. Once again, I realized I don't always know what's best for my parents.

Unfortunately, I wasn't finished making life difficult for the staff. On her eighty-ninth birthday, I had a party for Mother and wheeled Dad to A-Wing to join the festivities. It never occurred to me that I was opening Pandora's box. Dad quickly memorized the route to her room. The next day he wheeled himself to A-Wing and asked the head nurse about his wife's "condition." He wanted to know why he and Mother weren't living together in his room, and demanded that she return with him to B-Wing.

Mom was enjoying her independence and did not want to move. Dad wouldn't take "No" for an answer and began dragging her wheelchair down the hall while seated in his own. It was a scene worthy of reality TV. I got the first of several calls from staff members begging me to "do something about your dad." His behavior was driving them and Mother crazy. I agreed to drive to Georgetown and talk to him, though I had no idea what I would say. That's when six years of on-the-job training paid off.

The best way to approach my father is to use all the senses. Since I'm never sure what he hears, it's wise to employ both verbal and written communication. I wrote him a one-page letter printed in an extra-large font. I hoped that if I explained the rules of the nursing home, he would no longer feel responsible for Mother's care. For four years at the retirement home, it was his job to keep her from wandering. He needed to know that he was now officially off the hook. I wrote out the "rules" and brought a copy to Dad. We found a low-traffic spot in the hall, put in his hearing aids, and got out his glasses. I had him hold the letter as I read it to him loudly and slowly.

Dad,

I have talked with the administrator and gone over all the rules for the nursing home:

The administrator and nurses have assured me that Mother is absolutely safe to go anywhere she wants in her wheelchair. All the doors have alarms, and she can't get outside without someone knowing about it immediately. There is no reason for you to have to watch her or to stop her from going anywhere. Besides, it makes her happy to move around.

Don't try to bring her back to your part of the building unless she wants to because it upsets her.

The reason why Mother is in one part of the building and you are in another is because she gets special care where she is living. The nurses on A-Wing know how to handle her and like her very much.

The nurses would appreciate it if you would not come to visit Mother during dinner as they are very busy at that time.

Dad asked me to read it again. I did so and then had him read the letter to me. When we'd gone through it three times, he said, "Are you sure about this?"

I said that I was. That was almost good enough, but not quite. Dad handed me the letter and said, "I want this signed by the commandant."

I found the nursing home administrator and explained the situation. I brought him to my father, he signed the form with a flourish, and we made a copy for Dad's file. My father keeps the original in his nightstand. This letter eased my father's mind about his responsibilities and he never tried to drag Mother back to his room again.

Most parents cling to their independence as if to a life raft. My father no longer drives his Buick, but he still controls the speed of his wheelchair. If I go too fast he responds by dragging his feet, literally. The harder I push, the more he digs in his heels. Some days I feel stuck in a time warp: I am sixteen and Dad is teaching me to drive. Then I remember that I'm sixty and steering his wheelchair. Either way, I'm doing it wrong.

"Don't go so fast, Jim. You're going to hit someone. There's a lot of traffic at this corner." He is speaking of the notorious intersection of A-Wing and B-Wing.

Because of Dad's aversion to hearing aids, if I want to communicate with him, I have to yell. When we're on the street or in a restaurant, passersby wonder why I'm screaming at a helpless, wheelchair-bound old man. Their self-righteous stares used to bother me. Now I just keep bellowing.

When I'm with him, Dad wants me in his line of sight at all times. If I'm not visible for ten seconds, he hollers, "Where's Jim?" This is problematic when I visit the men's room. If I don't return quickly enough to suit him, Dad wheels into the john to make sure I haven't left. Despite everything, I prefer his prickly independence to docile resignation. Dad's feistiness and determination help to keep him alive and kicking, even if an occasional kick is aimed at me.

Since my father entered the nursing home, I've developed a routine for our visits:

1. Make a decision about using the hearing aids.
2. Ask the nurse on duty how he's been doing in the last few days.
3. Clean his electric razor.
4. Check the closet to make sure he has clean clothes.
5. See that he has at least $20 in the envelope kept by the receptionist.
6. Get him together with Mom.
7. Ask if he needs any toiletries.
8. Find his glasses and clean them.
9. Wheel him outside in the garden if the weather is good.
10. Tell Dad when I'll see them next.

During each visit, I check out their clothes. One time I opened Dad's closet to find it almost empty. That prompted my first visit to the laundry room. I introduced myself to the aides and asked about the missing garments. They did an immediate search and found two shirts in the wrong receptacles. Later they discovered several others that had found their way to another wing. More importantly, the aides knew my face and realized that I was keeping track of things. We didn't lose as many clothes after that.

I paid little attention to socks until the wife of his roommate, a kind and patient woman, told me that Dad was low on them. That was a genteel Southern understatement. He had one sock in his drawer. Not one pair: one sock. Grateful for her update, I bought five new pairs. Then I went through all his clothes and wrote his name on them with a magic marker. That does not guarantee pants and blouses won't get lost or delivered to another wing, but it improves the odds of a safe round-trip from the laundry room.

One subject of regular discussion is Dad's electric razor. He shaves every day, but no longer remembers to clean the razor. As a result, the shaver gets clogged and every two weeks he announces that he needs to buy a new one. When I open his Norelco, it is clogged with ivory colored whiskers. It looks as if Santa has been shaving. I give the head a thorough cleaning, but sometimes have trouble getting it back on correctly. When I'm stuck, I bring it to Dad, whose mechanical skills remain excellent. He pops it in place within seconds. With a little teamwork, we keep his razor operating smoothly.

Meals remain Dad's primary interest. He enjoys getting to them, waiting for them, consuming them, and commenting on their quality. No one appreciates structure more than my father. He arrives at his table in the main dining hall each afternoon at 3:50 P.M.—an hour and a half before they serve. He waves to the staff as if he was lord of the manor, and seems to think they could not set up without his benign presence.

For two years he shared a table with a tiny lady who had osteoporosis, a mop of white hair, and a sharp mind. She kept up with everything and was an excellent source of information on Dad's eating habits, health, and disposition. Though they were silent companions because of Dad's hearing loss, they got along beautifully. When she passed away suddenly, I felt a deep loss. She had become a friend and ally, and I miss her every time I walk into the dining room.

For six months they had a third tablemate who made involuntary "ooohwaah" sounds every eight seconds. I know it was eight seconds because I timed her, though I never learned the nature of her problem. Her noises could be heard by everyone within forty feet—except Dad. He missed at least twenty thousand vocal expulsions, thereby proving that deafness has an upside.

Several women have shared his table and later passed away or moved to the Alzheimer's unit. One night while I was visiting, his dinner partner began singing during the meal. The song was "Softly and Tenderly," a hymn from my Methodist youth. She was struggling with the tune and I felt impelled to help out. I surprised myself by recalling the words, and within seconds the dining room had quieted at the sound of our spontaneous singing. We sang two verses, got a big hand when we finished, and restrained ourselves from taking a bow. Where are those judges from American Idol when you need them?

I wish everything about caregiving was as easy as that dining room duet. A few years ago when Dad was in the hospital with a bladder infection, he became dangerously dehydrated. He was ordered to drink a full quart of foul-tasting, but essential, liquid and had refused to touch it all day. The nurses were extremely concerned about him by the time I arrived. They said he had to drink the entire quart or he would have serious problems, and assigned me the job of persuading him to down it. I walked into the room and said, "Dad, why aren't you taking your medicine?"

"It tastes terrible."

"The doctor says you have to drink it."

"Let him drink it."

"Come on, Dad, it's important."

"Why?"

With my back against the wall, I resorted to the truth. "Because they tell me you could die if you don't."

My father pondered that comment for ten seconds, made a decision, and said, "Okay. Let's get started."

It took an hour, but he downed 90 percent of the vile liquid. During his three days in the hospital, Dad was on the same floor where Mother's teeth had disappeared. Clearly aiming for the Guinness Book of World Records, the hospital staff defied the odds and managed to lose Dad's dentures as well. As Yogi Berra said, "It was déjà vu all over again." I didn't find out about the missing teeth until Dad got back to the nursing home, but this time I was not going to let the matter drop without a fight.

I stormed into the hospital, marched up to the fourth floor nurses' station, and demanded information about the dentures. Dad's teeth were missing and mine were gritted. The floor nurses remembered me from two hip operations and our unsuccessful search for Mother's teeth.

They told me that the head nurse was on break. I said I would wait as long as it took to get some answers. I contained my emotions, barely, and cooled my heels while the staff enjoyed a potluck dinner. After half an hour, they saw I was not leaving and invited me to share their meal. Righteous indignation is no match for fried chicken wings and potato salad. The food restored my blood sugar and good humor. After forty-five minutes, the head nurse returned and I explained the urgency of finding Dad's teeth. Two sets of dentures in the dumpster were simply not acceptable. I asked for an all-floor search and she agreed to conduct one. They found Dad's teeth four floors away and I was elated. I've learned to celebrate victories where I find them.

Parents of newborns don't debate whether to change diapers; they just get the job done. It's part of a package deal that includes helping with homework, attending school plays, and hosting sleepless sleepovers. Caring for parents is not all that different. Whether looking for missing teeth or wrestling wheelchairs, you do what it takes—sometimes more than it takes. The payoff is neither predictable nor certain. Sometimes it is captured in an offhand comment heard over your shoulder. As I headed down the hall after a visit, I heard a fellow resident ask my dad, "Who was that?" The pride in his reply was unmistakable, "That's my son."

Comer's Commandments

• Respect your parents' daily routine. It is an island of certainty in a world where they have little control.

• Remember that the quality of your parents' meals is more important to them than the quality of your conversation.

• Go to any lengths—even creating a form for the "commandant" to sign—to give your parents the feeling that they are still in control of major decisions.

• When you make a date for your next visit, show up.

Dad and Romelle do some "banking" at the Wesleyan reception desk.

16

Finances and Fundamentals

Banking is not among my strong suits. It's right up there with car repair and sewing. I'll never tune an engine or mend a garment, but parenting my parents has forced me to improve my fiduciary skills.

Keeping up with his investments and preparing his income taxes were essential components of Dad's sense of independence. He did not relinquish those duties until shortly before his ninety-first birthday. In January 2001 the retirement home receptionist told me that he'd given them a check for the newspaper subscription and mailed his rent check to the *Austin American-Statesman*. They thought it was time for me to get involved.

When I asked Dad if he would like me to start paying his monthly bills, I expected resistance. To my surprise he seemed genuinely relieved. Within the week I got check-writing privileges at his bank and had his few remaining bills routed to me. There was the newspaper, telephone, a Visa card he rarely used, and an insurance policy for Mother that cost $5.40 every six months. Their only major expenses were the retirement home and pharmaceutical company.

I took over their finances just after Mother went to the nursing home and four months before Dad broke his hip. During their years in the retirement home, they lived off their income and still managed to save money. When both of them had to move to the nursing home, they began running a $4,000 monthly deficit. I'm grateful Dad does not know that they are operating in the red. Recently he told me how lucky they were to be living at the Wesleyan for free, and I smiled and nodded in agreement.

At ninety-five, the only thing my father wants to know about his finances is that they are in good shape. When he asks, "How's our money holding out?" I reply, "Everything's fine." If he wants to know how much is in his account, I say "$10,000" and he smiles. After saving for seventy-five years, he deserves some peace of mind. His accountant takes care of his taxes. All he has to do is sign his name.

Dad's biggest financial worry is spending money, a subject that occupies much of our conversations. The front desk of the nursing home is high, wide, and paneled. It looks as if it belongs in a bank. The only thing missing is a touch of marble and a pistol-toting security guard. The receptionist Romelle is kindly and efficient, and she serves as Dad's personal teller. He thinks she works for the Union State Bank and regularly tries to withdraw funds. At first, she tried to explain that she did not work for a bank, but Dad brushed aside her explanations and pulled out his billfold.

No matter how many times we told him it wasn't a bank, Dad paid no attention to us. He has eyes and it looks like a bank to him. Eventually Romelle and I worked out a plan. I gave her $20 to keep in an envelope. When Dad wants cash, she gets out the envelope and hands him a few dollars. Each time I visit, I replenish the fund. In addition to his personal banker, Dad regularly asks me for money to cover his "expenses." Of course, there are no expenses. Haircuts go on his monthly bill and the staff removed the vending machine two years ago.

We don't know what happens to the money. Romelle thinks he stashes it in secret hiding places. She told me one of her neighbors died in his nineties and his children found thousands of dollars hidden between pages of books.

My guess is that Dad's money is being pilfered.

Once when he asked for cash, I foolishly replied, "Why do you need money?"

He replied sharply, "For the same reason you need it."

That shut me up and I handed him ten dollars in fives and ones, and then watched him slowly count it out and put it in his billfold. He likes the idea of having money he can hold and fold. Over time, I have come to realize that it's more important for him to have a little cash on hand than for me to worry about what happens to it. Bank balances are theoretical. Ten spots are tangible. Payback has come full circle. How many times in my youth did he slip me a ten or a twenty? Now I get to return the favor.

In the last year, Dad has developed a new concern. Like many Americans, he is worried that he is going to lose his job. The difference is that Dad has been retired for thirty years. Twelve months ago he was okay with being retired. Now he is convinced that he works for the nursing home. It started when they let him help pick up trays after meals. It made him feel useful and needed. He was so enthusiastic about this duty that he became impatient when residents dawdled over their food, and started to remove their trays while they were still eating. The staff had to keep him out of the dining area until after the residents finished their meals.

His volunteer duty may have given Dad the idea he was employed. Recently he told me that we needed to have a talk because he was not sure how long his position would last. He didn't know if the management was pleased with his work and whether he would keep his job. I listened to his comments without blinking an eye and said I'd talk to his supervisor and get him a full report. I walked over to the nurses' station and had a conversation with the head nurse, making sure that he could see us talking across the room. I wrote a note on a piece of paper, brought it back, and handed it to Dad.

> Your father is doing an excellent job. We are very satisfied with his work. He has no reason to worry about the job ending.

Dad read the note and broke into a big grin. "Well, that's a relief!" I could see his body relax, and I silently wondered if I could get someone to write a similarly calming note about my career.

Some readers may think that I've got it easy because I like my parents and get along with them. They may say to themselves, "Your parents have a sense of humor. It's not that way in our family." I am fortunate in many ways. I do like my parents and I get along well with them, but that does not mean there are no difficulties.

Christmas Eve 2002 comes to mind. It was a crisp, sunny day. The plates were piled high with turkey and dressing, my cousins' home was beautifully decorated, and everyone was having a good time. Then, ten minutes after finishing his pumpkin pie, Dad announced that he was ready to leave. We'd only been there an hour. I was shocked and ticked off.

"It's early, Dad. We haven't even opened presents yet."

He gave me a withering look and said, "If we must." Since he can't hear, a little family celebration goes a long way. We got through the gifts and it was time to exchange the white elephant presents that everyone except Dad enjoys.

"Jim, isn't it time for us to leave?"

I smiled and shouted, "Not yet!"

He wore a woeful expression as if he had been sentenced to the guillotine. Mother was eating candy, cracking one-liners, and rediscovering our two-year-old cousin, Luke, every few minutes. I continued to have fun as long as I avoided Dad's martyred gaze. He moaned intermittently, but we stayed until the end.

"Jim, I need to go now. It'll be dark soon." It was 3:15 P.M.

"Okay, Dad, we're going."

I had my marching orders and wheeled Dad toward the front door.

"Watch out for the step!"

"I see it."

"Where's your mother?"

"She's staying here with everyone else. You're the only one who wants to leave."

Although I was annoyed at our abrupt exit, Dad wanted to get back to his own world and that was his right. I got him into the car and drove back to the nursing home silently steaming. Eventually he noticed that the sun was not close to setting and picked up on my rigid body language. To my surprise, he apologized.

"I guess it's not as late as I thought it was. I'm sorry if I made you leave early."

I wish I'd had a tape recorder handy for that apology. "That's okay, Dad."

When we got back to his room, I unwrapped his new shirts and then used a felt-tip pen, borrowed from a nurse, to print his name on the inside collars in large block letters.

"What are you doing?"

"Writing your name in the new shirts."

"Do you have to do that now?"

I realized he was eager for me to leave because he wanted to take his usual spot in the dining hall an hour and a half early for dinner. A little thing like Christmas was not going to interfere with his schedule. I didn't have to understand his reasoning, merely accept it. I rolled him to the dining room and returned to his room to write JOHN COMER on his four new shirts.

Sometimes I forget that my parents are in their mid-nineties. I have to remind myself that they are doing the best they can—and so am I. In parenting, no one begins as an expert. Experience is the ultimate teacher. New moms and dads rarely have diaper-changing experience when they get home from the hospital. Within weeks, they can change those Huggies in their sleep. The same is true for those of us who must deal with more complicated messes.

My friend Anne Black, an only child who cared for her widowed mother, made a powerful statement about the dynamics of caregiving. She said, "Jim, you and I are lucky because we love our parents and have always had a good relationship with them, even if it's not perfect. That's not true for everyone. I have friends who have strained ties with their parents, and they face a much more difficult time caring for them. For some people, the process can be an incredibly painful experience." I paraphrased Anne's words and wrote them on the gratitude list I go over most mornings. "I'm a fortunate guy. I like my parents."

Each caregiver faces a unique set of circumstances. There is no one way to "do it right." You have to work out your own way, given the history and dynamics of your own family. You can't heal ancient wounds overnight or rewrite the past, but you can choose how you live the end of the story.

Comer's Commandments

• Encourage independence whenever you can.

• Never forget that ten dollars in foldable money may be more important than ten thousand dollars in a checking account.

• Don't burden your parents with too much information about their finances. Tell them that everything is fine and do your best to keep it so.

• If you have a good relationship with your Mom and Dad, be grateful. If it's less than ideal, then congratulate yourself for showing up anyway.

Jim and Mother at fiftieth wedding anniversary party, 1990

17

Going Gently

The last words of the great English actor, Edmond Kean, were, "Dying is easy. Comedy is hard." I hope Mr. Kean is right, although I'm not eager to find out. For six decades I have done my best to avoid the subject of death. Blessed with a long-lived family, I didn't attend my first funeral until I was twenty-five. In the early seventies, my parents bought cemetery plots and thought I'd be pleased to know that they got one for me. I fear my response was less than enthusiastic, and we never discussed the subject again.

Don't get me wrong: I have not ignored death. I have sung at funerals, delivered eulogies, and written scores of letters to the bereaved. Until I started work on this chapter, however, I had never picked out a casket, bought a burial plan, or planned a funeral service. Given my parents' advanced ages, I can't believe I stayed so uninformed for so long. Even though I'd written about denial, when it came to end-of-life issues I remained a practicing denier.

Then I watched a close friend go through the death of a parent and saw how unprepared he was, not only for the loss but also for the logistics of handling a death and preparing for a funeral. Finally, I got the message. Death is not a time to wing it, no pun intended.

Until recently, most people waited until a loved one died before making burial plans. In two or three days, families had to notify friends and relatives, select a casket, plan a service, choose pallbearers, order flowers, and deal with paperwork. And they had to do all that while grieving, receiving friends, and sometimes traveling hundreds of miles. Why would anyone want to put themselves under that kind of pressure? Certainly not me.

I wanted to make decisions about caskets or cremation, burial plots, and funeral services while there was time to think rationally and consider options without pressure or emotion. That meant having a conversation with my hearing-impaired father. Mother's Alzheimer's exempted her from this discussion. Even though I knew it was the right thing to do, it was not easy for me to bring up the subject of death. Inserting casket selection into a conversation does not come easy.

Because of Dad's hearing loss, I could not rely on the bellowed word alone. I wrote out ten questions and composed a tactful introductory paragraph. After numerous revisions and much deleting, I gave up on tactful and settled for direct. Not wanting to shout about funeral plans in a nursing home, I used a sixteen-point font to print out the questions so Dad could read them.

When I got to the nursing home, my father was sitting at his table in the dining room although it was not yet four o'clock. When he saw me coming across the room, he said, "Do you have something important to talk to me about?"

That comment stopped me in my tracks. Had he developed sudden psychic powers? How could he know I had come to talk about his funeral?

"Yes, Dad, I've got something I want you to read."

He looked at his watch and furrowed his brow. "It's awfully close to dinner."

It was 3:50 P.M. "You've got more than an hour before they start serving."

"Are you sure?"

"Positive. I'd like you to read this."

I handed him the questions. He put on his glasses, but they irritated him and were soon tossed aside. He took the page and began scanning.

Dad,

There are some important things we've never discussed. I know you bought cemetery plots, but I don't know what you want in your funeral service or what kind of casket you'd prefer. I think it would be a good idea to buy burial plans for you, Mother, and me. I've written some questions so I will know what you want and be able follow your wishes.

1. *What kind of casket would you like—metal or wood?*
2. *How much do you want to spend on the casket?*
3. *Do you want an open or closed casket at the service?*

4. What music would you like played?
5. Are there any special scriptures or readings you'd like included?
6. Who do you want as pallbearers?
7. Who should officiate at the service?
8. What would you like on your tombstone?
9. Would you like memorials sent to a special charity?
10. What would you like in your obituary?

"Metal."

I knew he wasn't talking about rock bands, but couldn't recall the first question. I peered over his shoulder and saw that he was referring to the type of casket he wanted.

He repeated, "Metal." From his tone, he could have been ordering cheeseburgers. Dad read each question aloud and answered them without hesitation.

"'How much do you want to spend on a casket?' I have no idea what they cost. Whatever you think is right."

"You don't care what kind?"

"Okay." In Dad-speak, "Okay" means he didn't hear me, but he wants to move on.

"'What music would you like played?' Nothing particular. Whatever you and Mother would like."

"'Any special scripture or readings?' No."

"'Who do you want as pallbearers?' I don't think we should have anyone from out of town because they would have to come from far away and spend a lot of money for no reason. But if you think that's wrong then change it because I won't know anyway." He broke out in a grin and we both laughed. This wasn't so hard after all.

"'What would you like on the tombstone?' Standard."

"You mean just your name and date?"

"Yes."

"'Obituary?' I don't know about that."

"I'll write it."

He handed back the questions and gave me a big smile.

"That was very well thought out, Jim. Add to it however you want. The funeral service is for the living. It's not for the dead because they are already gone. In fact, you might mention that in my service."

I left the nursing home almost lighthearted. I was armed with the necessary information and our conversation had not been uncomfortable at all. Why had I postponed it for so long? Clearly I was suffering from that old standby, *fear*. I wasn't sure what to say or how Dad would react to the conversation, so I just kept putting it off. The biggest problem had been my own procrastination. At the risk of sounding like a reformed smoker preaching to those who puff, I urge you to find out what your parents want and, while you're at it, get your own preferences in writing. *Don't let your last act be written by someone else.*

Although my father was not concerned about the details of his funeral service, many people plan their rites down to the last detail. My friend Liz Carpenter has definite ideas about her funeral and is not shy about discussing them. In the middle of her annual Christmas party, she announced that she wanted to hear "How Great Thou Art" because it was going to be sung at her funeral. She turned to her friend Ruben Johnson, who has been instructed to sing it at her service, and asked him to give us a dress rehearsal on the spot. You don't say no to Liz, so he sang.

One week after the discussion with my dad, I went to the funeral home next to the cemetery where my brother is buried. In less than an hour I chose caskets and burial plans for my parents. Selecting a casket is like picking out a suit you hope never to wear. The prices ranged from $500–12,000 and, following Dad's wishes, I picked ones on the lower side of the scale. I thought a casket would be the main expense, but soon that illusion was shattered.

Unfortunately, in the funeral business, the casket is just the beginning of the end. They want to sell you the "outer container" in which the casket is inserted. That's another thousand, if you choose to spend it. I did not. Ironically, the major costs are lumped under "minimum charges" and cover the funeral director and staff, preparation of the body, embalming, visitation, staff services for the funeral, transportation from place of death to the funeral home, and the hearse and flower car. The list goes on and on, though it covers only the basics. The cost for my parents' moderate burial plans, including caskets, was almost $6,000 each. I knew the price was high, but I was ready to get it over with and paid for their plans in full.

A few months after I'd written that $12,000 check, I heard about the Funeral Consumers Alliance. It's a federation of non-profit consumer information societies throughout the country. They have been around for forty years and provide consumers with information about how to choose meaningful, dignified, and affordable funerals. They told me I'd spent about twice as much as was necessary. You can contact them at 800-765-0107 or visit their fact-filled website at www.funerals.org.

Comer's Commandments

- Don't be afraid to bring up the subject of death. It's as natural as being born.

- Get your parents' funeral preferences down in writing. Don't let their last act be written by someone else.

- If your family does not have a pre-need burial plan, consider buying one.

- The Funeral Consumers Alliance may be able to save you thousands of dollars in burial expenses.

Dad, Jim, and Mother at the Wesleyan New Year's party, December 31, 2003

18

Unexpected Joys

If someone had told me I'd spend my fifties and early sixties hanging around hospitals, retirement facilities, and nursing homes, I would have questioned their sanity. I thought I had better things to do with my time. That premise turned out to be false.

When I moved to Austin, I made an unspoken commitment to my parents: I'm here for as long as you need me. I won't jump on a plane and return to my life in L.A. Like Cortés, I had burned my boats. *I was in Texas for the long run.*

After ten years of parenting, I've accumulated benefits that can't be found in even the most golden parachute. One of them is the joy of walking. In auto-crazed California, most people you find on sidewalks are homeless. In small-town Texas I discovered that you could walk for pleasure, exercise, and good company.

When they lived in the retirement home, my parents and I often took a six-block walk after dinner. Our evening stroll provided a simple activity we could share and repeat regularly. I suggested it to fill the time and give us some needed exercise. I never expected to enjoy myself, but soon I began anticipating these outings.

On our stroll, we passed the same white frame houses I'd driven by for years. Some were freshly painted, others badly needed a coat. Most yards were well maintained and a few needed mowing. I enjoyed architectural details that had escaped my eyes for years and I realized how much richness I'd missed from the windows of my car.

After a few days, I began to see things through my mother's eyes. Her vision and hearing remained excellent. Mother pointed out trees, plants, and flowers I would never have noticed. She commented on an oddly shaped branch here or an obscure blossom there, and brightened at the sight of redbirds flying overhead. She shook her head in dismay at toys littering a front porch.

"Someone is going to fall on that wagon and break his neck."

True to form, Dad plowed ahead oblivious to beauty but eager for signs of refuse. He scoured the streets for litter. If there was a piece of paper or an errant milk carton in his path, he nabbed it. He would have made a great New Yorker patrolling the streets, pooper-scooper in hand.

Later, when Mother moved to the nursing home, I was determined not to lose our walks. Now she rides in her wheelchair and I push, but the essential elements remain the same. We roll through the nursing home's gardens on a walkway that leads past rose bushes to a sculpture and erratically flowing fountain. Mother never ceases to exclaim over the colors of the flowers and enjoys each outing as if it was our first. Her only quibble might come if the temperature dropped below her accustomed seventy-two degrees.

"Jim, it's a little coolish out here."

"We'll only stay a minute."

"It only takes a minute to catch a cold. Oh, isn't that beautiful? Look at those yellow roses."

My father couldn't have cared less about the garden. He wanted to know where I'd worked last week. Dad always worried about my freelance lifestyle. Every time I visited he asked what I'd been doing to make "ends meet." He rejoiced with each new assignment and was eager to find out where I'd been last week and what I had lined up for the future. He was impressed that I get paid for giving speeches. However, when I told him I'd given a free presentation for publicity, he became concerned about my business strategy. The protective urge never ends.

I remember my first glimmer of what it was like to be a parent. I was eight. Mother was driving my five-year-old brother Chris and me back to New Orleans from a Christmas holiday in Texas. Dad had flown ahead for a business appointment. The year was 1953. The car was a Ford. The roads were narrow, pre-interstate, two-lane strips. My brother had just come down with chicken pox and loudly demanded calamine lotion every fifteen minutes.

After trailing slow-moving trucks all morning, Mother finally found a stretch of straight road in rural Louisiana. She gunned the engine, and we were cruising along at seventy miles an hour when a gigantic hog stepped from behind a roadside sign and began to meander slowly across the highway.

We were seconds from porcine destruction and there were no seat belts. Mother slammed on the brakes, throwing us to the floor. Our Christmas toys flew all over the car as we came to a stop one foot in front of Big Mama, who eyed us with disdain and lazily waddled on her way.

Chris and I screamed in terror for several minutes. I'm sure Mother was shaken though she tried not to show it. To quiet us, she promised ice cream cones. The bribe worked and we turned our attention to finding the

Chris and Jim, 1949

nearest Dairy Queen, which turned out to be an impossible task. This was twenty years before national franchises defaced America's highways. On New Year's Day in the rural South, almost everything was closed. We had to settle for Baby Ruths from a dingy gas station.

We got to Baton Rouge about nine and pulled into an all-night diner. My brother and I were excited because Mother was breaking her "We don't waste money on restaurants when we have your grandmother's tuna sandwiches" rule. Chris and I ordered cheeseburgers and fries. Mother had a large black coffee.

As I looked at her across the Formica table in the glare of the JAX beer sign, for the first time I saw not my mother but a person. She was a woman exhausted, responsible for two little boys, still reeling from a close call with pork-laden death, and with another eighty miles to drive.

For a passing moment I realized that it must be difficult to be a parent. I did not discuss this revelation, yet for a few seconds I actually understood. I wish I could say that as a result of this insight I became a better child, kinder brother, and more thoughtful eight-year-old. Unfortunately, my moment of understanding passed quickly. I asked for a nickel to play a Hank Williams tune on the jukebox. Chris and I finished our burgers, returned to the car, and promptly fell asleep. Mother got us home safely and tucked us into our beds.

She doesn't recall the story, but I will never forget her solo bravery on that long-ago day. Mother's courage remains alive in my memory just as

Mother and Dad on their
wedding day, June 8, 1940

children today observe their parents' unsung heroics, even as moms and dads least expect it.

The Gift of Your Presence

My friend Cindy Bragg is a talented musician who leads singing at four nursing homes each week though she doesn't have a family member in any of them. I asked her how she got involved.

"A woman from our church choir had a stroke and I started going to see her. Often I'd sing a hymn at her bedside, and she loved the music. I asked the nursing home director if I could take my friend to the activities room where they had a piano so I could sing to her there. He said, 'Please do. And if anyone else is around, sing to them, too.' That's how it got started. My friend died a few years later, but I've kept coming back, and now I go to two homes on Tuesdays and two on Thursdays, and have recruited a friend who comes with me." One year Cindy got laryngitis right before Christmas and persuaded me to lead the holiday sing-along. If nothing else, we made a joyful noise.

Cindy does a lot more than play for groups. She also makes rounds. "I enjoy visiting the residents in their rooms almost as much as the singing. The activities director told me that a number of patients were not well enough to come to the group singing, so I brought my portable keyboard and took it to their rooms. Many patients are confined to their beds and never see a visitor. Others speak no English, so I learned songs in Spanish, German, and Yiddish.

"One patient was a retired preacher who was extremely ill. When I asked him the name of his favorite hymn, he couldn't remember it. He was irritated with himself because he couldn't recall the name of the song. Then he said, 'It was written by a man who brought slaves over in ships.' When I sang 'Amazing Grace,' he got this wonderfully peaceful look on his face. The following week, I found out that he died less than twenty-four hours later. It was such a privilege to be with him on his last day."

If you are reading this book and have too much time on your hands—or if you don't have much time but can squeeze in one hour a week—I recommend that you find a nursing home and volunteer. Call the Area Agency on Aging where you live. You can find their number in the phone book or on the web at www.n4a.org/links.cfm. Better yet, find a nursing home in your neighborhood, walk in the door, and ask for the activities director. Every nursing home has a volunteer program, and they will welcome you with open arms.

If you don't have any musical talent, bring your dog or cat. If you don't have a pet, ask for the names of residents who never have any visitors and go see them. You don't need any special skills or training. A loving spirit is the talent residents need most. *Just show up.*

From the Algonquin to the Activities Room

One of my favorite moments at the nursing home happened in 2003 when my friend Steve Ross came to town and gave two concerts at the Austin Cabaret Theater. Steve is an internationally known performer who plays and sings at sophisticated clubs all over the world. He knew my parents were in a nursing home and asked if he could sing for the residents. I called the Wesleyan on Monday morning and they said they'd be happy to work him in to their schedule for that afternoon.

We walked into the activities room, where ten people were gathered over Bingo cards. The staff quickly ended the game and rolled out the beat-up piano. Before I could get my mother up from her nap, my elegant friend was going strong. His voice filled the dining hall and ricocheted down the halls. By the time I got Mother there, the crowd had grown to fifty and the wheelchairs kept coming. Steve had them singing, smiling, and tapping their toes for almost an hour. After seeing him so many times at stylish night spots in New York, I couldn't believe he was playing the Wesleyan in Georgetown, Texas.

I'll never forget when the tiny, bent woman who shared my dad's table got up spontaneously and began dancing across the floor, swaying in time with the beat. I never imagined she had those moves in her, but when Steve played she arose from her chair and danced three different times.

My friend was buoyed by the enthusiasm of the crowd, and that old upright piano never sounded like it did that day. Even my mother reached into a hidden chamber of memory and came up with long-forgotten lyrics. When Steve asked for requests, there were only two sought-after songs not in his repertoire: "Waltz Across Texas" and "San Antonio Rose." He promised to learn them both and make a return visit. I intend to hold him to it.

❦

A few years ago, I spent ten days in California. I sat by a perfect pool, enjoyed seventy-degree weather, and visited old friends. Then I flew to Santa Cruz to work on a video and stayed with my clients on a mountain surrounded by redwood trees, friendly dogs, and beauty at every angle.

Surprisingly, after a week I was homesick. I canceled a weekend with friends in Pebble Beach and paid American Airlines $100 to fly home early. As the plane approached Austin, I saw the Colorado River winding across the land and noticed minor elevations we call the Hill Country. When the captain announced that the temperature was ninety-six degrees, I didn't even flinch. As I took the first steps down the Jetway, humidity enveloped me like a blush. Much to my surprise, though, I did not want to be anywhere else.

I was returning to finish this book and look for a new house. In California, I could not afford a shanty in a slum. Here I could get three bedrooms and two baths in good neighborhood. I felt grateful not to be house shopping in the land of $500,000 sheds and million-dollar fixer-uppers.

Of course, there are trade-offs. I live in a state where liberals are an endangered species and evolution is considered a radical theory. Political correctness means having his and her gun racks. We execute more prisoners than any other state, but we do it with a smile. We drink iced tea in January and say, "Bless your heart" to cover everything from stubbed toes to amputations. Despite all that, I was glad to be back home.

I decided to drive to Georgetown and check on my parents. Mother would not know I'd been gone, but would greet me with a smile and unpredictable remark. Dad would want to know if I'd gotten some new clients.

At the airport tollbooth, I noticed the friendliness of the attendant. Heading toward the interstate, I took in the big, cloudless Texas sky and saw joggers running beside Town Lake. I turned the radio to a country station and sang along with the Dixie Chicks. Down deep I knew I was back where I belonged.

Comer's Commandments

• Create rituals that you can enjoy with your parents, whether it's a stroll through the neighborhood or watching Lawrence Welk reruns.

• A short visit is better than no visit at all.

• Let your parents know when you'll be coming back to see them. It gives them something to look forward to and provides you with a promise to keep.

• Find simple activities you can enjoy together: flowers, birds, movies, getting fresh air, riding through a park, or gossiping about the relatives.

• Don't just bring flowers or candy; bring an attitude that says, "I'm here and we're going to have a good time for the next half hour."

• If you have any talents, or know people who do, volunteer to entertain. You'll never find a more appreciative and less critical audience.

Mother and Dad at their fiftieth anniversary party, June 1990

19

Creating New Memories

When we spend time with our parents, it is only natural to dip into the past. The old days are familiar territory and we feel safe there—as long as we are careful about which memories we unwrap. While the past may be comforting, we must not neglect the possibilities of the present.

I miss no opportunity for a celebration. When my parents have a wedding anniversary or birthday, I make a big deal of it. On their fiftieth anniversary in 1990, we had a seated luncheon at a big hotel for more than a hundred friends and relatives. There were four courses, champagne, music, skits, songs, and laughter. I created a slide show from old family photos, compiled a memory book with letters from their friends all over the country, and had a video made of the entire event. Mother, who had fought the idea tooth and nail, said it was "the best day of my life."

History isn't something that happens to someone else. Everyone has stories worth telling and memories that should be shared. A few months before Dad broke his hip, I interviewed him on audiotape about his early days. He told me about his trip to Europe at seventeen on a tramp steamer. He was in Germany in 1930 and saw Hitler speaking at a street rally. For a few months during the Depression, he serviced slot machines that had been won in a poker game by the newspaper editor in Waxahachie, Texas. When Dad ran a service station in Corpus Christi, one of his best customers was the madam of the town's premier bordello. I have scores of letters Dad wrote Mother from England during World War II, when the casualty rate for airmen on his base was 80 percent. When Italy was liberated he stood on Mussolini's balcony in Rome and was asked to join a group of Catholic pilgrims who had a private audience with the pope. Despite the crowd, Pius XII noticed my father looking a bit uncomfortable and came up and introduced himself. When he learned that Dad was from Texas, the pope said, "Texas! I've always wanted to know something. Why do they pour concrete down the hole when they dig an oil well?" My father spent ten minutes telling the pope about oil fields. Not bad for a Presbyterian.

Dad holding Jim, 1945

Mining our parents' past is not expensive. It takes only time and energy. With a few taped interviews, vintage pictures, and period music you can create a homemade video that will honor and thrill your parents. If you have no technical abilities, get some help. Hire some clever teenagers with too much time on their hands, or look for professionals who provide this service.

Find out what's important to your parents about their past and get them talking about it. In our family, World War II has never really ended. I was named after two airmen, James Counce of Corinth, Mississippi, and George Balmore from the Bronx, Dad's closest friends on his bomber crew. They were in their early twenties when they said goodbye to my father on a cold January day in 1944 as he headed back to the states after completing the required twenty-five missions. Balmore and Counce had only a few missions to go until they reached twenty-five, and the three friends had big plans to reconnect in America. That reunion was not to be. Dad's two best buddies were shot down on separate planes on that same gray day.

During three years in the Army Air Corps, my father kept a journal that covered his training and combat missions out of England and Italy. We kept hundreds of handwritten pages in boxes that we moved with us from city to city. When Dad retired in 1974, Mother and I urged him to turn the journal into a book. It took five years to get him started and another five to complete the manuscript. I edited at least six drafts and, eventually, we honed it down to the best two hundred and twenty pages. In 1985 *Combat Crew* was completed. Dad contacted a local publisher, who said it would cost $15,000 to print fifteen hundred hardcover copies. For a conservative man, that sounded like $150,000. I assumed the book would remain unpublished. Surprising everyone, Dad spent the money. He was seventy-six and figured, "What the hell!"

When the books were delivered, I organized a party in Dallas and arranged an interview in the *Dallas Morning News*. They gave Dad a full page with a color picture. To our amazement, he sold all the books in six months. A friend sent a copy to New York literary agent Jane Dystel, who sold it to William Morrow & Company within weeks. Dad's book went through five editions, was published in England, and has been read throughout the world.

Dad in uniform, 1942

In 2000, when Dad turned ninety, I called the *Austin American-Statesman* and suggested they write an article about my dad and his book. Brad Buchholz, an excellent feature writer, came to Georgetown and had several long conversations with my father. The paper sent a photographer, who caught Dad standing in front of a painting of a B-17. Brad wrote a powerful and touching three-page article that ran on April 30, 2000. Soon my father began getting fan letters and unannounced visitors, and he found himself a local celebrity. Five years later he was still getting letters and email from readers around the world.

Each May there is a Central Texas Air Show that includes reenactments

Dad and *Corpus Christi Caller-Times* columnist Bill Walraven at a book signing

COMBAT CREW

THE STORY OF 25 COMBAT MISSIONS
OVER NORTH-WEST EUROPE

JOHN COMER

of World War II battles and an appearance by a B-17. Naturally, we never missed one. The field was hot, dusty, and crowded. There were screaming children and a blaring sound system. Within twenty minutes I was tired and cranky, but Dad was in heaven.

In the spring of 2000, Dad suffered a fall and had to use a walker. He was in pain and could barely make it to the dining room. I convinced myself that he couldn't handle the long trek from the parking lot to the runway and wouldn't be interested in going to the air show. I was silently relieved. As I walked him back to his room one night, we passed a huge poster on the bulletin board advertising the air show. I knew that Eagle Eye Comer could not have missed the sign. The event was the next weekend so I braced myself and yelled, "Do you want to go to the air show?"

Dad said, as he does so often, "What?"

I repeated the question at triple volume.

With exquisite timing, he replied, "Oh, I don't know . . ." There was a long pause, ". . . only if you want to go."

It turned out I was dying to go. We made a date for the following Saturday afternoon at one o'clock. When I walked into the retirement home that day, the receptionist said that my father had been pacing the lobby for almost an hour with his walker.

"He's so excited about going to the air show. He's been talking about it all week."

There he was wearing his Eighth Air Force cap and jacket. I reminded myself never again to get sidetracked by a literal interpretation of Dad's words. I had planned ahead and got us a reserved parking place and a ride in a VIP golf cart. I also brought folding chairs. Sure enough, when we got to the airport they had a spot for us close to the gate. So far, so good.

I got Dad's walker out of the back seat. Slowly we made our way to the entrance. When I told the ticket taker we needed a ride for a World War II veteran, he almost clicked his heels. I was impressed, but shouldn't have been. It took three walkie-talkie calls before they finally got the cart to us. By that time my ever-impatient father was griping about the wait.

I loaded Dad, his walker, and the folding chairs onto the cart and climbed in the front seat. The driver was a soldier from nearby Fort Hood. As we drove off, an enormous lightning bolt struck nearby. In my concentration on logistics, I had ignored the dark sky and ominous black clouds. I told the driver we wanted to go straight to the B-17. "Dad flew seventy-six combat missions in World War II."

"Seventy-six!"

"Yep."

"But didn't they send those guys back after twenty-five?"

"Dad volunteered for a second tour of duty. Mother almost divorced him."

"Seventy-six!"

The young soldier turned to my father and said, "Sir, you are my hero."

Dad gave him a smile and a kindly nod that meant, "I have no idea what you just said, but I'm sure you meant well."

"He can't hear unless you yell. He's deaf."

Our driver reached to the depths of his diaphragm for vocal support and screamed, "Sir, you are my hero!"

Everyone within a hundred yards heard him, even my father. The thunder was booming as we rolled on to the runway. For the first time I focused on the impending downpour.

"Get as close to the B-17 as you can."

"No problem."

He drove past the STAY OUT signs and headed for the Flying Fortress. Dad brightened visibly as he saw the plane's familiar outline.

"There she is! Isn't she beautiful?"

Lightning flashed again and I felt the first raindrop. Our driver was not deterred. He drove directly under the right wing just as the sky opened up. There was a twenty minute downpour of biblical proportions. All ten thousand air show attendees were soaked to the bone, but not us. As he had been sixty years earlier, Dad was sheltered by the wings of a B-17.

I jumped out, opened the walker, got Dad out of the golf cart, and prepared a folding chair as if it were a throne. For a moment I saw my father as he must have looked in 1943: lean, strong, blue eyes shining, and his whole future ahead of him.

Dad sat serenely as the rain swept around us. The plane's crew soon heard that a veteran of seventy-six missions had joined them. They climbed out of the plane and lined up to shake my father's hand. One of them asked for an autograph, and my father beamed as he signed his name.

When the rain stopped, we made our way slowly across the drenched field. We sat in our folding chairs amid the soaked grass surrounded by planes of his departed youth. We didn't say much because perfect moments don't require words. However, I couldn't miss the look of joy on my father's face.

And to think we almost hadn't come.

Comer's Commandments

- Celebrate everything. Make a big deal about birthdays, anniversaries, and holidays.

- No matter what they tell you, do something big for your parents' fiftieth anniversary and any birthday with a zero or a five at the end of it.

- Even if Mom and Dad tell you not to make a fuss about special occasions, make one anyway.

- Interview your parents on videotape and get them talking about their early days. It is the territory they may remember best.

- Ask questions while your folks can still remember the answers.

- Create a memory book of photos and mementos.

20

December 2005

This is the chapter I didn't want to write. A few months after his ninety-fifth birthday, Dad's health began to fail. His appetite, always hearty, declined suddenly. Instead of arriving for meals hours early, he sometimes skipped them altogether. He might show up late for dinner and eat a few bites, and then wheel himself back to his room and climb into bed, sometimes with his clothes on. Then he'd wake up hungry at midnight and think it was morning. The one constant was ice cream. He ate as much of it as he could wheedle from the staff though he had flagging interest in all foods that didn't come in small cold cups.

At Care Team meetings they reported that Dad was losing weight. I didn't need the staff to tell me that. My father was shrinking before my eyes. His face was drawn, the lines in his cheeks deepened, and his mental agility declined markedly. He still had a great smile and a firm handshake, but he was slipping.

I knew we were in dangerous territory when he stopped asking how my work was going. His lifelong concern about my income had never wavered— and with good cause. Each time I saw him I could count on the inevitable sentence: "How's your business?" Now weeks went by without that question. His concern for the outside world, even my precarious freelance fate, had faded. Much to my surprise, I missed the prodding.

The last time I recall Dad mentioning politics was the day after the 2004 presidential election. I walked into a dining room packed with residents and staff. My father saw me coming, beamed victoriously, and yelled, "Jim, Bush

117

won!" Although my enthusiasm about this news was muted, he was so joyous that I took a deep breath, forced a grin, and shouted, "Yes, Dad, he did!" I never heard him mention politics again.

In the summer of 2005 *something happened*. I wish I could be more precise, but the doctors and nurses were equally baffled. Was it dementia or the onset of actual Alzheimer's? Had he experienced a series of subtle strokes? Whatever shift occurred physiologically, it led to emotional outbursts.

Dad began to cry out, "Help me, help me! Please, help me!" He repeated that plaintive plea over and over from wheelchair, bed, or toilet seat. Like a child screaming for attention, he was relentless and unyielding. He might say the phrase several hundred times in one day. While his anxiety spun out of control, his vocal cords lost none of their strength. As always, my father had no trouble making himself heard. He did not discriminate in his requests, but talked to everyone within earshot. He would yell from his bed in the middle of the night or implore passersby in hallways or dining room.

"Help me, please!"

When I walked into the nursing home, often I heard that phrase in the lobby fifty yards down the long hall toward B-Wing. When he saw me, his eyes widened and the volume increased.

"Jim, help me!"

I gave him a hug, bent down, and shouted the same question week after week.

"What's wrong, Dad?"

He might stop for a moment, consider the question, and reply, "Nothing."

Seconds later, he resumed his mantra of supplication.

"Help me, please. Help me!"

An internal burglar alarm had been activated. None of us—doctors, nurses, or administrators—had the correct code to disable it. There was no help to be had. I would have given anything to relieve the anxiety that was haunting him. Hearing him call out day after day was heart-wrenching and humbling. I was supposed to do something, wasn't I? His vital signs were good. His will remained strong. The staff assured me over and over again that he was not in pain, yet he demanded help with ever-growing intensity.

While I knew the non-stop pleas were not my father's fault, they were— as the months dragged on and they continued unabated—maddening. I'll admit that I sometimes broke my cardinal rule and did not go into his world, but tried to force him into mine. More than once I heard myself saying, "Dad, you're okay. There's nothing wrong. Everything is fine."

What a stupid thing to say. Everything was *not* fine. Something was terribly wrong; I just didn't know what it was. My father was almost ninety-six, deaf, incontinent, had been stuck in a wheelchair for five years, and was losing his grip on reality. Of course he was agitated, anxious, and depressed. I would have called for help, too. Only I wouldn't have said "please."

The staff remained amazingly patient. They heard his cries from one dawn to the next. Frankly, I don't know how they stood it. The nurses' aides would hold his hand, give him hugs, and offer orange juice or his beloved vanilla ice cream. Mostly they gave him their attention, providing far more than our money's worth of kindness and affection, even though Dad was just one of many needy residents on his wing. Some of his peers cried. Others yelled. A few talked non-stop nonsense. I tried my best to tune out their misery.

I got in the habit of requesting "help me" updates from the staff whenever I visited.

"How has the yelling been today?"

"Not too bad this afternoon. He's only hollered about five times. But yesterday he never stopped."

Dad's doctor requested permission to give him medication for anxiety and depression. I told them to do *anything* that would relieve his fears but not leave him drugged and half-asleep. They assured me they would give him small doses of Ativan and see how it worked.

Dr. Benold, the home's highly respected medical director until the end of 2005, had monitored my father's health for five years. One day I stopped him in the lobby and let him know how concerned I was about Dad's weight loss and precarious mental state.

"Jim, I want to be frank with you. Your father is beginning to go downhill. If he doesn't start eating more, his body will eventually begin to shut down. He won't let the staff members feed him. Of course, we can be more aggressive and feed him intravenously if you want."

"No, Dad would hate that." I was putting it mildly. My father would rip out the tubes and curse out the nurses. He did not want to be kept alive by any artificial means and had put that in writing long ago.

When Thanksgiving 2005 approached, my cousins asked if I planned to bring my folks to the family dinner. I said, "Absolutely." Mother loved the candy and the kids. Dad had always been good for at least two hours, especially if they served wine. I didn't realize how profoundly things had changed. I would have to work hard to be thankful on this Thanksgiving. My father was yelling for help when I arrived and his cries never wavered. Clearly he wasn't feeling grateful and soon neither was I.

For once, I couldn't get him into the car by myself because he was so frightened about moving from his wheelchair to the front seat of my Camry. We'd done this transfer successfully scores of times, but now I had to call on the staff for help. That should have been an omen of things to come, but I remained oblivious to the obvious, rooted in my determination that we were going to have a good time, damn it!

My cousin David, a freshman at the Coast Guard Academy, picked up Mother. Normally that would have made things easier as I only had one wheelchair to handle. However, Dad's fear was more challenging than fifty pounds of foldable steel. He was unhappy about leaving the nursing home and his attitude did not improve during our brief ride across town. When we arrived at my cousins' home, I had to call for reinforcements to get him out of the car and into Bill's house.

Surely he would calm down once he saw the family, turkey, and Chablis. Wrong again: he became even more agitated. Wine didn't help. Small children didn't garner his attention. Greetings and hugs had no impact on his mental state. During the middle of the blessing, Dad interrupted our host and addressed his Creator directly: "Help me, help me, please." His prayer was not answered.

I got him a full plate of food and placed him at a table next to younger cousins. Let them have a preview of things to come. I sat with my mother at the end of another table as far away from Dad as possible. Mother was happy and quiet, which was what I needed for a few minutes. Dad quieted down while he ate his sweet potatoes and I began to feel a false sense of security. Maybe the food would calm him down. For the first time in an hour, I relaxed. Unfortunately the respite was short lived.

Before dessert was served, Dad began his familiar chant. No words from me would quiet him and finally I realized that a strategic withdrawal was in order. Without further debate, I wheeled him out of the house and headed back to the nursing home as quickly as possible. On the drive back, I accepted the fact that his days at family gatherings were over. Things had changed even though I had not wanted to acknowledge it. Despite all evidence in front of me, I'd been practicing denial once again.

Sunday, December 18

One week before Christmas, I stopped by the nursing home after church and found Dad slumped over in his wheelchair. He often snoozed in that chair, but he never slumped. He looked more fragile than I'd ever seen him.

When I tried to get his attention, he slurred his words as if he was drunk. I knew his protein shakes weren't spiked and that something fundamental had gone wrong. I got two nurses aides to help me get him into bed. Although his breathing was labored, in a few minutes he was asleep. I had the nurse call the doctor and let her know there had been a marked change in his condition. After hanging around for another half an hour, I realized that there was nothing more I could do.

Monday, December 19

After leaving a 6:45 A.M. Toastmasters meeting, I had three messages on my cell phone. The nursing home and both cousins had called to say that Dad had taken a sudden turn for the worse, was on oxygen, and might have to go to the emergency room. By the time I got to the nursing home the administrator, head nurse, and social worker were at his bedside. Two doctors were on their way. Dad's oxygen level had reached dangerously low levels during the night. He was not able to eat or take liquids and his level of ureic acid was rising. When Dr. Shepherd arrived, she said his condition was critical and that he probably had only a day or two to live. Dr. Benold said, "Your father may have a week."

Although I took in the words, they did not fully register. Other people died, but not my Dad. Didn't those doctors know that he'd flown all those missions over Germany and lived? Couldn't they see those portraits of B-17s on his wall? This man was a survivor. Last week he was rolling himself down the corridor raising a ruckus. Now he had "a day or two to live."

We agreed not to send him to the hospital, but to keep him in the nursing home, where the staff knew him and his surroundings were familiar. My cousins said they would help me take turns staying with him at the nursing home. Bill, a master of organization, offered to make out a schedule for us.

That morning my world changed as abruptly as it had when I got the call about Dad's stroke a decade earlier. This time there would be no miraculous recovery. I walked slowly to A-Wing and brought Mother to Dad's room. When we arrived, I told her that he was very sick. She said, "Bless his heart. I sure hope he gets better." She was her usual sociable self and had no idea that the man in bed, struggling to breathe, was her husband of sixty-five years.

By noon everyone had left the room and I was sitting alone with my father. Suddenly Dad roused himself and began trying to get out of bed. He managed a feeble, "Help me, help me." For the first time that phrase sounded good to me. By afternoon he had rallied, loudly demanded to get out of bed, and was sitting in his wheelchair in front of the nurses' station.

At five o'clock, one of his favorite nurses' aides, Jackie, determined that Dad would eat something. Even though he said "No," she would not be deterred. She coaxed, persuaded, and demanded that he take "just one spoonful" and then another. I watched her feed him slowly, bite by grudging bite. She held the spoon one inch from his lips, willing him to open his mouth. I was touched by her concern and amazed by her ability. I'd never seen anyone feed my father.

Once again, I saw how much the staff loved my father and how concerned they were about his condition. All afternoon, nurses' aides and senior staff members had stopped by the room to see how he was doing and tell me how much they liked "Mr. Comer." Over and over I heard them say how much they enjoyed his smile.

I looked at my watch. It was five-thirty and I'd promised to take my younger cousins to see the Trans Siberian Orchestra. A night on the town was their delayed Christmas present from a year earlier and I couldn't disappoint them. Besides, I had $140 worth of tickets in my pocket. I headed to town at rush hour and met them for dinner, and we got to our seats just in time. Despite the ticket price, we were seated nearer the roof than the stage. The place was packed with twelve thousand fans and I did my best to focus on the extravaganza before me. Despite the music, lasers, and fireworks my mind kept returning to a hospital bed twenty-seven miles north.

Tuesday, December 20

I told the nurse to call me if Dad got any worse during the night and she took me at my word. At 4:00 A.M. the phone rang. She was worried about his breathing. After three hours of sleep, I pulled on jeans and dragged myself to Starbucks, arriving as they opened the doors. With a cup of over-priced caffeine in hand, I aimed the car for the nursing home. By the time I arrived, Dad was doing better. His oxygen level had stabilized and his color had improved.

A few hours later, Dr. Shepherd said her previous day's prediction was wrong. Dad might last a week or two. She suggested that we bring in hospice care and I said that was fine with me. She called Hospice Austin and forty-five minutes later they called me. That was the quickest medical response I'd seen since being rushed to the hospital by ambulance after a car wreck. The hospice worker wanted to know if they could send a social worker to the hospital for an intake interview. I said, "Sure. What day will they come?"

"In an hour."

"An hour?"

"Is that too soon?"

"No, that's amazing."

While Dad slept, I remembered that I needed to check on Mother. I walked thirty seconds down the hall where the annual nursing home Christmas party was in full swing. It is one of the major social events of the year, and there was no sign of impending doom in the dining room. It was filled with smiling residents, family members, administrators, workers, and volunteers. The energy, laughter, music, and buzz of life stood in stark contrast to the room I'd just left.

The staff had worked for weeks to transform the large dining area with colorful decorations. Each table had a festive centerpiece and an array of refreshments was served to the residents. I found Mother at the back of the room and sat down next to her. Since there was chocolate cake on her plate and two cute children visiting a grandmother at the next table, she was in excellent spirits.

"Where's your cake, honey?"

Good question. I walked to the front of the room to get my sugar fix when suddenly the holiday spirit overtook me—or maybe I just lost control. Two guitars were playing a catchy Latino tune. Without plan or warning, I began dancing around the middle of the room, making up the moves as I went along. Soon there was clapping, so my steps got bolder. Quickly I recruited an unsuspecting staff member as a partner and we began improvising across the floor. I'm sure we looked like failed reality show contestants, but a little dancing was just what the party needed. We added a touch of unscripted wackiness not included in the official program. I laughed out loud for the first time in three days.

After the dance, which got an unexpected round of applause, the administrator handed me a microphone and said, "You've got to sing." I looked at the elderly pianist and said, "How about 'O Holy Night'?"

"What key?"

"Your guess is as good as mine. I don't read music!"

"Don't worry, honey, I've heard it all. We'll fake it."

She gave me a good introduction and must have found my key because it appeared that I might hit the high note at the end of the song. As I belted out "O ni-ight di-vine" I saw that Mother had been wheeled up front and was smiling at me. When I finished the song, I went over to her. A woman standing next to her said, "When your mother heard the first line of your song, she said, 'That's my boy singing!' So I brought her up close so she could see you."

Mom hadn't known who I was for a year, but she recognized my singing voice from a hundred feet away. That was the best Christmas present I could get; I received the gift of recognition. Her temporary moment of memory restored my perspective. Dad might be terribly ill fifty yards away, but Christmas was coming with its joy, possibility, and hope.

Thirty minutes later a hospice social worker walked into Dad's room. I was stunned by the speed with which her agency had moved. I'd seen police departments respond less efficiently. She asked what kinds of services we needed. I told her I wanted Dad's last days to be as peaceful as possible. She told me that they would have a nurse there the next day to work with the staff and to make sure he remained pain-free.

Wednesday, December 21

The following morning the nurse arrived promptly, checked my dad's vitals, talked with the doctor, and arranged for morphine to be administered orally when needed. Later that day I got a call from the hospice chaplain, who had come by the room that afternoon. I began to understand why so many friends had told me how hospice care had been a blessing to their families. Hospice responded quickly and thoughtfully, and were there when you needed them.

The most powerful image of Dad's last week was the time I spent alone with him, sitting by his bed, forced to face the fact of his impending death. I'd lost a brother in a car wreck and seen friends waste away from cancer and AIDS, but I'd never kept watch by the bedside of a parent. This was new territory for me.

On the table by his bed was a large photo from my New York actor days. That youthful, unlined face stared at me all week, a stark reminder that my eighties are closer than my twenties. Encased in a broken frame, my optimistic image was propped up by a Bible. Someone had spilled water on the Good Book, baptizing the pages and leaving them crinkly to the touch. I opened the New Testament and began reading. By Wednesday I had set a personal record and gotten through Matthew, Mark, and most of Luke. My father would have been pleased.

Thursday, December 22

Dad had stopped talking, though his presence remained powerful. Lying there, eyes wide open, he gazed intensely at the ceiling. As I stood above his bed and looked down, he stared through me at a landscape beyond my range of vision. I held his hand, amazed by the strength of his grip, and told him loudly that I loved him. I wanted to believe that he heard me, though I doubt he did. Dad was focused on only one thing: his next breath.

After four days, I had the nursing home routine down pat: temperature taken, oxygen level measured, food offered and refused, Dad's dry mouth swabbed with water, and morphine administered every four hours. Doctors, nurses, aides, and housekeepers came and went, did their jobs, and offered me kind words. Dad was turned regularly to avoid bedsores. My cousins' families came through for me as they always do, taking turns keeping watch while I went home to sleep.

Saturday, December 24

Christmas Eve arrived on a Saturday, five years to the day that Mother had broken her hip. Mother was in house shoes and excellent spirits for our family's traditional dinner. I bought candy and flowers for her, two of the few tangibles she still enjoyed. The most powerful fact of this holiday was the absent faces. My cousins' parents, Aunt Gene and Uncle Bill, had died that year, just eight months apart. Now Dad was holding on by a thread. Sadly, we wouldn't have to worry about his wine intake this year.

The real fun was after dinner when white elephant monstrosities were traded with gleeful malice. Since my Reynolds-wrapped contribution was usually poorly received, this year I brought a $75 gift certificate to a spa that I'd gotten for singing at a celebrity roast. I hoped it would make up for ten years of spatulas and bad art.

Sunday, December 25

On Christmas Day, I went to church, ate yet another high-calorie, artery-clogging feast at a friend's home, and then headed for the nursing home. As I drove up I-35, I tried to calculate how many times I'd driven the twenty-seven miles from Austin to Georgetown in the last ten years. I figured between twelve hundred and fifteen hundred round-trips.

As I walked down the hall of B-Wing, I could see bright boxes being opened and families gathered around beds doing their best to import joy. At the nurses' station, lights were twinkling, decorations glistened, and the atmosphere was resolutely cheerful. As I walked into his room, I realized that for the first time since grade school, I had no present for my father. This year my gift was being there.

I sat with him for hours, thinking of Christmases past: the time he couldn't get my electric train set up and the year of the yapping puppy hidden in the basement. I recalled long trips in big cars crowded with presents. There was the difficult Christmas after my brother died when my folks came to see me in New York to break our usual routine. As my mind swept over the past, I wondered what Dad was thinking about or if he was thinking at all.

Little had changed in a week. His mouth remained wide open and held an oxygen tube to keep his breathing steady. His eyes were glassy, fixed on the ceiling. He hadn't said a word in three days, nor did he respond to what was said to him. His hand no longer gripped mine. Nevertheless, he was still here. My cousin, Bill, arrived at ten to take the late-night shift. I told him I'd be back at eight in the morning.

Monday, December 26

I arrived at eight as promised, Starbucks in hand, and found my twenty-five-year-old cousin, Kim, sitting by Dad's bed. She's a fourth-year med student home on holiday break and this was a chance for us to catch up. We talked for two hours as Dad slept peacefully. There was nothing to suggest anything unusual was happening. He looked the same as he had the night before. Kim left at ten to get some sleep and a nurse came in to check Dad's vital signs.

I went to get Mother so she could visit the husband she no longer knew. I hoped this time she might recognize him. Five minutes later, when I brought her into his room, the nurse was bending closely over Dad's face, checking his breathing. I walked over to the bed to see how he was doing. The nurse checked his pulse. Half a minute went by and she said, "I think he just took his last breath."

Dad had died seconds after Mother and I walked into his room. We had no warning. Nothing dramatic happened. There was no gasping for breath or sound of a struggle. He simply stopped breathing and tiptoed out of our lives.

I'd never seen anyone die, much less a parent. Even though I heard the nurse's words, they didn't register fully. I stood there looking at him, trying to take in what had just happened. I'm sure there was conversation, though I don't remember what was said. I only knew that Dad was gone. I felt sad, relieved, exhausted, and grateful that his struggle had ended.

After a few minutes, I called my cousins and told them the news. Staff members began to come into the room: Tim, the administrator; Vanessa, the social worker; Dean, the chaplain. Someone asked if I wanted them to call the funeral home. I figured that's what you were supposed to do next so I said, "Yes, please call them."

I saw Mother sitting there calmly amid the hubbub. I needed to tell her what had happened and searched for the right words, even though she wouldn't remember them. I put my arms around her shoulders.

"Mom, Dad has gone to heaven."

"He has?"

"Yes, he's not sick any more."

"That's good."

She seemed to have no trouble with the concept of death for the few seconds she considered it. As we headed back to her room, she had forgotten the news before we passed the nurses' station. Part of me envied her.

Within less than an hour two employees from the funeral home had arrived. They didn't waste any time getting there. I asked for a few minutes alone with Dad. As I stood there looking at him, I realized I was no longer in the room with my father. He had departed.

I told the funeral home people to come in. Within minutes, Dad was covered with a sheet and wheeled out to the waiting ambulance. I was unsure what came next. There is choreography to death and I didn't know the steps. My cousins, who had gone through this experience twice in the previous year, suggested that I have lunch at their house before dealing with the avalanche of decisions and details about to descend on me. Bill said that going through the paperwork at the funeral home would take three hours.

"That's impossible. I've got a pre-need burial plan."

"Trust me, it will take three hours."

He was right.

21

Funerals Are for the Living

Three hours after my father's death, fortified by lunch at my cousin's house, I drove ten miles to the funeral home. It was located next to the cemetery, which had been chosen fifty years ago as our family's final resting place. It was not the wisest choice. The "memorial park" is directly adjacent to I-35, the traffic-laden main corridor from the U.S. to Mexico, which handles tens of thousands of smoke-belching trucks and speeding cars every day. Though the cemetery is well kept, the backdrop is non-stop noise, pollution, frequent sirens, and the occasional multi-car collision.

Within minutes of my arrival at the corporate-run facility, I was escorted into a conference room to meet with the funeral director and her assistant. They offered me a soft drink as we surveyed the mountain of documents I had to review and sign. The last time I'd seen that many forms was when I closed on a house. The good news was that this paperwork had nothing to do with mortgage payments. The bad news was that I had to read it.

As we reviewed paperwork, the director pointed out how much money I'd saved by planning ahead. She said that prices had escalated dramatically in the last few years and told me how fortunate I was to have bought the plan in 2003. Somehow this information did not cheer me, nor did I find it in good taste. I wasn't there to celebrate a bargain but to talk about burying my father.

The only major "add on" was the headstone for my parents' graves. I planned to buy something simple and inexpensive, as my father had instructed. I was informed that there was an arbitrary standard of marble below which the cemetery would not descend. Even if I had been a latter-day Michelangelo, I was required to go with a predetermined design deemed appropriate for the park. The least expensive headstone, lying flush with the ground, was $2,200.

Despite our detailed pre-need burial plan, I had many decisions to make. Fortunately, I'd talked to my father about his wishes and was clear about my own preferences. These are a few of the questions I was asked:

Did I want a public visitation?

No, I wanted friends to attend the memorial service, not to view the body. I preferred them to remember Dad at his best, not the diminished figure of the last six months.

Did I want to use the funeral home chapel for the service?

I preferred a simple graveside service for the immediate family and close friends. Dad died on Monday, so I chose to hold the burial service on Thursday at ten. Because it was in the middle of the Christmas holidays, I decided to hold the memorial service on the first Saturday after New Year's Day. Having it on a Saturday afternoon made it easier for friends and relatives from out of town to attend and did not require anyone to take time off from work.

Did I want a military honor guard?

Because Dad was a veteran we could get an honor guard to cover the casket with the flag, play "Taps," remove and fold the flag at the end of the ceremony, and present it to Mother. This was an excellent idea that I knew Dad would have liked. Unlike everything else about a funeral, the honor guard is free. All we needed was my father's military service number, which I could not find. Weeks later I discovered it in the lockbox at the bank.

I had his medals, pictures of him in uniform, and a nationally published book he'd written about his service in World War II, but no service number. The funeral director said the missing number might be a problem in getting the honor guard, but that she would try to arrange it.

Who did I want as pallbearers?

I gave her a list of healthy, young relatives. Caskets are not only hefty in price, but in pounds. I wanted no coronaries during the service.

Who would officiate at the graveside service?

I chose ministers who were close to my father and me, even though their theological views did not mesh seamlessly. My own minister, the chaplain from the nursing home, and a friend from Hospice Austin agreed to participate. Since it was December, I asked the clergy to keep their comments brief.

What did I want in the death notice that would be faxed that afternoon to the Austin newspaper and appear in the next day's edition?

We wrote a simple three-line announcement of Dad's death and the two services we had planned. The death notice is free. The obituary would be costly and run several days later with Dad's picture.

In what papers did I want the obituary to appear and how many days should it run?

I wanted it to run on Sunday, when the readership is higher, in the *Austin American-Statesman*. I also felt it should appear in the *Dallas Morning News* because my parents had lived in Dallas for thirty-four years. I knew that friends and neighbors there would want to know of Dad's passing.

Would I like the funeral home to write the obituary?

Definitely not. I wanted to write it myself so I could include personal details and make the tone consistent with my father's personality. I did not want a cut-and-dried notice that came from the funeral home template.

How many death certificates did I want to order?

The funeral director explained that these would be needed by banks, insurance companies, and courts in order to probate the will. She suggested I get at least four copies. Since I knew nothing about death certificates, I went along with four.

Did I want to buy a guest book from the funeral home that would be personalized with pictures and details of my Dad's service? That would cost an additional $55.

At first I said "No" because the same book would cost $20 at Hallmark. Two hours later, as my energy was fading, I changed my mind and bought it.

Would I like to see the gravesite?

Absolutely. It had been several years since I'd visited the cemetery. The assistant director drove me to the site where our family's plot was supposed to be located. We got out of her car and spent ten minutes trying to find the gravesite. It became apparent that the funeral home map was incomplete. She radioed for help and a man in a van showed up. He could not find our plot either, so they drove back to the funeral home to find accurate information.

I was left standing alone listening to eight-wheelers whiz by at eighty miles an hour just a hundred yards away. I vowed silently that my ashes would never be interred by this interstate, but scattered in a more serene locale. At last the funeral director returned with a new map and we found the spot where my father was to be buried. With a little too much enthusiasm, she pointed out the plot where my ashes would be interred. I eyed the grass warily. I might die, but my ashes would not be going there. I'd be flung into a lake or off a mountaintop and my relatives could sell the plot to the highest bidder and donate the proceeds to a worthy cause.

We returned to the funeral home and I scrawled my name on at least fifty pages of forms. I was so bleary-eyed by the time we finished I might have signed over my house. When I left the funeral home it was 4:15 P.M., three hours and five minutes after I'd arrived. My cousins' estimate was right on target. I drove home and fell into bed with my clothes on.

The Graveside Service

My greatest surprise about my father's death and the days that followed was my state of exhaustion. I had no idea how tired I would be. The week spent at Dad's bedside had left me physically and emotionally depleted. And yet there was no time to recover. I had two services to plan, an obituary to write, many calls to make, details to oversee, and a eulogy to compose. All the while I felt as if I was operating in slow motion.

My solution? I drank many triple grande mochas, an intestinally challenging concoction that I had "given up" with great fanfare several months previously. Eating crow, even hyper-caffeinated crow, was a small price to pay for a little boost to get through the next few weeks.

I practiced what I preach in this book: I asked for and received help from friends and relatives. Most importantly, I got out of bed each day, put one foot in front of the other and—as they say in twelve-step programs—tried to do "the next right thing."

The graveside service was relatively simple to plan. I chose three of my favorite readings from the Bible and asked a talented French horn player to play as people arrived at the cemetery. Along with close relatives, I invited the staff of the nursing home to attend because I considered them to be family.

The only hitch was getting the honor guard. The funeral home director did not succeed in getting one lined up so I went to my congressman's office carrying Dad's medals and air force pictures in hand. No luck. It was four days before New Year and the office was closed until January 3.

From there I went to Tim Stuteville, Wesleyan's efficient and likable administrator. I told him the situation and he said "No problem." He knew the person I should call at Fort Hood, the army base in nearby Killeen, Texas, that would supply the honor guard. Within five minutes Tim had the number and invited me to make the call from his office. I got through immediately to a kind woman who scheduled the honor guards, and told her my situation.

"You don't need that number, just a picture of your father in uniform."

"I have that photo in front of me."

"Fax it to me and I'll take care of the honor guard. Where is the cemetery and when is the service?"

I faxed a photo immediately and called her back. She said that the guard would arrive two hours before the service on Thursday. Problem solved.

On the morning of the service I got to the funeral home an hour early. The funeral director asked if I'd like to see my father's body before they took the casket to the gravesite. With some serious misgivings, I went into the viewing room hoping I was not making a big mistake. I was not.

Dad looked twenty years younger. He face was full, unlined, and peaceful. I was amazed at the transformation. I don't know how they did it—and don't want to know—but he looked once again like the father I had known. I would not be forced to remember him with oxygen tubes and a sunken face. Momentarily, I regretted not having a formal viewing, but only for a few seconds. This time was for me.

They'd put his air force cap in the casket as I had instructed. At the last moment, I had a change of heart and decided to keep it. Nothing symbolized my father's spirit better than that cap he wore night and day. I would take it home and keep it where I could see it every day.

The morning was beautiful, with clear skies and a temperature in the high sixties. I went over the order of service with the ministers. My cousins Bill and Bonnie brought Mother from the nursing home. She didn't seem aware or concerned about the event she was attending. She was just glad to be out and about on a pretty day.

The French horn played, the honor guard waited in the background and at ten o'clock Mother and I took our seats in front of the empty grave. The casket was carried in without incident and the service flowed beautifully.

"Taps" was played and the flag was folded and handed to us. My minister ended the ceremony with a beautiful prayer.

When the service was over, I invited the entire family for lunch on my father at a local steak restaurant. He always said I liked to spend his money, and I couldn't think of a better way to prove him right.

The Obituary

It was important to me that Dad's obituary not only reflect basic information about his birth, death, and survivors but also that it be an authentic overview of a remarkable life. I worked on it for hours to hone ninety-five years into twelve column inches.

John Smith Comer

John Smith Comer, age 95, passed away peacefully on December 26, 2005 at the Wesleyan Nursing Home in Georgetown, Texas with his wife and son by his side.

John was born in Ennis, Texas on March 1, 1910 and graduated from Gatesville High School in 1927. He attended Trinity University in Waxahachie, Texas and transferred to the University of Texas, where he worked three jobs and studied journalism.

He moved to Corpus Christi in 1935 and married Anne Haynie of Smithville, Texas on June 8, 1940. He and his wife were looking for their first house on the Sunday Pearl Harbor was attacked. John enlisted in the Army in January 1942 and volunteered for the Air Corps. He served in the 381st Division of the 8th Air Force and was a technical sergeant and top turret gunner on a B-17.

When his crew arrived in England in July 1943, the casualty rate on his base was 80%. He completed his first twenty-five missions in January 1944, returned to the states and was assigned to flight school in Gulfport, Mississippi. He claimed that combat was safer than training new pilots and - much to his wife's chagrin - volunteered to return to Europe. In Italy, he completed fifty-one additional missions for a total of seventy-six.

After the war, he began a career in sales. In 1949 he joined the Sherwin-Williams Paint Company where he became an award-winning salesman and in 1954 was appointed regional sales manager in Atlanta responsible for thirteen states. In order to help care for aging relatives, he transferred his office to Dallas in 1962.

He retired in 1975 and served as a consultant for Sherwin-Williams in Asia and South America. He mentored young business people through the SCORE program, was active in Casa View Methodist Church and gave weekly tours at the Frontiers of Flight Museum at Love Field in Dallas.

Using hand-written journals from World War II, worked for six years to turn a thousand pages of notes into a book. Combat Crew was self-published in 1985 and sold out in six months. It was sent to a New York agent who sold it in two weeks to William Morrow and Company. Published in the United States and England in both hard cover and paperback, it sold more than fifty thousand copies.

John was a true renaissance man who could take apart an engine, discuss philosophy or quantum physics, teach a Sunday School class, enjoy season tickets to Dallas Cowboys games for thirty years and travel the world. He worked his way to Europe on a tramp steamer at twenty, traveled to Tibet at seventy-eight, visited five continents and had a lively conversation about oil wells with Pope Pius XII.

He was preceded in death by his parents, C.C. Comer and Jessie Smith Comer; son, John Christopher Comer; sister, Gene Comer Stump and brother-in-law, William Stump, Sr.

He is survived by his wife of sixty-five years, Anne Haynie Comer of Georgetown; son, James Balmore Comer of Austin; sister, Mary Beth Comer of Georgetown; niece, Marguerite Sanderson and her husband, Tommy of El Paso; nephews, William Stump, Jr. and his wife, Bonnie of Georgetown; Randy Stump and his wife, Donna of Georgetown.

Private burial services were held at Cook-Walden/Capital Parks Cemetery on December 28, 2005.

A memorial service will be held at St. Andrew's Presbyterian Church, 14311 Wells Port Drive, Austin, on Saturday, January 7, 2006 at 2:00 p.m. with a reception following.

In lieu of flowers the family request memorials be sent to the Wesleyan Homes Building Fund, 1105 Church Street, Georgetown, Texas 78626.

COOK·WALDEN
Capital Parks · Funerals & Cremations
14501 North IH-35
251-4118

Because I'm a writer, composing the obituary was easier for me than it might have been for others. However, every family knows the key moments in their parent's life. They understand what was important to their loved one. They have someone among their circle of acquaintances who can take these facts and turn them into a fitting account of their parent's life.

If you don't have a friend who can write the obituary for you, hire a professional. There are freelance writers listed in every phone book and on the Internet. Don't have the obituary written by the funeral home or by a sibling who made a C- in English. We pay a professional florist to provide the flowers for the service and ask trained singers to do solos. It only makes sense to find someone who writes well to craft an obituary that actually reflects the life and spirit of your parent.

At least fifty people who never met my dad told me that they felt they knew him from reading his obituary. That's not because of my talent, but because he had an interesting life and I took the time to share it. You owe that to your parent as well.

Many people have the mistaken impression that papers run obituaries as a public service. Would that were the case. Newspapers are not charitable institutions, and obituaries are a steady profit center. In major metropolitan papers, obituaries are expensive.

We wanted Dad's to run in the Sunday edition of the *Austin American-Statesman,* which has a circulation of 240,000. Papers charge by the column inch or line. Our obituary ran twelve inches plus a two-inch picture and cost $700. That was longer than the average obituary, but not nearly as long as many. *The Dallas Morning News*, with a larger circulation, charged $690 after I cut several paragraphs. The total for the two obituaries was around $1,400 and I feel the money was well spent.

Unfortunately, there was a miscommunication between the funeral home and the Dallas paper, and the paragraphs listing the survivors and the time and date of the memorial service were omitted. Much to their credit, the funeral home ran the entire obituary again the next day and paid for it.

The Memorial Service—Getting the Word to Friends

Although the obituary is important, many people will not see it because they don't read newspapers or may have missed that day's edition. There is a growing group of people, mostly under thirty-five, who don't read newspapers at all and get their news from TV and the Internet.

That leaves two choices: telephone or email. If I'd had the time and energy, I would have called every friend and acquaintance personally to tell them about Dad's death and invite them to the memorial service. That was not possible. Even though I asked friends in several organizations to spread the word, I still had hundreds of people to contact.

I called relatives and out-of-town friends who might want to come to the service, and then bowed to reality and composed an email for everyone else. Using the computer allowed me to get the word to people all over the country in a manner of minutes. Because I waited several days to send the message, I was able to attach the obituary that ran in the local paper.

Here are a few thoughts on letting people know about a parent's death:

- Err on the side of telling too many people rather than leaving out those who would want to know.

- Don't rely on your memory in deciding who you should tell.

- Use your address book or database *and* your parent's address book.

- If your parent was active in a church, call the church secretary so an announcement can go in the Sunday bulletin.

- Talk to people from each of the organizations to which your parent belonged so they can make announcements or phone members.

- Tell people who enjoy spreading news—good or bad.

- Tell your own friends. They want to be there for you, but can't show up if they don't know about your loss.

Know What You Want Before You Meet with Your Minister

Don't expect your minister, priest, rabbi, or funeral director to tell you how to organize the service. Do your homework, consult with your family, and be prepared to let those who will officiate know what you want the service to include.

I realize that some religious traditions are more flexible than others, but the family has a lot to say about music, eulogies, and the general tone of the service. You also get to choose the minister who conducts the service; this individual can make all the difference. If your family is not religious, you may choose to celebrate your parent's life through secular readings, music, and personal tributes. The more personal and authentic you can make the service, the better.

I met with my minister and choir director five days before the memorial service, and I had done my homework. I brought them an outline of the service as I saw it, including:

- Three scriptures and poems I wanted read and by whom

- The people I wanted to do tributes

- The solos I wanted sung and by whom

- The music I wanted playing as the congregation entered: Samuel Barber's "Adagio for Strings"

- I planned a slide show with pictures from my father's life and wanted Pachelbel's "Canon" to play under the slides. I needed to find out if they had the appropriate audio/visual equipment in good working order

- I asked for advice in choosing the two hymns the congregation would sing and went along with the choir director's selections

- Most importantly, I briefed the minister on the key events, challenges, and achievements of my father's life. I gave him two typewritten pages about Dad, along with his obituary

My minister, Rev. Jim Rigby, had met my father but did not know him well. I wanted him to understand and appreciate the person he was going to eulogize. We spent half an hour talking about my dad's life. Jim got a real feeling for my father and the obstacles he'd overcome: living through the Depression, having Pearl Harbor hit on the day he and Mother were looking for the first house, dedicating almost four years of service in the Army Air Corps, and starting a new career in sales at forty and turning himself into a top salesman. In each case, my father met and overcame adversity. Jim's eulogy reflected the insights I gave him.

I asked for what I wanted. I called Jim and Carol Norris, wonderful singers and musicians in Dallas, and requested that they sing at the service. I asked my friend Jennifer Harvill, who has a gorgeous voice, to sing "The Lord's Prayer."

I went to Keith Knight, a professional who had edited a video for me, to help put together the slide show. I supplied the scanned pictures; he edited the DVD and put in the song underneath. And Keith wouldn't accept payment for his work. The day before the service, David Marks, our choir director, assembled the projector and we did a technical rehearsal of the slide show.

To give tributes, I chose three people who had totally different experiences of my father. His next-door neighbor in Dallas, Gean Smith, looked on

Dad as a surrogate father and was awed by his service in World War II. My cousin, Randy Stump, knew my father as an uncle, friend, and, finally, as a client. He also has a great sense of humor and was privy to family tales. Last, I asked the administrator of Wesleyan Homes, Chris Spence, to talk about the last decade of Dad's life.

I included members of the family in the service. My cousin Wren Stump sang "Amazing Grace" with great poise. Jessica Haynie read St. Francis's prayer. Kim Stump read St. Paul's powerful passage on love from I Corinthians. Her father, Bill, read my favorite passage from Paul that ends with the affirmation, "Nothing can separate us from the love of God."

Finally, I added a personal perspective in my tribute and talked about the gifts my father had given me. He endowed me with racial tolerance in the segregationist south of the fifties and encouraged me to discuss subjects from politics to religion to philosophy. He demonstrated an inquiring mind that was not bound by conventional ideas. Most importantly, Dad gave me the gift of unconditional love.

I led a life that was not the one he would have picked for me. I lived in New York and Los Angeles for thirty years. I tried to be an actor for ten years and made little money when my contemporaries were buying houses and settling down. I didn't get married and produce grandchildren. I had problems with sobriety in my forties. Dad stood with me when times were rough and loved and supported me through them all. I ended by giving him the last word and reading the final page of his book, in which he talks about the death of his best friends—the men after whom I'm named—and his belief that they will meet again.

My church family could not have been more loving and supportive. The deacons put on a beautiful reception with excellent food and punch in the foyer of the church following the service.

At 10:00 A.M. on the morning of the service, my friend Kathi Miller created posters with pictures of my father for the church lobby as I finished writing the eulogy which I'd changed drastically a few hours before.

A few things almost slipped through the cracks. I called the nursing home to have them do Mother's hair on the Friday before the Saturday service and found out that was the day the hair salon was closed. However, they said they'd find someone from the town to come in and do Mother's hair and for me not to worry about it.

The night before the service I remembered that Mother had not worn anything but house shoes for five years in the nursing home. I called my cousin's wife, Donna, and asked her to buy Mother a pair of real shoes on the morning of the funeral. Donna got those shoes at 11:00 A.M. and mother was wearing them at 2:00 P.M.

Mother received her old Dallas friends and relatives in the church library before the service. She did not remember a single one of them, but she faked it with grand southern style. She told them how good they looked and how glad she was to see them again. She couldn't have been more gracious if she had actually remembered them. Her social skills and ability to improvise continue to astound me.

The result of the preparation paid off. The service was just what I'd hoped it would be: an authentic, loving, positive celebration of my father's life. Many friends who didn't know my father before the service knew him when they left the church. His friends and family experienced a memorial service that matched the man. It was one of the few events in my life that more than met my expectations.

Comer's Commandments

• Be gentle with yourself. No matter how prepared you think you are, the death of a parent will bring up feelings you don't expect.

• Get as much rest as you can. The last few weeks of your parents' life will be physically and emotionally exhausting.

• When friends and relatives volunteer to help, say "Yes."

• You do not need to be at the hospital or by your parent's bedside every moment.

• You do not control the timing of birth or death. While you may want to be in the room when your parent passes away, that may not happen, and it is okay.

• Your presence at the moment of death is not as important as your presence in the months and years leading up to that moment.

• Patience is not only a virtue but a requirement.

22

I Got More Than I Gave

I've found that patience is the currency of love.
I'm a little less selfish, most days.
I've gotten good at folding wheelchairs.
I know my relatives on a non-holiday basis.
I realize how much I have in common with the
eighty- and ninety-year-olds who share my parents' lives.

In the last decade my view of life has changed immeasurably. I understand that dignity comes in a variety of shapes, including bent, wrinkled, and walker-assisted. I realize that parenting is not a part-time job but a full-time commitment. Mine is not a cameo appearance; I'm here for the long run.

Mother likes to tell people that Seton Hospital only charged her $4 a day when I was born—*and that I'm worth every penny of it*. I hope I've lived up to her investment. When people ask me how my folks are doing, I'm happy to say that I know the answer. I can look in the mirror without flinching. Every time I walk into the nursing home and see their faces light up, I know I'm in exactly the right place.

Before she broke her hip, Mother always walked me to the elevator of the retirement home. Despite all the years, her parenting instincts needed no prodding. As the doors opened, she would hug me and say:

"Jim, do you need a little folding money?"

"No, I'm fine."

"Well, if you ever need help, we're always here for you."

Good parents always are. Now it's my turn and I wouldn't have missed it for the world.

PART TWO

A Guide to Parenting Your Parents

Do *not* close the book until you have answered
the following questions in writing

23

Fifty Questions That Will Save You Time, Money, and Tears

There is no way to assign a dollar value to peace of mind or to put a price on being prepared. Families who talk to each other openly—who ask hard questions and face difficult answers—will be better prepared when a crisis comes. And, eventually, it will come. I learned from experience that ignorance is *not* bliss. Because I had not done my homework, I paid the price of denial and felt the fear of the uninformed.

If you and your siblings will take the time to answer these questions— *and it may take you weeks or months to get all the information*—I guarantee that you will be in much better shape to deal with your parents' care. Make copies of the following questions, share them with your siblings, and then go over the appropriate questions with your parents.

Have a family discussion in a relaxed atmosphere, not in the middle of a holiday celebration, birthday, or anniversary. These questions deserve a time slot of their own. If the family is geographically dispersed and you can't have the discussion in person, arrange for a conference call. Using the phone is better than not talking at all. The most important words in this book are: *Communicate Now.*

When Roles Reverse

1. When is the last time you talked with your parents about their plans for the future?

_____

_____

2. What decisions have they made?

_____

_____

_____

3. What specific plans has your family made for a sudden parental illness or emergency?

_____

_____

_____

4. How frankly—and how recently—have you talked with your siblings and other family members about the realities of caring for your parents?

_____

_____

5. If a parent becomes ill or incapacitated, who will be the primary caregiver, or will it be a shared responsibility?

_____

_____

6. Which other family members can you count on to be involved in your parents' care?

_____

_____

7. If you will be the primary caregiver, how do you feel about that responsibility?

_____

_____

8. If you are married, how does your spouse feel about your commitment to your parents?

_____

_____

9. What are the names and phone numbers of your parents':
Primary care physician:

_____

Eye doctor:

_____

Dentist:

_____

Specialists:

_____

_____

Lawyer:

_____

Accountant:

_____

Financial planner:

_____

10. When have you last talked to your parents' doctors?

_____

_____

11. Are your parents signed up for Medicare?

_____

12. Have they signed up for Medicare Part D, the prescription drug benefit, and how do they feel it is working for them?

_____

_____

13. Do they have supplemental Medicare (Medigap) insurance and what does it cover?

_____

_____

14. Do you know the differences among care facilities? Can you briefly define the following:
Independent living/retirement home:

_____

Assisted-living residence:

_____

Skilled nursing home:

_____

15. What is the monthly price range for care facilities in your area?

_____

_____

16. What is your parents' monthly income including social security, pensions, investment, and interest income? If you don't know, find out.

_____

_____

17. If your parent needs nursing care and does not have savings or long-term-care insurance, do you know how to apply for Medicaid?

_____

_____

18. Do your parents have long-term-care insurance and, if so, what does it cover?

_____

_____

19. What are the options for home health care in your area?

_____

_____

20. Do you see your parents often enough to adequately assess how they are doing?

_____

_____

21. If your parents need ongoing care, would one of the children move near them, or would they move near one of the children?

_____

_____

22. If your parents refuse to move from their hometown and none of the children can move near them, what are your plans?

_____

_____

_____

23. How would you describe your relationship with your parents?

_____

_____

_____

24. If there are major issues, what can you do now to help resolve them?

_____

_____

_____

25. Do your parents have any of these problems?

    Physical limitations:

    _____

    Inadequate diet:

    _____

    Memory loss:

    _____

    Isolation:

    _____

    Substance abuse:

    _____

26. Are your parents still driving?

    _____

    _____

27. Should your parents be driving?

    _____

    _____

28. If one or both of your parents should not be driving, what can you do to get them to stop?

    _____

    _____

29. Do your parents have wills and do you know where they are kept?

    _____

    _____

30. Have their wills been updated recently?

    _____

31. Where are their financial documents kept, and have you reviewed them with your parents?

_____

_____

32. Do your parents have a safe-deposit box?

_____

33. Is your name on the box, and do you have a key to it?

_____

34. Do you or one of your siblings have durable power of attorney that allows you to act legally in your parents' names?

_____

_____

35. Do you or one of your siblings have health care power of attorney that allows you to make health care decisions in your parents' names?

_____

_____

36. Do you or one of your siblings have co-signing power at their bank?

_____

_____

37. Do your parents have a directive to physicians (living will) that states their preferences for end-of-life decisions such as being placed on a feeding tube or ventilator?

_____

_____

38. Have they signed a do-not-resuscitate order that would serve as direction to the medical staff?

_____

_____

39. What are the name and phone number of the family minister, priest, or rabbi?

_____

_____

40. Would your parents prefer a traditional funeral, memorial service, graveside ceremony, or no service at all?

_____

41. If they want a service, would they prefer to have it in a church or a funeral home?

_____

42. What specific readings, music, or scripture would each like to have included in his or her service?

    Music:

    _____

    _____

    Scripture/readings:

    _____

    _____

    Photos and/or videos:

    _____

    Who would they like to give eulogies?

    _____

    _____

    Who would they like to be pallbearers?

    _____

    _____

43. Do they want an open or closed casket?

_____

44. Do your parents have a pre-need burial plan that includes burial plot, casket, and funeral service costs? Where are these documents kept?

_____

_____

45. What do they want inscribed on their grave markers or tombstones?

_____

_____

46. If your parents prefer cremation, do they want their ashes buried or scattered?

_____

_____

47. If they want their ashes scattered, when and where do they want that done?

_____

_____

48. Do they want to be organ donors and have they signed the forms to make that possible?

_____

_____

49. In case there is a disagreement among family members, do you have their funeral preferences in writing and where is this document kept?

_____

_____

50. Do you have the biographical information and photographs you will need for your parents' obituaries?

_____

_____

John and Anne Comer;
wedding portrait, 1940

Caring for Your Parents:
There's No One Right Way

Although I have dealt with emergency rooms, intensive care, four operations, three rehab centers, a retirement home, assisted living, a skilled nursing home, and hospice care, *my experience is limited*. I have no idea what it's like to deal with squabbling siblings, argue over money or mementos, change diapers, or be responsible for meals and medications. My folks never moved into my home and I never moved into theirs. I have not balanced raising children with the pressure of parental care. All in all, I've had it easy.

To provide a wider perspective and a variety of viewpoints, I have interviewed full-time caregivers, home health-care agencies, geriatric care managers, and administrators of retirement homes, assisted-living residences, and nursing homes—as well as critics of the industry. I've spent hours talking to elder lawyers, long-term-care specialists, staff members of Area Agencies on Aging, funeral directors, and chaplains. These professionals have worked with thousands of families from varied backgrounds, ethnicities, income levels, and religions. I won't say they've seen it all, but there is very little they have missed. Their experiences and insights will help you negotiate the legal, financial, and emotional issues you are likely to face as you care for your parents.

24

Home Care

Contrary to popular opinion, the vast majority of caregiving takes place in the home. Despite the tremendous growth of retirement communities, assisted living, and nursing homes in the last twenty-five years, most seniors live at home or with their children. The great majority of parents want to stay in their own homes as long as possible, even sometimes when it's not the safest setting for them. When stay-at-home-till-they-carry-me-out parents become ill, a child or relative may move in to care for them. If parents have the financial means, they might hire home health care workers or even get around-the-clock nursing care.

Among those parents whose health or isolation finally causes them to leave their home, most move in with one of their children. Taking in—and taking on—an elderly parent is a loving act on the part of the family members who care for them, but it is not always an easy experience. Of course, neither is raising teenagers. One-on-one caregiving requires sacrifices of time, money, and energy. It may bring up emotional and psychological challenges, but millions of American families would have it no other way. I want to begin with the greatest care facility of all: a loving home.

I've known Richard and Elizabeth Hess for six years and have been amazed at their commitment to caring for their parents at home. I met with them in February 2006 and talked candidly about their experiences in providing hands-on care for more than a decade. Their words are so honest and direct that I

want you to read them as I recorded them. Their love and commitment are clear, but so are the difficulties they faced.

Elizabeth: This is the first time in eleven and a half years that Richard and I have been together in this house without a parent living with us. Dad is visiting my brother in California. We had both of my parents with us for ten years until Mama died in November of 2005. While Mama was still alive, we had Richard's dad, Sidney, with us for ten months. At one point we had three over-ninety-year-olds in one 1,800-square-foot house. To put it mildly, it was a very lively home.

My mom and dad were living in southern Arizona when Mother had two strokes in her early eighties. The second one was a serious brain-stem stroke and she was having a lot of difficulty. Dad was doing his best to help her, but she wasn't getting the kind of care she needed and he wasn't getting the support he needed.

I have a brother in California, a brother in North Carolina, and a sister here in Austin, and we were living in Ithaca, New York. My parents had lived in Austin for five years in the early eighties and liked it, and my sister had been living here for many years. So we made an agreement with my parents. We said, "If you'll move back to Austin, we'll leave Ithaca and come there, too." With my sister here we felt we would have plenty of family support. My parents said, "Okay, we'll do it."

When I told her that we were all coming to Austin, my sister said, "Great." She had a husband and grown children and was in the last years of a high school teaching career. However, I made a big mistake right up front. I didn't ask her a key question. I didn't say, "What's your vision of taking care of our parents?" I assumed that she had the same ideas that I did.

We moved my parents to Austin in the spring of 1994 and they went into a retirement home in south Austin, the Continental. It was independent living so they had their own apartment, but they went to the dining room for meals. My dad hated the place. He was in excellent health and didn't have anything to keep him busy. Mama disliked it for other reasons. She didn't like having to get dressed and go to meals at a set time.

When Richard and I arrived in town, I got a job working near their retirement home. Soon I found myself going there before work, at lunchtime, and after work. Mama needed help bathing and getting dressed. My sister would come only once a week and timed her visits to arrive ten minutes before my parents had to go to a meal.

Jim: Did you and your sister talk about this?

Elizabeth: I'm afraid we're not a family that talks about things. When it became clear that the retirement home was not working out for my parents, Richard and I suggested, "Let's just rent a place together and see how it works. We'll see how we all do and if it feels good." We started looking at rentals and couldn't find what we wanted.

About that time this house was being built right across the street from where we were living. It has a master bedroom and bath on one side and a master bedroom and bath on the other side. We thought, "Maybe this wouldn't be too bad." We brought my mom and dad to look at the house and they liked it. So my father bought this house.

The four of us moved in together on Labor Day of 1995. I was going to cook wonderful meals and make everybody healthy and happy, but food turned out to be a major issue. Richard and I are not big meat eaters and our idea of a good meal was quite different from that of my parents. I cook a lot of rice, vegetables and stir fries, and things like that. My folks were not interested in that kind of food.

One night my father, who's usually a nice guy, looked at my plate and said, "What's that crap you're eating?" They wanted "real food" and that meant meat and potatoes. Meals were a real struggle until I realized finally that I would have to make two different meals, one for them and one for us. It was hard for me to accept that we were sitting down to two different meals every night. But that's what we did.

Richard: It made things much harder on Elizabeth and she was still working full time.

Elizabeth: I worked another year or so. Then I told my dad, "I can't do this. I'm cheating everybody. I'm cheating my job. I'm cheating myself. I'm cheating you because I try to get meals together when I am exhausted." At that point we weren't getting any money for feeding them or taking care of them. My father bought the house and paid the bills. So he said, "Okay, I can pay you $500 a month." That was $6,000 a year, plus $1,500 a month for the mortgage, home insurance, and utility bills. I said, "I'll do that." Richard was bringing in additional money from teaching pottery classes.

My father is not a wealthy man, but he was getting a good deal. He was paying $2,400 a month at the Continental and was unhappy. Here he was content, had more space, meals, and full-time care for much less money. My parents knew that they could no longer live independently in a house without somebody there. Occasionally they acknowledged that we were filling that void for them. Like many caregivers, I thought I'd receive more gratitude. I believe they felt it, but didn't express it very often: maybe once or twice a year.

Caring for my mother was hard work. I bathed her every day because she was incontinent.

Richard: Elizabeth asked her sister, who had retired from teaching, if she would relieve her one day a week. She wasn't working, but she wouldn't come. She just never showed up.

Jim: And you never talked about it?

Elizabeth: No, and that was not smart.

Richard: All of us should have talked about what's going on.

Elizabeth: After another year, I asked her, "Would you come one morning a week and bathe her so Richard and I can be gone for half a day? She said, "Well, I guess I could do that." She never showed up once.

Jim: Did you call her on that?

Elizabeth: No. I'm willing to own my part that I never said anything. My brother in California was always wonderful—and still is—about calling and coming every three months. I have another brother in North Carolina. His family would come once a year for their vacation.

Richard: One of the most important things both of us learned is that the family needs to have a real honest, detailed discussion about who's going to do what *before* anything takes place. You need to make sure you are all on the same page. We've spent much of the last ten years saying to ourselves, "We shouldn't have all lived in the same house. We should have lived upstairs, downstairs, next door, or across the street. Four adults living together is a very difficult situation, but we would have never changed our decision to care for them. We would not put our parents in nursing homes unless we couldn't deal with it here. *The caring part we would do again. The particulars of how we arranged the care we would do differently.*

Elizabeth: For those who are considering caring for their parents at home, don't underestimate how difficult it will be on all involved. As much of a strain as it was for Richard and me, I'm sure it was just as hard for my parents. We were giving up our privacy and they were giving up theirs. We all needed to maintain that privacy and it was impossible to do that while living in one house. We did the best we could.

Richard: It would have been better if there had been a physical separation like a duplex.

Elizabeth: That would have been perfect.

Richard: You could have a door between the two and still have your separate spaces. You need to do those personal things that you just can't do with someone else around. Especially if that someone is a parent—or in our case, two or three parents!

Elizabeth: This house has two bedrooms. We had a small bedroom and used the front room as a sitting room and to watch TV. So we had a separation. My parents had a bedroom and bath on the other side, but Mama liked being out in the living room. She went to bed promptly at nine o'clock and Dad would stay up for a few more hours. So if Richard and I were having a disagreement and needed to have a fight with each other—as most couples do from time to time—there was no place to do it.

Jim: What if you wanted to go out at night?

Richard: We did that sometimes, but not often because Elizabeth came home in time for her mother's bedtime.

Jim: Did you know other people in town?

Richard: We met a lot of people through my pottery classes.

Elizabeth: But we didn't really like having people here for dinner because we felt that we had to include my parents. We couldn't feed them early and say "Go to bed." With Mama's early bedtime we couldn't make noise after nine. Sometimes she would say, "Have your friends over." Mama meant well, but that was uncomfortable for me because my parents were always here and it felt odd. Later, when there were three parents here, we never had anybody over.

Jim: What got your father to Texas, Richard?

Richard: I always promised Sidney on my life that I would never have him go to a nursing home. It was his worst fear. I told him that if he wanted to come to Texas I'd work it out. And he said, "I can manage on my own." Even when he stopped driving he said that. At ninety-five he was hospitalized three times for congestive heart failure.

The last time I was down in Florida taking care of him, I fed him lunch and he said, "You know, nobody is going to feed me like that." And I said, "Come to Texas and I'll feed you." And he said, "I'd do it in a heartbeat." And I said, "Okay. It's a one-way ticket and once I make the phone call, there's no coming back. Elizabeth has got to get the sitting room ready." So I put him to bed and kissed him good night. And he said, "I'm not sure." And I said, "Tomorrow morning you make up your mind. Either we get full-time care for you here or you come to Austin."

The next morning he said, "Okay."

I said, "Are you sure?"

He said, "Fine."

Elizabeth asked her parents if it was okay if he came and they were very gracious and said, "Fine, he can come live here." I had him on hospice down in Florida because of his heart condition. Before we got him to Texas I transferred him to hospice here. He had a wonderful nurse who came once a week and loved him. But once he got to Texas, in a few months he went from being an incredibly sweet guy who you would absolutely adore to being an incredibly angry guy.

He'd say things like, "I don't have control any more" or "You're taking my money." He would refer to Elizabeth's father, Randy, as "the landlord." He gave him $200 a month because I suggested it. Eventually I realized that I couldn't make a living doing pottery and take care of him full time. Since Sidney had an $800 social security check coming every month, we used that to help with living expenses. One day he said, "I'm paying you too much."

"Paying me?"

"When we left Florida I thought I'd give you $15 a week. That's $60 a month."

I said, "You keep your money. I don't want your money." Then later that day he came out here and said, "Just forget what I said."

He was angry because he was declining and being taken care of. I would make him his bagel and egg every morning. When I did that in his home, he was incredibly appreciative, but it was still his home and he was in charge. Once you take away a person's independence, you'd better watch out. He was on somebody else's turf and he didn't like that. Once he said to me, "I guess Randy has cut back on the food."

"Why do you say that?"

"Well, we didn't have many potatoes last night."

Elizabeth: I'd told all of them the night before, "This is leftover night, guys," but he thought we were cutting back on his food! Sidney had a benign tremor and when he ate he made a lot of noise, clanging his fork. My mother, who had choking issues caused by dementia, was sure that Sidney was making all that noise on purpose, which made her crazy. Dinner time was always an adventure.

Richard: My father turned ninety-six while he was here. He needed a walker to get around but was able to bathe himself almost to the end. He needed to be cooked for, but he ate more like Elizabeth and me than her parents. The bathroom here was the main issue. I could see the light go on and his door shut and I would race to the bathroom and make sure I did what I had to do because he was in there for an hour.

Jim: What was he doing for an hour?

Elizabeth: We never knew.

Richard: What a ninety-six-year-old does for an hour. It takes longer to go to the bathroom, or to take a shower. And he had to wipe down the shower with his shaking hand so the glass doors just rattled like crazy. After almost ten months, he said to me, "I can't do this anymore." And I said, "Well, whatever I can help you do."

Elizabeth: Sidney wanted to live to be one hundred. Every morning he got up early, closed his door, and did exercises. One day he came out of his room looking angry and said, "I'm not doing these anymore. It's not helping." He was almost ninety-seven but exercise hadn't helped. It wasn't going to make him live any longer. So he quit doing his exercises. And he must have been right, because two weeks later he died.

Richard: We had hospice in place and that was a good experience for all of us. We were with him when he died here in his bedroom. His death was terribly hard on his buddy, Max, who lived in Florida. He would call Sidney every week and they would talk on the phone. When he hung up, Max told his brother, "Sidney is still alive!" When he heard that my father had passed away, he said, "Now that Sidney is dead, what's the use?" Max died a couple of months after Sidney did, just like in a marriage.

Elizabeth: Mama died last November so now we're down to one parent. My father is ninety-two and goes to the gym twice a week. He's remarkable.

Richard: He does a mile on the treadmill and looks like he's seventy-five. He learned the computer in his seventies so when we have computer problems we go to him. He was a professor of forestry at the University of Illinois at Urbana and now he's writing his memoirs. After all these years, we all get along well.

Elizabeth: He knows that we've been here for him.

Jim: Eleven years! A fifth of your life.

Richard: Both of us want to say that we are grateful that we took the time to care for those who cared for us. They didn't always do it perfectly, and neither did we. However, if we had to take on this responsibility again, we would. But, we would do some things differently. With the benefit of hindsight and eleven years' experience, we've learned a few things worth sharing.

Richard and Elizabeth's Commandments

• Create a caring community of friends to help you as life gets tougher.

• Talk openly about what is bothering you.

- Say "thank you" often.

- Learn to accept things as they are, not as you wish them to be.

- Keep a sense of humor.

- Recall how good it feels to have someone listen to you.

- Never forget that privacy is important.

- Be generous with your money when you can.

- Understand that it's important for all of us to feel needed.

- Remember that it isn't easy to take care of someone else, nor is it easy to be cared for.

Maryanne Longenecker of Austin, Texas, wrote this memory of caring for her father.

I am an only child whose parents lived in upstate New York. When Mother came down with Alzheimer's, Dad was her sole caregiver. Living in Texas I couldn't be much help. I went home twice a year, at Christmas and Easter, and observed Mother's steady downward spiral. After seven years, my father reached the end of his rope. He called and said, "I can't do it anymore."

There was a pause and I heard myself say, "Okay, I'll come home and take care of you."

Many of my friends thought I'd lost my mind. I left a good job with the State of Texas and moved back to a town where it snows six months a year. My three children were grown and I was divorced, so I had nothing to keep me from going. My son lived on one side of the duplex I'd bought and covered the mortgage while I was gone; otherwise, I would have lost the house. Of course, I had little income while I was in New York. There are zeros in my social security statements from those years, but I wouldn't hesitate to do it again.

A care facility was never an option in my father's mind. The idea of putting his life partner in a nursing home was out of the question. Of course, that's not how he explained it. He said, "I don't want to lose all my assets." We had someone from the Department of Aging explain to him how he could save his home and preserve his assets. He didn't want to hear it. When he talked about preserving his assets, he really meant preserving his independence. It was hard to argue with that.

By the time I arrived in New York, Mother was at the end stages of the disease. I was there for her last nine months. When she died, Dad gave up. He was not ill, but he needed emotional care. I soon discovered that caregiving is a twenty-four-hour-a-day job.

Eventually I found part-time work at the Area Agency on Aging. It was the perfect place for me. I had lots of questions and they had the answers. That job not only helped me survive emotionally, it led to a position with the Texas Department of Aging. Caring for my parents opened the door to a career I love.

I must be like my dad because I don't intend to go to a nursing home when I'm old. I want to stay home. If I blow everything on paying for my care, that's okay with me. I've taken out a life insurance policy for my children and told them, "If you want that money, you'd better take care of Mom while she's here!"

25

The Continuum of Care: Overview of Long-Term-Care Facilities

As a child in the fifties I visited aging relatives and family friends in what were called "rest homes." That term sounds comforting, but it belied a grim reality. Rest homes were catch-all facilities that dealt with everything from broken hips to broken lives. Residents might have serious physical problems or merely need help bathing or getting dressed. Many had nowhere else to go. Some suffered from memory loss, but we didn't call that condition Alzheimer's back then. In the Eisenhower era, the term "Alzheimer's" was as foreign as "cyberspace."

In the 1960s, things began to change. Sun City, the first major retirement community, was opened by Del Webb on January 1, 1960. It included a golf course, a shopping center, recreation facilities, and five model homes from which residents could choose.

Soon independent-living retirement homes began to spring up all around the country. Medicare and Medicaid were passed in 1965, and within a few years elder care became a big business and major expenditure for state and local governments. Rest homes evolved into skilled nursing facilities, which today are home to more than one million Americans in sixteen thousand licensed homes. The concept of assisted-living facilities did not arrive until the eighties, along with Alzheimer's units. Seniors—another term that didn't exist in the fifties—have a wide array of options on the continuum of care.

Despite all of the changes in the last fifty years, many families still confuse retirement homes, assisted-living facilities, and skilled nursing homes. Too often they lump them all together. Clearly they've never observed dinner on A-Wing of my mother's nursing home, where many residents are unable to feed themselves. They would never confuse that with the lush carpet, linen napkin, and waiter service Mom received in the six months she spent in an assisted-living facility or the tempting buffet line at her retirement home. Each stop on the continuum of care is distinct in what it provides and costs. That's why it's important to be armed with information and options when you decide what is right for your parents.

Retirement Communities

Many retirement communities, such as Sun City, are subject to age restrictions and a number of other regulations. Homes are for sale only to those fifty-five or older. No person under nineteen may be in permanent residence and grandchildren may visit only up to three months a year. Property must be strictly maintained and changes to outside paint color and ornamentation must be approved.

- These communities are designed for active, healthy seniors who want to live independently and enjoy a wide range of activities.

- Retirement communities may include private homes, condos, and/or apartments.

- Most senior communities offer amenities such as maid service, activity centers, swimming pools, tennis courts, restaurants, and golf courses.

- Activities may include golfing, tennis, swimming, exercise classes, yoga, clubs, dances, and lectures.

- Prices range from moderate to very expensive.

Retirement Homes

The key factor that separates a retirement home from an assisted-living residence or a skilled nursing home is that residents must be ambulatory and able to care for themselves.

- Retirement homes *do not* provide help with activities of daily living, although residents may hire someone privately to assist them.

- Most retirement homes offer one- and two-bedroom apartments with private baths. Some have living rooms and full kitchens.

- Facilities usually include a dining room that serves three hot meals a day, as well as public reception areas, activity rooms, hair salons, and exercise rooms.

- There is a wide range of social activities, classes, and entertainment.

- Most provide buses to take residents shopping and to and from special events.

- Someone is on duty twenty-four hours a day in case of emergencies.

- Residents typically range in age from the seventies to nineties.

- Costs vary from around $1,500 to $3,500 a month or more, depending on location, number of rooms, and amenities.

Some residents may spend the rest of their lives in a retirement home. Others will eventually require more care and move to an assisted-living or a skilled nursing facility. There is a growing trend for retirement homes to be located on a campus that may include assisted-living facilities, a skilled nursing home, and an Alzheimer's unit.

Assisted-Living Residences

Assisted-living residences bridge the gap between a retirement home that provides no care and a nursing home that offers full-time medical care.

- Assisted-living residences provide help with the activities of daily life, not medical care.

- Assisted-living residents don't require nurses, but may require help in getting dressed, taking baths, getting in and out of bed, or taking medications.

- Residents may remain in assisted living for years, or they may need more care and move to a nursing home.

- Because of the larger staff, assisted-living facilities cost more than retirement homes. *Nursing homes and Alzheimer's units are covered by Medicaid, but assisted-living residences and retirement homes are not covered.*

Skilled Nursing Homes

Nursing homes are medical facilities licensed by the state and are designed to care for residents who have chronic and severe health problems.

Many residents suffer from dementia or Alzheimer's disease. In addition, nursing homes provide short-term rehabilitation treatment for those recovering from broken bones, strokes, and serious surgeries.

- A medical director and physicians are on call to give residents regular checkups and to closely monitor their health.

- They employ a full staff of nurses, physical therapists, occupational therapists, social workers, and nurses' aides.

- Many nursing-home residents have serious health problems such as diabetes, broken hips, stroke, cognitive disorders, emphysema, and dementia.

- Nursing homes provide rehabilitation facilities and are able to help many patients regain their mobility and return home or move to an assisted-living facility or retirement home.

- Nursing homes offer residents a full range of activities and entertainment, from sing-alongs and pet therapy to crafts, card games, wheelchair exercises, and chapel services.

- The cost of nursing-home care varies greatly depending on geographical location and the local cost of living. According to the MetLife Mature Market Institute, in 2005 the national average for a semiprivate room was $169 per day or $61,685 per year. For a private room, the national average was $203 per day or more than $74,000 a year. As with other long-term-care facilities, some states and cities are much higher than others. In 2005, my father paid around $46,000 for a semiprivate room.

Alzheimer's Units

As Alzheimer's disease has become more prevalent, there has been tremendous growth in specialized units to handle the needs of Alzheimer's patients. These may be stand-alone facilities or part of a continuous-care retirement community.

- Alzheimer's units have strict security precautions so residents can't wander away from the facility without supervision.

- Because Alzheimer's patients need more care, these units have more staff members per patient than nursing homes.

- Nurses and aides are trained to deal with the specific issues facing Alzheimer's patients and provide individual care.

- Because of the increased staffing, Alzheimer's units are more expensive than skilled nursing homes. A typical cost for semiprivate room in an Alzheimer's unit is $5,000–7,000 per month.

Hospice

When I began my research, I thought hospice was a place people went to be cared for when they had a terminal illness. I learned that hospice is not primarily a building, but a concept of care.

- In many communities in-patient hospice centers provide a caring place for terminally ill people to spend their final days, but these centers serve only a small percentage of hospice patients.

- Most hospice care is provided in a patient's home, a nursing home, or a hospital setting.

- The theory behind hospice is simple and profound: compassionate caring, not curing. They are there to help individuals have a death that is natural, pain-free, and surrounded by caring people.

- Hospice works closely with families to help prepare them for the loss of a loved one and make the necessary arrangements for burial and funeral services.

- Hospice also offers bereavement counseling and support groups.

- Hospice is covered by Medicare, Medicaid, and private insurers. No one is turned away for lack of funds.

Wesleyan Nursing Home, Georgetown, Texas

26

Retirement Homes

My aunt and uncle lived one block from the Wesleyan Retirement Home in Georgetown. Since we often spent Christmas with them, my parents saw the building being erected and knew people who lived there happily for years. It was the logical place for them to retire. Even Dad agreed that this retirement home seemed a "nice place for old people" and that he might *someday* consider living there. As is often the case, "someday" did not come by choice but by necessity. When Dad recovered from his stroke, the Wesleyan was his first choice. Because we knew firsthand about its reputation, our decision was easy. Most families are not so lucky.

Choosing the right long-term-care facility is a decision layered with apprehension and emotion. Some parents resist leaving home until their dying day—literally. Others make the move gracefully because they realize it is in their own best interest. Most families find themselves caught somewhere in between.

Every family wants a home that fits its parents' needs, has high standards of care, and is convenient to visit. To find the right place requires research, referrals, and footwork. While personal preferences may differ, there are fundamental qualities that every well-run care facility shares. *This chapter is about knowing what to look for—and what to avoid.*

This section is based on interviews with two men who worked closely with my family over the last decade. They are experienced, professional, and caring. They don't just talk a good game; they live it.

Chris Spence has worked in the long-term-care indus-try for more than twenty-five years and has been president of Wesleyan Homes, Inc. in Georgetown, Texas, since 1989. A non-profit facility associated with the United Methodist Church, the Wesleyan includes a retirement home and the largest nursing home in Central Texas.

Chris McCormick was development director of Wesleyan Homes from 1986 until August 2002. He not only raised funds, but he also shared residents' joys and problems and listened to their stories.

I will share their forty-five years of experience by letting them speak for themselves.

When Should Families Start Planning?

Chris S: Families should start thinking about a long-term-care facility long before they need one. Pre-crisis planning is essential. The difficult days follow-ing a stroke, heart attack, or broken hip are not the best time to make a deci-sion, yet that's when many families choose a facility. When faced with a medical emergency, families are under pressure to act fast, and they may have only a few days to move their parent from the hospital to a long-term-care facility.

To avoid last-minute decision making families should become familiar with care facilities in their parents' community as well as their own. Parents may not want to leave their hometown, friends, and church—even if they're hundreds of miles from their nearest child. On the other hand, they may choose to move near one of their children. It's best to check out several possible sites where they live *and* where you live.

Tour the facilities as if you were about to move in yourself. That will make you take a closer look. Speak to the administrator and ask tough questions. Compare costs and ask for a copy of their latest survey, which is the annual rat-ing they receive from state regulators, or get it off the Internet from the website of the National Agency for Area Agencies on Aging at www.n4a.com.

Chris M: Families should walk all over the place and see what's going on. Don't go only where the administrators take you. Go where they don't take you. Use your five senses.

• Is the facility clean? If not, turn around and leave.

• Do you see respect and kindness in conversations between staff and residents?

• Are the residents involved in activities or staring at a TV?

• Do you hear any laughter?

• Do most residents look relatively happy?

• Are the residents' clothes clean and do they appear well groomed?

• If something doesn't seem right to you, it's probably not right.

Chris S: If you like the facility, find out if there is a waiting list. If you think your parents may need a care facility in the near future, you might want to get their names on the list now. The more you know about what's available, the better prepared you will be to make decisions when the time comes. If there is a sudden need to move into a care facility, you won't be starting from scratch.

Give the On-Site Caregiver a Break

Chris S: One of the most common problems in caring for aging parents is that often the children no longer live nearby. They may live in four different states or a foreign country and be totally unaware of how their parents are actually getting along day by day.

The child who lives closest to the parents will likely become the primary caregiver by default. Sometimes this works out beautifully; often it leads to resentment and misunderstanding among the other siblings. The on-site, daily caregiver may be criticized by more distant siblings. She—and it is far more often a she than a he—makes decisions with which the others don't agree. The child providing daily care rarely does anything well enough to suit far-flung brothers and sisters.

Just as the parents of teenagers rarely hear "thank you" from their offspring, on-site caregivers may not receive much gratitude from their parents. Children who are there regularly are the ones saying "you better not do this" or "you need to do that." Siblings who live far away may remain comfortably in denial. The last time they saw the folks—maybe last Christmas—they seemed fine. Of course they were. Most of us can sparkle for a day or two. The family was together and Mom made her famous sweet potatoes. Dad played the piano. How could they need to be in a retirement home or assisted-living facility?

It's only natural for those far away to tell themselves that things are going well. They don't consciously choose to be in denial; it's just so much more comfortable than reality. If a parent begins having memory problems, children who live out of town have difficulty understanding the actual level of confusion in a short visit. Mom or Dad may have social skills that hide their true condition.

The primary caregiver should do whatever it takes to get the other siblings to spend a chunk of time alone with the parents. This should not be a holiday or vacation, but real caretaking. Ask them not to stay in a motel, but with their parents so they can see what things are like moment to moment. After they've experienced a few days of reality, talk to them about what they have observed.

If they still don't get it and won't join in making the necessary decisions, go ahead and take action on your own. Your siblings may get upset, but your first responsibility is to take care of your parents. Your initiative may prod other family members to face facts and deal with the situation. It also helps if the primary caregiver has power of attorney.

No one needs to hire a private eye to know if Mom and Dad are holding their own. You can use your own eyes and focus on a few key areas:

• Get in their car and let them drive. Fasten your seatbelt. Stay off interstates.

• Go through their medicine cabinet. Are they up-to-date with their prescriptions? Check the dates to see if they are current.

• Look through their clothes closets and take a whiff. If you find that their clothes are not as clean as they should be, there could be a problem. Our sense of smell decreases with time, as do sight and hearing. They may not be able to see or smell that their clothes are dirty.

• Examine the refrigerator closely. Is the milk sour? Have the perishables perished? Check the dates on cartons. Throw away anything from 2003.

• Go through the kitchen shelves and pantry. Do they have a balanced assortment of groceries? Are potato chips and pretzels considered a food group?

• Drop by unannounced for lunch or dinner. Are they eating balanced meals? How does the food taste?

• Are they behind on utilities, credit cards, insurance, or doctor's bills?

Bringing up the Subject

Chris M: It's difficult for some children to realize it's time for their parents to move to a retirement home because it brings home the fact that Mom and Dad really are getting old. They can no longer pretend that their parents are in their mid-fifties and everything is fine. It forces the family to consider what's going to happen if their parents continue to decline and need more care.

When we come to grips with the gradual decline and death of our parents, we also realize that those things are going to happen to us eventually. That realization frightens many people. When we deal with grief and sadness over our parents, we begin to deal with our own mortality.

Often the children's sense of security is deeply tied to the house where Mom and Dad live. We want to be able to go back once or twice a year and revisit our past. In our minds, things remain frozen in time. That illusion is easier to maintain for children who don't see their parents regularly. They may refuse to accept that things are as bad as they are. I can't tell you how many times I've heard people say, "I was there at Christmas and my parents were fine. Things can't have changed that much in just six months." Oh, yes, they can.

Elderly people can go downhill dramatically in a matter of months or even weeks. After a broken hip, stroke, or heart attack their condition can alter irrevocably in a matter of seconds. About 80 percent of the time, parents get to a retirement home because a child shows up at their home unexpectedly and finds things are not going as well as he or she thought they were. Or the child gets an emergency phone call from a friend or neighbor, as you did.

Move in on a Trial Basis

Chris S: Of course, sometimes even the most persuasive children can't get their parents to talk about moving into a retirement home, much less touring one to see what it's like. When Mom and Dad won't consider moving out of their home, even when it's time to do so, you need to visit facilities on your own.

Children must help their parents understand that no choice is irrevocable. They don't have to make final decisions on anything. It's easier on everyone if parents consider the move to a retirement home as a trial run. After all, it is a rental facility. Retirement homes don't ask potential residents to move in for the rest of their lives. They say, "Are you willing to try it for a month?"

When your aunt began having memory lapses, she and your uncle moved one block from their home to the Wesleyan. Even though they only traveled a hundred yards from their front door, the psychological distance was enormous. Your uncle had lived in that house for eighty-two years.

They moved in on a trial basis and walked home every day to feed the cat. They liked their room, the staff, and especially the food, but after three months they moved back home. It was their option and they exercised it, even though your cousins were not overjoyed by the decision.

Later, as your aunt's condition worsened, they moved back to the Wesleyan. They still kept their house intact and looked down on it from the windows of their room. Naturally, they kept feeding the cat, a feline whose care added years to their lives. Only after spending a year in the retirement home did your uncle agree to have the home placed on the rental market. Still he called the shots and made decisions when he was ready to make them.

Don't attempt to do everything at once. Moving into a retirement home and selling your parents' house don't need to happen simultaneously. Take one step at a time. In most cases there is no pressing need to shut down your parents' house. They can keep it as long as they want. Only if they like the retirement home and decide to stay there will they need to think about putting the house on the market. Let them keep their options open.

Chris M: It's absolutely essential to understand what possessions and mementos are important to your parents, and what is not. In his book *It Was on Fire When I Lay Down on It*, Robert Fulghum talks about the box he keeps on the top shelf in his office. It holds what he considers his most prized possessions: a hair ribbon from his little girl, a worn softball, a letter from a dear friend, a family Bible, photos, and a favorite book. It doesn't contain gold or diamonds, but this box is what he'd take with him if the house caught on fire.

Children need to know what their parents' good stuff is. If it comes time to go into assisted living or a nursing home, where space is often limited, there may not be room for more than a few boxes of possessions. If the kids don't know what means the most to their parents, they might throw away their greatest treasures or consign a yellowing book of much-loved poems to Goodwill.

That's true with furniture as well. I recall seeing a son and his mother going at it in the hallway because she wanted to move a beat-up old love seat into her room. The son was furious because he couldn't talk her out of it.

I said, "Have you asked why she wants to keep it?"

"No."

"Well, maybe you should ask her."

The son came back later with a sheepish look on his face and explained that his mother told him the love seat was the first piece of furniture that she and his dad had bought after they married. It may have been weather-beaten, but it embodied fifty years of memories. Once he understood her feelings, there was no problem. The love seat remained in her room in a prized spot by the window.

A common error is to make choices *for* our parents instead of involving them actively in those decisions. It's important to include them at every step along the way. I've seen well-intentioned families pick out a room for Mom and even hire a decorator so everything will be perfect when she arrives. But they fail to involve their mother in the process. When she moves in, there is nothing of her in the room and she is miserable.

Ask what pictures and paintings she wants on the wall. What knickknacks should be on the dresser? Her choices may not be yours, but she has the right to make them. Your parents will face enough changes without having to move into a room that does not reflect their own tastes.

When people over seventy think about a retirement home, they often picture a nursing home full of people who are ill and infirm. That false image has to be shattered and the best way to do it is to have lunch with a friend who is living happily in a retirement home. Your parents will see that independent living is just that: it is for people who can take care of themselves. When you walk in the door, you may think you are in an upscale hotel. There are exercise rooms, recreation facilities, beauty shops, and daily maid service. One of our residents told me, "No one ever made the bed for me in my whole life." She felt like she'd moved into the Waldorf.

While the decision to move to a retirement home may be difficult, the ultimate result is often freeing for parents and children alike. The parents will have balanced, nutritious meals three times a day. In most facilities, there is a staff person on duty twenty-four hours a day in case of an emergency. Residents have transportation to the doctor, shopping, and church. There are a variety of planned activities as well as entertainment and social events. The best part for many residents is an end to isolation. Now they have a comfortable setting in which to form new friendships.

Once they get used to the routine, your parents will be the same people they were before they moved in, for good or bad. People don't change because they get old. If your parents were happy and agreeable before they went to the retirement home, they will be happy and agreeable in it. If they were worriers and complainers at home, they will be worriers and complainers at the retirement home.

Sometimes people who have been isolated for years come out socially in a retirement home. In the majority of cases, the wife outlives her husband. There are many widows in retirement homes, some of whom had domineering husbands and are now alone. Watching a woman discover her independence and reclaim her individuality is like seeing a person reborn.

Fixing Our Parents

Chris S: One of the most common mistakes families make is believing that we can fix our parents. We can't stand to see them down or depressed. We waste energy trying to keep them from crying when we need to let them weep for as long as it takes and be okay with it. If they've made the move to a retirement home or care facility, we need to step back and let them adjust. We can't do it for them. Our parents must choose to adapt to their new surroundings. They will either join in the life of the community or they will not.

Our parents are much more resilient than we realize. Their generation has been dubbed "the greatest" for good reason. Many of them survived both economic depression and war. They have lived through seventy or eighty years of change and upheaval. They have dealt with a lifetime of struggles, and most of them know how to cope and adjust. Who are we to think they won't be able to survive moving to a retirement home? Give them the credit they deserve.

There are clear signs when it's time for a resident to move from a retirement home to an assisted-living or skilled nursing facility. Usually it's a question of moving to the next level of safety. That's the bottom line. A care facility should provide a safe place to live, but not more care than is needed. More care is not always the right answer. For example, if nursing home residents have trouble walking, they can be put in a wheelchair and may stay there the rest of their lives. Or the staff can give them a walker and encourage them to keep walking step by step.

The best nursing homes do their best to encourage independence. If someone is in a wheelchair, it's easy for a nurses' aide to push the chair for them. If the resident has a "giving up" nature, they may start asking to be pushed instead of making the effort to push themselves and stay as self-sufficient as possible for as long as possible.

The Unasked Question

Chris M: Most people wonder whether retirement home residents have love lives, but they don't know how to ask the question. Well, the answer is yes. There is romance in retirement homes. There are love stories and remarriages and occasional hanky-panky. The residents are fully alive; they are not saints. You might be surprised at how much tiptoeing across the halls goes on after nine at night.

What About Cars?

Christ M: Only about 20 percent of the Wesleyan residents still own a car. Some haven't driven theirs in a year. Nevertheless, they like knowing it's in the parking lot. They may not use it much, but know they could. A few years ago the staff was getting ready to repave the parking lot and sent out a notice asking the residents to move their cars for a few days. All the cars were moved except one. No one knew who owned it. Finally the administrator called the police and they ran the plates through the Department of Motor Vehicles. The owner had died nine months earlier and her family had forgotten about the car because she hadn't driven it in five years. They donated her four-wheeled security blanket to charity.

For many residents, the idea of having a car is more attractive than the reality of driving it. Most of them are happy to use the shuttle bus and let someone else drive. They are picked up at the front door, do their errands, and then the bus brings them back. There are no problems with parking, traffic, or bad weather. If they need to go to the doctor or dentist, transportation is arranged for that as well.

Nursing home residents can't have cars, but occasionally the home will stretch the rules. There was one gentleman at the retirement home who knew he needed to move over to the nursing home, but he owned a pickup truck that he loved dearly. He was willing to come to the nursing home but not willing to get rid of his truck, even though he rarely drove it. So we struck a bargain. He parked the truck in the nursing home parking lot, but the vehicle was fixed so he couldn't drive it. Nevertheless he kept the keys and could open and close and lock the door. Every day he would sit in his truck for about an hour. That made him happy and we were pleased to make it possible.

How Do Family Members Judge the Quality of Care?

Chris S: There are a number of simple ways to judge the quality of any care facility:

• Be there at mealtime and check out the food. See how it's being served and whether most of the residents are eating it.

• Look at the posted menu for the week. Does it seem balanced and interesting? Never underestimate the importance of food in a care facility. It is probably the number one concern of residents. Food that is appealing, tasty, and has real variety goes a long way toward making residents content. If the food is bad, no one is happy.

• Look and listen carefully to the quality of interactions between the staff and residents. Those relationships are the greatest concern of most family members.

• Many homes are designed to market themselves by external grandeur. The lobby chandelier makes families feel that they are putting Mom and Dad in a "nice" place. Like the swimming pool in an apartment complex, it is there to make an impression but has little to do with the quality of life.

• Adult children should spend less time worrying about the décor or age of the building and more time getting personal recommendations and references from people who have had family members live there.

How Often Should You Visit?

Chris M: If you live nearby, once or twice a week is enough. Then there are children who come every day and some who almost never visit. The frequency of visits is up to each family, but children must realize that they are going to be involved in their parents' care for the foreseeable future. In a retirement home, where daily care is not provided, someone needs to come around regularly to make sure Mom and Dad are going to meals, bathing regularly, and doing their laundry. A family member may choose to wash their clothes, but that's not necessary. The staff can help find a person to do laundry for a nominal fee.

Of course, there can also be *too much* family involvement. Children don't need to be babysitters and they don't have to be there every day or sit with their parent for hours. I remember one of my mother's friends saying, "I'd like to go on the bus trip to the mall, but my daughter is going to be here again this afternoon so I can't go." I suggested that she call her daughter and tell her she had plans for the afternoon. There needs to be a balance between too much and too little family involvement.

27

Assisted Living

For five months in 1996, while my father was learning to walk again after his stroke, Mother lived in an assisted-living facility. She was in the same building that housed Dad's skilled nursing unit so they could see each other daily. Her room was large and the furniture came from her own home because I hired a truck and drove it down from Dallas. She ate in a well-appointed dining room with waiters, real china, and cloth napkins. Her building was located on a hill overlooking the skyline of Austin. There were days I wanted to move in. There were days I'm sure I qualified.

Just fifteen years earlier, Mother would not have had that option. She would have had to stay with relatives, get full-time care at home, or move into a nursing home. Because of the advent of assisted-living facilities, she had an opportunity to live in a beautiful setting that fit her needs, cost less than nursing care, and was only two floors away from her recuperating husband. We were very fortunate.

I strongly support the assisted-living concept because I know that it works. Unfortunately, many elderly people think assisted living is a nursing home with better wallpaper. Therefore they won't even give it a try. Believe me when I say there are vast differences between assisted living and skilled nursing homes. Assisted living is not *nursing home life.* It offers a completely different experience.

Jamison Gosselin is Manager of External Communications for Sunrise Senior Living, a company that helped to pioneer assisted living across America and is now the largest provider of senior living services in the country. His words make it clear why Sunrise has been so successful.

From a Rock Band to a Renovated Boarding House

Jamison: In 1981, Paul and Terry Klaassen were members of a Christian rock band that volunteered at nursing homes in northern Virginia. They were surprised to see how many people in their audiences did not need full-time skilled nursing care, but nevertheless were living in expensive institutional facilities. Many nursing home residents needed only daily care assistance, not nursing care. At the time, there was nowhere else for them to go. Retirement homes were for healthy seniors and nursing homes were for everyone else. There was nothing in between. Even though they lacked professional experience in health care, Paul and Terry decided to create a living environment for seniors who did not need nursing care.

They bought an old boarding house in Oakton, Virginia, renovated it themselves, and opened an assisted-living residence in December 1981—a time when most Americans had never heard the term "assisted living." Their idea was to create a comfortable, homelike atmosphere for those who needed help with activities of daily living, but not twenty-four-hour-a-day nursing care. They created a living environment that was warm and inviting, with real plants, cookies baking in the kitchen, and a friendly dog wandering the halls. Their goal was to make the residence look and feel like home, not an institutional setting. Each resident was assigned a designated caregiver to whom they could form a close bond.

Senior Living Success Story

Through common sense and a concern for the elderly, the Klaassens and others like them all over the country began to change the face of senior care. The results have been dramatic. By 1996, that converted boarding house had grown into Sunrise Senior Living with forty-two senior communities. In the last ten years it expanded into the nation's largest provider of senior living services with more than forty-five thousand residents in 420 senior living communities in thirty-seven states, the District of Columbia, Canada, the United Kingdom, and Germany.

Our average assisted-living residents are in their eighties, and at least two-thirds of them are female. The average stay is about two and a half years. Most residents need assistance in at least two activities of daily living. The most common needs are help in bathing, getting dressed, and taking their medications on schedule. While staff members provide whatever help is needed, they encourage residents to be as independent as possible. If they can get them out of the wheelchair, even though it may take longer to get around on a walker, it's a better option.

Short-Term Stays

Many assisted-living facilities offer short-term stays for caregivers who are burned out, need a break, or must go on a business trip. This respite care may last a week or a month, and it gives the senior time to get a feel for the residence and the community. It is an ideal way for a parent who has been considering assisted living to experience what it's like. Often they enjoy the activities and friendships of the assisted-living residence so much that they decide to move in permanently.

Visitors and Volunteers

When Sunrise develops new communities, its neighbors are concerned that there will be a steady stream of cars coming and going all day. They always ask, "How many people will visit each day?" Unfortunately, our answer is "Not nearly enough." That's why there are volunteer programs in every residence and why the staff tries to match the talents of the volunteers with the interests of the residents. It doesn't require special skills to be a volunteer who makes a powerful positive impact on residents' lives. The best volunteers know how to give a hug, share a smile, and listen. Sometimes it only takes half an hour to make someone's day.

Long-Term-Care Insurance

Whether the facility is large or small, an independent home or part of a chain, only a small percentage of assisted-living residents have long-term-care insurance because few from their generation bought it. Although policies have been available for thirty years, most current residents did not sign up for them. Today's generation will be different. Baby boomers have had to care for their parents and often watched them go through every penny they had. As a result, they are much more likely to buy long-term-care insurance for themselves.

Alzheimer's Patients Often Do Best in Assisted-Living Environments

Those in the early to middle stages of Alzheimer's disease don't necessarily need nursing care. They need oversight and activities structured specifically for them. Too many people with Alzheimer's disease are in costly nursing homes that don't have a program specifically designed for their individual needs. In the Reminiscence Program, residents are provided with reminders of what they used to enjoy doing. When a staff member puts a paintbrush in the hand of someone who hasn't painted in twenty years, they light up and reconnect to something they always enjoyed. The Sunrise philosophy in our memory care/Alzheimer's program is to create a pleasant day for residents. If they only have the moment, let that moment be a good one.

Todd Hyde co-owns two small independent assisted-living residences in east Texas. One of his residences has sixty-four beds. The other is a mix of thirty-two assisted-living beds and sixteen independent-living apartments.

Todd: Assisted living is the fastest-growing segment of long-term care. The industry has mushroomed in the last twenty years and there are now approximately one million people in assisted-living facilities throughout the United States, and the number increases each year. There are actually more assisted-living facilities than nursing homes, though the skilled care facilities are larger and have about twice as many residents.

Nationally, the median cost for an assisted-living facility is around $2,500 a month, or $30,000 a year, although the price increases each year. In small towns in east Texas, costs are considerably less, often around $2,200 a month. The rate is higher in cities just a hundred miles away.

Geographic location is a key factor in cost. Rural areas and small towns are usually less expensive than large metropolitan areas. Southern and midwestern states are usually much less expensive than the northeast and much of California. Rooms or apartments that have more square feet cost more. In a high-end assisted-living residence you will pay for the pools, paneled dining rooms, and concierge service. Some assisted-living facilities charge $4,000–6,000 a month or more.

What comes as a surprise to most people is that assisted living is not covered by Medicaid. This is a painful shock to many families. Nursing homes and Alzheimer's units are covered by Medicaid, but retirement homes and assisted-living facilities are not.

Medicare and Medicaid Are NOT the Same!

Medicare and Medicaid sound alike, but the resemblance ends with the first two syllables.

Medicare is a federal health insurance program for Americans sixty-five and older.

Medicare Part A covers hospitalization.

Medicare Part B covers physicians' visits and other outpatient care.

Medicare Part D, introduced on January 1, 2006, covers prescription drug benefits.

Norma Almanza of the Texas Department of Insurance put it succinctly when she said, "Medicare is like the back of a hospital gown. It's open-ended. Middle-income families need to find out what it does not cover so they can get a supplemental policy for those costs."

Medicaid is a joint federal/state program established to cover medical care for low-income Americans. Payments are made directly to the providers of services on behalf of those who are eligible. Thousands of formerly middle-income older people who have exhausted their financial resources now rely on Medicaid to pay long-term costs not covered by Medicare or private insurance. Approximately 80 percent of all nursing home costs in the United States are paid for by Medicaid—and that number is growing each year.

If a person needs to be in assisted living but doesn't have the money to pay for it, in most cases they will have to rely on personal financial resources, family support, or long-term-care insurance that covers assisted-living facilities.

There is one exception, a Medicaid waiver program called Community Based Alternatives (CBA) that is available in some states. The term "Medicaid waiver" means that the usual Medicaid rules are waived and the state may offer alternatives to institutional care in nursing facilities. Among these services may be:

• Adult foster care

• Assisted living/residential care

• Home-delivered meals

• Minor home modifications

• Personal assistance services

• Respite care

• Physical therapy

There is a tremendous demand for the limited number of openings in CBA residential-care assisted living. The program has long waiting lists that range from one to five years. In classic doubletalk, the Texas Department of Aging and Disability Services refers to these waiting lists as "interest lists" because so many seniors are interested in getting on them. That sounds like senior spin to me.

Not every state offers assisted living as one of its community based alternatives. You can find out if your state provides this option by calling your state Department of Human Services and asking, "Do we have a Medicaid Waiver Community Based Alternative program for assisted-living facilities?"

If they have such a program, ask how you go about getting on the CBA waiting list. A friend or relative can make the call if your parent is not able to do so. The caller most likely will need the name, social security number, date of birth, and Medicare number of the applicant, as well as the name of a contact person. When the state gets that information, your parent's name will go on the waiting list in their computer.

Of course, that is only the first step. You must get your parent qualified, and that typically takes three months. You'll need to prove both medical and financial necessity for care as outlined in your state. If your parent meets the financial qualifications, a home health worker will come to the home and do a medical assessment. Be sure to have a family member present during the interview because many older people don't want to admit that they have trouble taking medications, bathing themselves, using the toilet, or eating properly. Your parent may tell them that everything is fine and thus not qualify for the program. If a relative is there, the interviewer will get the straight story.

In Texas, there is one alternative that might help in avoiding the waiting list. Someone who is already living in a nursing home may apply to transfer to an assisted-living facility after thirty days *without going on the waiting list*. Therefore, if your parent needs an assisted-living facility but doesn't have the money to pay for it, the family can place the parent in a regular nursing home and immediately apply for CBA benefits as a nursing home resident.

It takes six to eight weeks for the paperwork to be processed, but the resident may qualify to be transferred from a nursing home to an assisted-living facility without going on the long waiting list. Instead of paying $25,000–35,000 a year for an assisted-living facility, the family will only be required to pay for a few months in the nursing home.

Of course, the children may have a hard time getting a parent to go into a nursing home even for a short time. If they can convince their parent to make this decision, the family may avoid the waiting period and be able to qualify for Community Based Alternative benefits in an assisted-living facility.

I strongly urge families who can afford it to invest in long-term-care insurance plans that cover assisted-living facilities and retirement homes, as well as nursing homes. One year in a retirement home or assisted-living facility may be worth ten years or more of insurance premiums. If you buy long-term-care insurance, it's important to know the policy's *day rate*. If the policy was taken out fifteen years ago, the day rate may not cover the full cost of assisted living today.

I was told of a resident who bought her long-term-care policy in the mid-1980s, when it paid $30 a day for assisted living. That sounded like enough to her at the time but, with inflation, the policy now covers only half the cost and she has to pay the other half herself. *It's essential that a long-term-care insurance policy be adjusted annually for inflation.*

What I like best about running an assisted-living facility is that we get to live up to our name and actually assist people in *living*. For instance, there is a couple in one of our facilities who make me appreciate my job every time I see them. The gentleman has Parkinson's and had been living in a trailer park, but realized that he needed more care. He got a private room in our older building while the new one was being built. In the meantime, a lovely woman moved into the same facility and they quickly became close friends. Very close.

In six months, when it came time for him to move, they appeared in my office and said they wanted to get a suite together in the new facility. I said it was fine with me but wondered how their daughters would respond.

Sure enough, both daughters hit the roof and were extremely critical of the idea, but that didn't stop the older folks. They told their kids, "We don't care what you think. We're happy and we're going to stay together." They've done just that for the last three years, supporting each other emotionally and having a wonderful life together. When I see them, I realize what "happily ever after" really means.

Doug Hall and His Dad

Recently, my friend Doug and his sister went to dinner with their dad, who is almost eighty-five and in failing health. Naturally, he insisted on driving to the Red Lobster. He let them out in front of the restaurant and then went to park the car. But he never came into the restaurant where they were waiting. Doug scoured the parking lot but could not find his dad. Finally, he called him on his cell phone and his father answered. Doug said, "Dad, where are you?"

"I'm at the Red Lobster."

"You are? Well, we're there, too, and we didn't see you come in."

"I'm definitely at the Red Lobster."

"Dad, would you do me a favor and go outside and see what the sign says?"

"Sure."

Thirty seconds later, Doug's dad said, "I don't understand. It says Olive Garden."

He'd parked the car in the handicapped zone and gone into the nearest restaurant. Unfortunately it was not the Red Lobster, where he was supposed to meet his children. Doug went next door to the Olive Garden and got his dad, who seemed totally unfazed by the entire experience. They laughed about it and went on to have a pleasant dinner.

The following week, Doug's father promised to take a memory test, but was worried about remembering how to get the doctor's office. Doug showed him the route and they did two practice runs. He figured that if his dad did not make it to the doctor's office, the test would be redundant.

As Doug flew home to Austin he was worried about his dad, who lives alone in Phoenix. He began talking to the woman seated next to him and told her that he was trying to get his dad to move into assisted living in Dayton, Ohio, where his sister could look in on him. Of course, his father was resisting this move. Then synchronicity struck. His seatmate told Doug that she had run assisted-living facilities and had a suggestion that worked for the families of many of her former residents.

She suggested that Doug say, "Dad, it's so good of you to have agreed to move to Dayton and live at the assisted-living center near Julie's house. It makes things so much easier for all of us and we've already made plans to have your own furniture in your room."

Most likely, his father will not remember having had this conversation and may go along with the "agreement." Yes, it is bending the truth; however, in dealing with dementia, sometimes the truth needs bending.

❦

Although those of us who have parents with memory loss may despair at their altered condition, we need to remember that they live in the moment, just as we do. The difference is that their moments don't come with the burden of the past or the fear of the future.

Two weeks after my father's death, I stopped by Mother's room to check on her. I'd been running from the lawyer to the bank and had placed several calls to two insurance companies. Mother was sitting in her room with a smile on her face and eating a piece of Russell Stover candy from the box I'd brought her at Christmas.

"Mom, how are you doing?"

"I don't know. Why don't you tell me?"

"You're doing fine!"

"Good. I'm glad to hear it."

Although that dialogue could fit into a sitcom script, it was real and brought a smile to my face. Mother wasn't worried about dealing with finances or settling Dad's estate, but focused on enjoying a delicious piece of dark chocolate candy. There are worse things.

28

Nursing Homes: The Good

I interviewed two owners and one administrator of skilled nursing homes in states as diverse as New York, Indiana, and Arkansas. Together they have seventy-five years of combined experience in this growing field. Because they know the industry inside and out and have strong opinions on how it works—and sometimes doesn't work—I'm not going to edit their words, but let them speak for themselves.

Neil Chur, Sr. served as CEO and Chairman of the Board of the Park Associates in East Aurora, New York. He bought his first nursing home in 1976. Twenty-two years later his company had grown to 120 homes with more than eleven thousand beds and eight thousand employees, and has provided more than twenty million days of patient care.

Neil: The biggest change I've seen in the nursing home industry is the severity of the residents' illnesses and the multiple diagnoses many of them have. I was a hospital administrator in the seventies and many of our nursing home residents today are as sick as our hospital patients were thirty years ago. When I had my first nursing home, we had residents who would go to the country club for a fish fry on Friday night. Today many of them don't know where the country club is or whether it's Friday night or Monday night.

Many changes are a result of economics and the expanding elder population. Costs have risen dramatically and that has affected the way we provide care. Instead of having a patient in a hospital at $500–1,000 a day, they are placed in a nursing home or skilled facility at $150–200 a day. Healthier people who might have once been in nursing homes are now in assisted living, where it might cost $65 a day.

Nursing homes face a tremendously difficult environment. The number of private-pay residents used to be 50 percent, and now it's approaching 10 percent. The reliance on state and federal legislatures for the majority of our revenue subjects the nursing home industry to political whims and budgetary constraints.

In the last few years, a large number of states faced huge budget deficits. Where did politicians look to balance the budget? They cut Medicaid payments to nursing homes. In state after state, Medicaid payments were slashed. State governments are paying less and demanding more. In many states Medicaid payments already do not adequately cover the cost of care.

In many ways our situation is like "the perfect storm." We face four factors that are converging at the same time. Our patients are more acutely ill. The costs of provider care are rising at double-digit rates. Consumer and state health department expectations are higher than ever. And demographic trends show an increasing demand for skilled nursing services.

There's No Substitute for a Caring Staff

The number one factor in a good home is a caring environment. For one thing, that means that the facility is clean and you aren't hit by odors when you walk in the front door. Then the family needs to get a sense of whether the employees are genuinely concerned about the welfare of the residents. Often you can look at the residents and get a feel for that.

If you go into a facility and the residents don't have on matching clothes, their hair is uncombed, or the men are unshaved, that tells you something. If a resident's eyes are runny and red, it may be that their fingers and fingernails are not clean and they've been rubbing their eyes and gotten them infected.

After almost thirty years in this business, I can tell you that the quality of the staff makes the difference, not brick and mortar. We owned a large, older facility in Illinois that had a great administrator. She ran that old building with the skill of the captain of an aircraft carrier. Everything about it worked beautifully and the residents were cared for and happy.

Not far from there, we owned a modern facility that was only ten years old. We had great hopes for it, but we were never able to find the right people to run it. No matter what we did or who we hired, we couldn't get the leadership we needed. After much effort and frustration, eventually we sold it. The bottom line for a good nursing home always comes down to the leadership and commitment of a caring staff.

As a nursing home owner, my biggest concern is the quality of our top administrators. The director of nurses is a very important person. If you have a weak director of nurses and a strong administrator, you may have some problems in the facility. But if you have a weak administrator and a strong director of nurses, you are probably okay. Ideally, you want both to be outstanding. Of course, it's not just the top people. The quality of the entire team is important. That includes nurses, social workers, physical therapists, occupational therapists; and dietary, laundry, and nurses' aides.

We have a quality assurance system of clinical professionals whose job is to make sure we are doing everything we are supposed to do. The last thing we want is for the state to come in and tell us we are doing something wrong. Of course, even with our best efforts, sometimes we make mistakes because we are human. We are people taking care of people, primarily the oldest and frailest people.

The most common misconceptions about nursing homes are largely based on lack of personal experience. A national survey found that among people who had personal experience with nursing homes, *70 percent were favorably impressed*. Among those with no personal knowledge of nursing homes, *70 percent had a negative perception*.

I have been in hundreds of nursing homes and seen some lousy ones; however, the vast majority of homes are well run. Most staff members work hard and are there for the residents, even though their jobs are physically and emotionally challenging.

Turnover: A Four-Letter Word with Eight Letters

One of our biggest challenges is turnover in staff. It takes a special kind of person to do this work. Some people get a genuine sense of satisfaction from caring for others and can do it for thirty years. But if an employee is not that kind of person, he or she will be out the door in six months. We have the largest turnover at the entry-level positions: nurses' aides, dietary aides, and laundry aides. Sometimes new employees are excited to get a job but don't realize how hard it will be. They have to dress and feed the residents, lift them out of beds, and sometimes wipe their bottoms. It's difficult, demanding work.

We also face challenges in dealing with the families of some residents. Sometimes they have unrealistic expectations about what a nursing home can do. If a resident is ninety years old and has serious health problems, we can't turn back the clock. In most cases, our goal is to maintain the resident where he is, rather than to rehab him so he can go back to the community. We do our best to keep the residents at their present level, but in time their condition may deteriorate.

I'm sorry to say that many residents rarely or never get visits from their families. Then if something negative occurs, relatives who haven't been there in a year start yelling, "Why did you let that happen?" Those who are not active caregivers are often the first in line to file a frivolous lawsuit. In today's litigious society, there are hundreds of ads on TV urging relatives to sue. Don't get me started on that!

Communicate Early and Often

The most important thing families can do to prepare for the possibility of long-term care is to *talk to each other*. When families are willing to discuss what's really going on and be open about the situation, it's better for everyone. Encourage your parents to talk to you about their finances. They might have a checking account at a bank that you don't know about. It's important for them to discuss who is going to get what, whether it's clothing, homes, furniture, money, or stocks. And, of course, they should put everything in writing.

The best time to bring it up is when there is no problem and the parents are still healthy. Today is not too early. Most people do just the opposite. They delay and delay. They don't want to approach the subject because they are afraid it won't be easy to talk about. That may not be the case at all. I know I'm getting older so I've already talked to my kids about finances, funerals, and what Barb and I want done. I'm fifty-nine and in excellent health, but people can have accidents or get a chronic disease at any age.

On January 2, 2005, Neil Chur, Sr. died suddenly of a heart attack. True to his word, his affairs were in perfect order and he left a legacy of service to many thousands of families.

Tim Stuteville was named administrator of the Wesleyan Nursing Home in 2005 at thirty-three. At a young age, he's already had ten years' experience as an administrator. He changed his career course and chose to focus on long-term care because of a personal experience.

Tim: I planned to be a police officer and went to college as a criminal justice major. Then my grandmother had congestive heart failure and went to a nursing home in Fort

Worth. When I visited her I was disgusted by the conditions I saw. I called in several complaints about the nursing home and made life holy hell for the administrator. As a result of that experience, I changed my major to health care administration. I thought then—and still do—that I could help to change things. For me, it's a personal journey. I feel it's a calling.

After I received my degree, I relocated to Houston to pursue postbaccalaureate work in long-term-care education but was eager to work in a nursing home. When I learned that there was an opening for a nursing home administrator in the town of Bertram, Texas, I bought a J.C. Penney suit and drove two hundred miles to interview with the board of directors. When I arrived, I was told that the board was too busy to meet with me that day. I said, "Don't worry. If they can't meet with me, I'll meet with them." I tracked down every member of the board individually. I had an interview with one woman in her kitchen while she cleaned her toaster. I climbed through a barbed wire fence, walked through mud, and jumped on top of a tractor to interview with a rancher. I ruined my suit and shoes, but the next day I got a call from the board. They told me that anyone who would interview on top of a tractor was their man. I got the job.

Why I Like My Job

The greatest satisfaction of being a nursing home administrator is getting to know people who have lived rich lives but who are often are discounted because they are no longer actively involved. To have the ability to look them in the eye, give them a hug, and listen to their stories is moving to me. Today, working at a large facility, I feel as if I'm surrounded by 215 teachers and that if I pay close attention I can learn from their examples and become a better person. I believe that when you give yourself over completely to working with others, you really can make a difference.

At the Wesleyan our goal is not just to stay where we are, but to expand our services and move in new directions. We just opened a new wellness center that triples the size of our rehab facilities. Last year we returned 120 residents to the community, more than double the previous year. We have hired a full-time hospice director who is going to make a tremendous difference in our service to residents and families. This year we break ground on a Continuous Care Retirement Community (CCRC) where we'll have independent living, assisted living, skilled nursing, and Alzheimer's care on one campus. Our architectural designs for the new campus include exploration of an innovative concept which focuses on smaller clusters of residents cared for by a health care professional who is cross-trained among many disciplines, from nursing to housekeeping. The advantage of this new approach is to provide a homelike atmosphere for both residents and employees.

It's All About the Staff

What's most important to me is the quality of our staff and their loyalty to the Wesleyan. Many of them have been here for ten, fifteen, twenty, and twenty-five years. That longevity is exceptional in any industry, especially this one. And it didn't happen by accident. In most nursing homes, you don't find a registered nurse on every wing who serves as a mini-director of nurses. We call them clinical supervisors, but they are RNs.

If I got on the public address system and asked to see my clinical supervisors, assistant directors, admission directors, hospice nurses, and training nurses, I could pull ten registered nurses into my office in a matter of two minutes. Many nursing homes operate off the minimum requirements: "Thou shalt have one registered nurse as Director of Nurses and one on the floor."

Quality care is a result of investing your resources in the right people and the right number of people. When you say you are going to provide exceptional care, you've got to be willing to spend money to make that happen. Our nurses' aides start at $9–10 an hour, which is very competitive for central Texas. On top of that, we fund their 401(k) 100 percent and give them full benefits. We cut down on management tiers and let all our employees know, "You are important to us."

Of course, turnover of nurses' aides is a problem for every nursing home. Our turnover rate is in the high eighties, which is considered good, and it's coming down. Part of the problem is that many nurses' aides are single moms who may have no support at home. They are giving at work and then they go home and give there. They are giving to others eighteen hours a day and sometimes the cup runs dry. Then they recharge and come back and do it again.

With more than two hundred residents, staying on top of things is an enormous challenge. I appreciate families who tell me when they have a problem. If they have a question, a complaint, or need help I want to know about it. When I arrived last year, I sent out a note on our billing statement that said, "I'm Tim. I'm the new guy here and if you ever have a question or concern, please call me. Here are all my phone numbers. You can reach me any time." And I tell my staff the same thing. My biggest frustration is for people to be upset over something and keep it to themselves. I want them to make me aware of the issue before it becomes a crisis.

I hear so many family members say, "I don't mean to complain . . ." or "I don't want to be a nag . . ." If I had a dollar for every time I heard that I could take my family to Disney World. People are entitled to be concerned or upset when something goes wrong. They don't have to preface it with an apology. I want to know what's happening now, not later, so I can do something about it. Too many families don't complain when they ought to because they don't want to be perceived as griping or be pigeon-holed as a problem. Some even fear that if they raise an issue, it will be taken out on their loved one. Nothing could be further from the truth. We want to know when something is wrong. Period.

Diane Rules!

I have no illusions about my importance to the nursing home. My job is to help Diane Malia, our Director of Nursing, keep this home running smoothly. Diane has been here for twenty-three years and has worked almost every position in the home. But she still comes in the middle of the night if there's a problem because she cares passionately about our people here. She isn't casual about her responsibilities. If something is wrong, she tackles the problem head-on and will not accept anything less than what our residents deserve. She treats our nurses fairly, but will not tolerate those who do not provide proper care. I see my role as supporting what she does so well and making sure she gets what she needs.

I Wouldn't Be Anywhere Else

Jim, one day your Dad was yelling out, "Help me," as he did in his last year. One of our young nurses' aides—someone who had never really experienced strong family love and support—said, "Mr. Comer just keeps on yelling. What are we going to do?"

I was in the hallway and heard her ask that question. Immediately I thought about your dad and my grandfather and all they did for our country in World War II. I said to her, "If you knew Mr. Comer and the sacrifices he made, and the close calls he had, you'd know it's a miracle he's still with us today. Then you would understand that as long as Mr. Comer has a voice, I hope he yells out because he deserves to be heard." That's how I really feel about it. One of the great satisfactions of this job is to be there at the end of a good life. I get to be part of that final chapter and that's a real privilege. It makes me realize my purpose and that I will have more opportunities to make a difference.

Jim Santarsiero administered nursing homes in New York, worked for a large health care corporation in Baltimore, and now owns and operates several nursing homes in Arkansas.

Have Clear Priorities

Jim S: My philosophy of running nursing homes comes straight from my friend and mentor, Neil Chur. He always said, "Keep your priorities clear. First and foremost, you must take care of the residents and patients. Secondly, you must take care of your employees. And if you do those two things correctly, and in that order, you will have a financially successful business." Neil practiced what he preached and I do my best to follow his example.

I've been in the nursing home business for almost thirty years. In the last five to ten years, the structure has been changing. From the seventies through the nineties, the concept was "bigger is better." Now you see more regional operators like me. That change happened within the last three years.

I don't believe nursing home companies should be publicly traded corporations. There is a major conflict of interest there. A publicly traded company is earnings driven and responsible primarily to its investors. We're in the health care business, taking care of frail, elderly folks who are often in the last stages of their lives. That's 70 percent of our business. The other 30 percent deals with people, many of them much younger, in our rehab units and outpatient clinics.

Cost-Effective Rehabilitation

The cost of acute-care hospitals has skyrocketed in the last twenty years. As a result, we are doing a lot of rehabilitation in nursing homes that traditionally took place in hospital or specialized rehab centers. Clearly this is financially motivated. Everybody wants the best care, but nobody wants to pay the price for it. If we set up a rehab unit in our nursing home, we can get the same quality of successful outcomes as a hospital or rehab center at a much lower cost.

If you have a knee replacement, whether you go to an expensive hospital or rehab center or to a nursing home, they still need to strengthen your muscles, start you walking, and get you to be totally independent. We get the same results using physical therapists and podiatrists who specialize in physical medicine and rehabilitation; however, we don't have to support a fifty-thousand-square-foot medical complex, a staff of forty physicians, and millions of dollars of equipment as does an acute-care center.

The Market Is Changing

Today's consumers are more savvy than they were ten or fifteen years ago. In 1990, most people didn't know anything about quality surveys. They were concerned about cost, getting a private room, and whether the place was pretty. Pretty is not important. I knew a nursing home operator who used to say, "I hang my marketing money on the walls." When you went into his facilities, everything looked great. But if you asked him about staffing ratios or quality control, those things were not important to him.

The baby boomers are going to be more demanding. They will shop around and demand quality care delivered in a courteous, consistent manner. On top of that, they are going to expect to be treated with compassion. That's one requirement you can't put in a job description. I can teach my employees to be courteous, but I can't teach them to be compassionate. That has to come from their hearts.

We have a hospice unit in one of our facilities with thirty beds in it. It was so successful that we increased the number of beds to sixty. We are known for the caring and compassion of our employees in that location. I believe if I raised the number to 120 beds, we'd still fill it. We get letters and testimonials from families with specific examples of how our staff made a difference to them. We might read a note that says, "When the nurse came in to give my medication, my wife broke down and was in tears, and your nurse didn't say a word. She just sat on the bed and rubbed her shoulders."

The biggest challenge for the long-term-care industry right now is to figure out how to do more with less. Funding is a national issue and it's not going away. We have to meet the rising cost of health care and get outcomes that meet people's expectations, and do it more efficiently. In addition, we have to do a better job of combating staff turnover. If I knew what to do to lessen the turnover, both at the top and especially among the certified nurses' aides, I would have written a book and be living on a beach somewhere. Turnover is 200 percent at some places. If you're under 100 percent you are doing well. Eighty percent turnover is considered fantastic. To be honest, I don't know the answer. It's a huge problem.

If a facility has a high occupancy rate it can provide more financial resources and can pay higher salaries. If you go into any marketplace and visit five nursing homes and you rank them in terms of how they pay nurses' aides, those paying lowest will run 50 to 60 percent occupied. The ones that pay best will be at 90 to 95 percent occupancy.

What I Would Look for in a Nursing Home

If my mother had to go into a nursing home and I didn't know anything about the facility, I'd go in and ask for their survey history. I'd want to know their track record in terms of delivery of care. I wouldn't be interested in taking a tour or talking to the administrator. I'd want to speak to the person in charge of the unit that my mother is going to be on. I'd want to know the charge nurse and meet the people who are going to take care of Mom. They're the people who will ensure that she gets the care she needs.

Advice from the Experts

Chris Spence: I highly recommend pre-crisis planning. The difficult days following a parental health crisis are not the best time to choose a long-term-care facility, yet that's when many families make their decision.

Chris McCormick: I can't tell you how many times I've heard people say, "I was there at Christmas and my parents were fine. Things can't have changed that much in six months." Oh, yes, they can.

Todd Hyde: If you buy a long-term-care policy that covers assisted living, make sure that the day rate is adjusted yearly for inflation.

Jamison Gosselin: A short-term stay is an excellent way for parents who have been considering a move to an assisted-living residence to find out what it's like before they make a decision.

Neil Chur: Families need to talk to each other. When they are willing to discuss what's really going on and be open with each other, it's best for everyone. The time to start planning is when there is no problem and the parents are healthy. Today is not too early.

Tim Stuteville: If families have a problem, concern, or complaint they shouldn't apologize or beat around the bush. They need to tell the administrator immediately so she or he can do something about it before the problem escalates into a crisis.

Jim Santarsiero: I can teach my employees to be courteous, but I can't teach them to be compassionate. That has to come from their hearts.

29

Nursing Homes: The Bad and the Ugly

Having devoted a number of pages to those who own or administer long-term care facilities, I also want to present another side of the story. I spoke at length with a highly respected attorney who has worked on numerous cases of nursing home abuse and headed two statewide investigations into the nursing home industry. Just as I did with the nursing home executives, I'm going to quote him directly.

David Bragg is a partner in the Austin law firm Bragg Chumlea McQuality. A former Peace Corps volunteer, he graduated from Baylor Law School at the top of his class. From 1979 to 1982, he headed nursing home investigations for the Texas Attorney General's Office. In 1991, Governor Ann Richards appointed him Citizen Trustee to investigate Texas nursing homes.

David: In 1978, I became Chief of the Consumer Division in the Attorney General's office. Soon after I took the job, the *Lufkin Daily News* ran a Pulitzer Prize-winning series on nursing home abuse in East Texas. The stories were shocking. In one facility, they were beating old people with coat hangers. In another they were using three chickens to make soup for a hundred residents. The Attorney General,

John Hill, called me into his office and said, "Make me a nursing home task force."

I had never been in a nursing home in my life. Within a few weeks, we created a twenty-five-person task force composed of lawyers, CPAs, nurses, and social workers. In two years, we physically inspected more than 250 nursing homes.

We divided into six teams, each composed of four people. The team leader would go into a nursing home first, find the administrator, and keep him or her busy while other team members fanned out through the facility. One of us would ask a resident for permission to go into his room. Unseen by staff members, he would push the call light and time how long it took the nurse to arrive. We wanted to see how things were actually run. By the time we left we had a good idea of what each nursing home was like. Ultimately, we were able to prosecute twenty of the worst facilities and close down ten of them.

When Ann Richards was elected governor ten years later, part of her platform was to investigate nursing home abuse. There had been another series of scandals and the usual temporary outcry. Since I knew the territory, she asked me to conduct an investigation of the industry and those who regulate it, and to report to her on what could be done.

After several months of work, I could see that things hadn't changed much from my investigations twelve years earlier. I wanted the governor to see some of the homes for herself. It was difficult to convince her to make an unannounced night visit because she didn't want it to be seen as a publicity stunt. When she agreed to go, I picked out a really bad home and an excellent home because I wanted her to see the stark contrast. Both homes were located in Houston, only twenty minutes apart, but they could have been anywhere in the state.

First we went to a home that was mostly Medicaid funded and that had many AIDS patients. The moment we walked in the door our eyes started watering because the urine smell in the air was so strong. It was midnight and the place was dimly lit. Nurses had left notes about patients written on pieces of cardboard. The place was filthy and stank. Naturally, the governor was appalled.

A few hours later, we walked into a private-pay facility across town that was sparkling clean and had a pleasant, homelike atmosphere. When we looked into residents' rooms, we saw furniture from their own homes. It was two in the morning and the facility was quiet and peaceful. All the residents were sleeping so soundly that the cynical lawyer in me was suspicious. We checked the charts to make sure the residents weren't being drugged. It was not chemically induced sleep, just a well-run nursing home. The difference between the two facilities was striking, but there was one amazing similarity: the nurses' aides in both homes were paid the same salary.

The governor wanted to know why one home was horrible and the other excellent. I told her it was the leadership—or lack of it. In the private-pay facility, the staff would have killed for the administrator. In the other one, they barely knew her name. Over and over, we found that frequent turnover of administrators is a clear indicator of problems. Continuity is important and the staff needs a sense of loyalty to the person at the top. If a home has a history of losing an administrator every year, something is wrong.

The quality of the administrator makes a tremendous difference. So does the director of nursing. If either is a strong leader, the home will work. But at least one of them has to be an effective administrator in order to run a quality facility.

As far as I can tell, conditions have not changed significantly. There are some excellent homes, some mediocre facilities, and some terrible ones. The same thing that was wrong with the bad ones when I did my investigation is wrong with them today. *Every serious problem in nursing homes, with few exceptions, can be traced to inadequate staff, either in number or in training.* The reason staffing is such an enormous problem is that nurses' aides, who provide 85 to 90 percent of the hands-on care, are paid low wages and have little opportunity for career advancement.

Entry-level employees may come from McDonald's to the nursing home and in six months move on to Taco Bell. Finding and keeping good employees to do hard work at low wages is difficult. Many nursing home facilities have a turnover rate of 100 percent or more each year.

Nursing home staff turnover is high for every job position including directors of nursing. However, the frontline workers—the nurses' aides—have by far the highest rate. These figures were published in the May 2003 edition of *Provider*, a monthly publication of the American Health Care Association. These are the latest figures on nursing home turnover that have been published.

Highest Annual Turnover Rate of Certified Nurses' Aides, Based on the Six Months Ending June 30, 2002

Oklahoma	135 %	New Mexico	109 %
Missouri	123 %	Louisiana	108 %
Arkansas	114 %	Texas	105 %
Idaho	110 %	Arizona	104 %
Utah	110 %	Massachusetts	100 %

When you are considering a nursing home for a loved one, ask the administrator for the turnover rate for nurses' aides in the last year. They know the number and you have a right to know it as well. The lower the turnover in staff, the better the care is likely to be.

I believe the reason there is so little public awareness about nursing home abuse has to do with ageism. If some of the abuses we saw in nursing homes had happened in day-care centers, the public would be up in arms. When it comes to the elderly, people don't seem to want to know the truth. If we don't know about it, we don't have to do anything about it. Nursing home scandals happen over and over again, yet the public loses interest quickly. As soon as the six o'clock news finds a sexier scandal, the blinders go back on.

There were nursing homes where you could walk in the door, apply the smell test, and know it was a bad place. I wondered why the families of residents didn't demand change. There were church groups that had services amid the squalor and never reported it. There were friends and family who visited regularly, yet seemed oblivious to the conditions.

Some people wanted us to create a rating system for nursing homes or award stars like critics do for movies or restaurants: excellent, good, fair, or poor. I didn't want to do that because I was afraid it might give families a false sense of security. I know how fast the quality of care can change because I've seen it happen. A home that rates five stars one week might deserve no star the next. A facility can go south in a matter of days—even hours. Without the proper staffing, a good facility can become a bad one. On any given day, if three or four key people call in sick or don't show up, the quality of care suffers tremendously. If a nursing home loses a top-notch administrator or director of nursing, it's like an acclaimed restaurant losing its celebrated chef.

Sometimes vital staff positions will be eliminated because of budget issues. Most nursing homes are for-profit institutions and may cut positions in order to achieve their profit targets. Then there is the tremendous, ongoing difficulty of finding and keeping staff members in low-pay, physically demanding positions. Staff turnover, especially in entry-level positions, is a never-ending problem. It's important for families to stay involved on a daily basis because things can change so quickly.

Do you realize that up to 60 percent of nursing home residents get no visitors ever? No one (outside of the nursing home staff) checks up on them, attends Care Team meetings, or takes them out for holidays or special occasions. Remember, the average resident is an eighty-two-year-old widow who will live in a nursing home for two years. Fifty percent of them have no close family members. That number is not an estimate. It came from a statewide survey conducted by the Texas Department on Aging.

Nursing Homes: The Bad and the Ugly

The fact that so many residents were not getting visits from loved ones was one of the reasons we came up with the Adopt-a-Nursing-Home program. We knew how successful the Texas Department of Highways had been in getting groups to adopt highways and keep them clean. We asked ourselves, "Why not have groups adopt nursing homes?" The goal was to involve the community in nursing homes through volunteer groups. It has been successful beyond our wildest expectations and is making an enormous difference in the lives of residents and volunteers.

The Texas Department of Human Services administers the program with only four full-time staff people in a state with more than 1,100 nursing homes. The program was started in 1992 and has grown to almost 4,000 volunteer groups with 40,000 volunteers in 700 nursing homes throughout the state. Almost two-thirds of the nursing homes in Texas are involved.

We have volunteers ranging from second-grade classes and Girl Scouts to Rotary Clubs and Veterans of Foreign Wars. To create an Adopt-a-Nursing-Home group, you only have to visit the nursing home at least four times a year. You don't even have to be a person: fur and feathers count. There are pet therapy groups who bring their animals. Some volunteers visit residents who have no family members. Others help with activities, entertainment, crafts, singing, or church services.

Texas originated the concept and Florida tested a program based on our model. The idea is spreading and I hope every other state will follow suit. The cost is minimal and the payoff is enormous. You can find out all about it by going to the website at www.adoptanursinghome.org.

If someone in my family had a massive stroke and had to go to a skilled care facility, first I'd go on the Internet and do some research. In Texas, the Department of Human Services has a website where they actually give information about the regulatory history of every nursing home in the state. If you live in other states, call your Department of Insurance and ask where you can find records of a facility's scores from the last few years of inspections.

Medicare also has an excellent site that gives the regulatory history of each nursing home in the country: www.medicare.gov/NHCompare/home.asp. It doesn't rate the quality of care—and it's not foolproof—but gives a statistical snapshot of the facility for a short period of time. Of course, that picture is subject to radical change.

If I had to put a loved one in a nursing home, I'd start off by doing research on the web. Then I'd talk to people who have family members living in the nursing home and find out what their experience has been. The more specific personal information you have, the better. I'd also make several unannounced visits.

I can tell a lot by walking in the front door and taking a deep breath. In many ways, assessing a nursing home is a sensory experience. It's about looking, smelling, hearing, and tasting. I'd want to see the bathrooms and check them for cleanliness. What's so deceptive is that the prettiest homes may not be the best homes. A beautiful lobby is a poor indicator of the quality of care.

What matters most is the quality of the staff and their relationship with the residents. Does the home have enough staff members on duty? Does it offer ongoing training for employees? Do staff members provide genuine care and concern? I'd stop by the day room and see how many residents are sitting with their chins on their chests. I'd want to see if there are activities going on.

I'd visit the home at least two or three times and at different hours of the day. The morning shift is the most active because they have to get everybody up, bathed, and dressed for the day. If you come when that is happening, you get a good idea of what the home is like. I'd go at night as well. The night shift is the least accessible because good nursing homes don't want people wandering around at midnight, but it's important to see if the residents are sleeping well and that the level of care remains attentive.

Comer's Commandments

- Use your five senses when judging a nursing home. How does it smell? How well-cared-for do the residents look? What tone of voice do staff members use when they speak to residents? How does the food taste?

- Find out the percentage of staff turnover for the last year, especially the rate for nurses' aides. Lower is better.

- Be wary if the facility has a history of going through administrators every year or two. Continuity breeds loyalty among the staff.

- Check out www.medicare.gov to get a regulatory history of the home's last few inspections.

- Volunteer! If you participate in the life of the nursing home, you will do yourself, your loved one, and the other residents a world of good.

30

Hospice: A Compassionate Approach to Living and Dying

This chapter forced me to confront my own mortality. I asked myself what I'd want to do if I had a terminal disease. Would I want to be hooked up to monitors, pumped full of chemo, willing to do anything to buy a little more time? From the comfortable perspective of health, I don't believe I'd go that route. If I found out tomorrow that I had cancer, I might change my mind.

One thing for sure: I want hospice care when my time comes. Hospice helps those who have made a decision—along with their doctors and families—to shift direction from cure to comfort. Many patients have endured months or years of painful medical treatment and do not want to spend the last days of their lives hooked up to machines. Quality of life is their

 principal concern, as it would be mine. They prefer to be alert and free of pain, and to spend time with those they love. Hospice care makes that possible.

To learn about hospice care from a professional, I interviewed Michael Turner, who has worked in the field for the last

ten years and was recently appointed as the first Director of Hospice Care at the Wesleyan Nursing Home.

Michael: The year I got accepted to nursing school, I was taking care of my great aunt in Kansas City and one day she said, "I think I have swallowed a toothpick. I have a sharp pain in my throat every time I swallow." We went to the hospital and found that a malignant tumor had totally engulfed her esophagus.

The doctors wanted to put in a feeding tube and we were going to do it on a Monday morning. I came to the hospital before the procedure and my aunt asked me, "Will we be able to put a chicken fried steak in the feeding tube?"

I said, "No, you don't understand. That's not how it works."

"Well, if I can't enjoy my food, then why am I bothering?"

"The tube will to keep you alive a little bit longer, but the tumor is going to continue to grow."

"I don't want to live like that."

"So what do you want?"

"I want to go home and be with my cat."

I asked the nurse what to do and she said, "We'll send her home on hospice." We took her home. When the hospice people arrived, they were wonderful. I explained that I took care of her, but was about to start nursing school.

They said, "You're going to be a hospice nurse when you get out."

"Oh, no, I could never do this."

"You wait and see."

My aunt died two weeks later.

The hospice nurses were prophetic: My entire nursing school experience revolved around geriatrics. When it was time for me to choose a field of specialization I said, "Hospice." I was one of four students chosen to follow a hospice team for a full semester.

You don't get a hospice job right out of nursing school because it's essential to have nursing experience first. I worked for a year at Texas State Hospital, and then went to Children's Hospital, where I did pediatric acute care. When I'd been there for three months, I had to turn over one of my kids to Hospice Austin. When the admitting nurse showed up, I told her I was interested in working with hospice. She invited me to meet the staff at Hospice Austin and see the facility. They said I didn't have enough experience. On top of that, they didn't have any openings. Two weeks later they offered me a job. Those nurses back in Kansas City were right, after all.

I worked with hospice for five and a half years as a case manager and in admissions. Along the way, I realized that patients in nursing homes and assisted-living facilities didn't get the same level of hospice care as our other patients. Since they had nursing care on site, hospice work was often done by a part-time nurse. I didn't feel that was right, so I started pitching the idea of a specialized hospice team for long-term-care facilities.

Finally our administrator said, "Let's try it and see what happens." We put together a specialty team that worked specifically with nursing homes and assisted-living facilities. I took care of patients at the jail and at Doug's House, an AIDS hospice, for two years.

I have a deeply held conviction that health care, especially death and dying, should not be something from which you make money. I was never interested in working with a for-profit agency. Because I share their philosophy, when the Wesleyan asked me to direct their new in-house hospice program, I agreed immediately.

At first we talked about taking over part of a wing, and then decided against that approach. Residents' rooms or apartments become their homes. Moving them to a new wing for our convenience would be like taking them from their home and moving them to a strange place. It does not make good sense to uproot Alzheimer's patients from familiar surroundings and force them to have a new roommate, surroundings, and caretakers. So, we changed our minds and decided to work with residents where they live throughout the facility.

Many people who hear the word "hospice" think it's somewhere you go to die. Most of the old hospices were like that. They began in the 1800s in Europe as facilities run by nuns primarily for the poor.

We've come a long way since then. Dame Cecily Saunders, the mother of the modern hospice concept, founded St. Christopher's House in London. She charted new approaches in the treatment of the terminally ill based on her belief that no human life should be denied dignity and love. A true innovator who viewed pain relief as a vital component of a "good death," she wrote *The Care of the Dying*, a book that has influenced caregivers around the world.

In the United States, the hospice movement took off in the fifties and sixties, with the establishment of facilities where the terminally ill could receive care. In the 1970s, it became more of a home-based, home-care model. There are still a large number of in-patient hospices, but not in most smaller communities.

The advantage of an in-patient hospice is that symptoms can be managed more effectively. Patients may get to a point where pain, nausea, agitation, or restlessness cannot be brought under control at home. Sometimes a family has been dealing with these issues for so long that they are totally burned out and patient care begins to suffer. That's when in-patient hospice is the right place to go: they provide twenty-four-hour-a-day care with trained staff and nurses.

Physicians are available to determine which medications are working and when it's time to try others. Once the symptom is under control, the patient may be able to return home because most patients want to die at home.

In order to receive hospice care, there must be a doctor's prognosis that the patient will die within six months. Cancer patients are one of the largest populations in hospice. We also work with those who have Alzheimer's, dementia, and heart disease. We had a large number of AIDS patients until the protease inhibitor "cocktail" was created in the mid-nineties.

We see a lot of patients in end-stage kidney failure. Many have gone through dialysis for years and are tired of being hooked up to a machine three times a week for hours, leaving them exhausted the next day. They feel this is not a good quality of life. Sometimes they'll say, "I'm tired of this." They choose to stop dialysis and have hospice care at home.

Many people are under the misconception that hospice will medicate their loved one out of this life. That is not hospice's goal. Hospice is not there to prolong life, but not to shorten it either. Our goal is to provide comfort and quality to whatever time is remaining.

Some patients—and their families—believe that hospice is going to provide enough morphine to put them to sleep and they won't wake up again. And that's not true either. We give morphine only when it's appropriate, when a patient has intractable pain that we cannot get under control. If someone has bone cancer, morphine doesn't help. Instead we use high doses of ibuprofen and steroids.

Sometimes dying people are so miserable and uncomfortable that they can't relax. They can't allow a natural progression to take place. They are so tense and tight, and hurt so bad that they are constantly restless. If a patient is having respiratory difficulties, we use morphine. The drug tricks the body into thinking that it's getting more oxygen than it really is, so the patient takes slower, deeper breaths. Morphine also helps the diaphragm relax so that the lungs can open more fully. It doesn't make people pass away but allows them to be more comfortable. Often, once that comfort level is reached, a patient is able to let go.

The problem is that most patients don't start on hospice early enough. When someone gets a cancer diagnosis, physicians want to do all they can to fight it, to prolong the life, to "win" the battle over the cancer—or whatever the disease may be. In many cases, they get to a point where they know they can't win. The cancer is spreading and the battle is lost. That's when a physician will call in hospice.

The average hospice patient is on service for less than fourteen days. I believe it should be much longer. I would like to see patients on hospice care for three to four months. That gives our staff time to win over a patient's trust and provide both spiritual and social support to the families. We need to get the family ready to accept the death and make funeral arrangements. We have people ready to help them get through that process.

Hospice care is paid for by a variety of sources: Medicare, Medicaid, private insurers, long-term-care insurance, and private-pay patients. However, the great majority comes through Medicare and Medicaid on a day rate, which varies from state to state. Patients are rarely turned away from not-for-profit institutions like Hospice Austin, and many for-profit hospices also take charity cases.

I feel grateful that I've been able to work with hospice. I've experienced it both as a provider and a caregiver. I've had hospice care for those I love and know that it works. My idea of a good death is one that is peaceful, calm, and pain-free, surrounded by love and with a family that is supported and prepared.

To learn more about hospice care, visit www.hospicefoundation.org.

My friends Ed and Barbara Dickinson of Pebble Beach, California, were the first people who told me how much hospice care meant to them.

Barbara: In 1995, when I lost my mother, and in 2004 when my husband, Ed, lost his mom, hospice played an enormous role in the process, as well as the processing. They led us through each stage explaining—in terms we could understand—what was happening, what we could do, and what we could expect in the days to come.

At the same time, they provided the physical care our mothers needed: bathing them, giving them medication, massaging their aching limbs, and, most importantly, encouraging them. They made us aware when the time had come to call our siblings and what we could do as a family to ease the transition from this life to the next.

Hospice workers were there when they said they would be, called to follow up, took care of the practical details following the death, and supported us throughout with kindness and consideration. We are so grateful that because of hospice our mothers were allowed to die with dignity in their own homes and surrounded by their children.

Ed: When my ninety-year-old mother suddenly made the conscious decision to stop eating or drinking, I was at a complete loss, with knots in my stomach and fear in my heart. I telephoned hospice and they sent someone over immediately. I assumed this person would "fix" Mom and get her to start eating and drinking once again. Instead, she explained to me lovingly that my mother had chosen to complete her journey on earth.

When Roles Reverse

Mom was tired, aware of how quickly she was failing, and ready to move on. Through the gentle guidance of the hospice worker and her careful explanation of how different people cope with dying, I was able to understand and accept my mother's wishes. From that moment until Mom died, hospice became part of our lives. Because of their work, I was able to spend the time we had left sharing the blessing she was in our lives and then lovingly let her go.

SECTION TWO

What You *Don't* Know Will Hurt You:
Legal and Financial Issues

31

Elder Law Attorneys

For four and a half years, my parents lived on the fourth floor of a retirement home and paid a monthly rent of $1,950 for two rooms and two baths. They had a view of oak trees and church spires and enjoyed three hot meals a day, maid service, transportation for shopping, and many group activities. With their combined social security, Dad's pension, and investment interest they actually *saved* money while living there. Then their circumstances changed abruptly. In just seven months between December 2000 and July 2001, both of them suffered broken hips and required the full-time care of a nursing home. Suddenly they went from a positive cash flow to a sharply negative one. Their combined expenses jumped from $2,100 a month to $7,500.

While costs more than tripled, their monthly income remained the same: $3,000. Do the math. They faced a yearly shortfall of $50,000 and the gap widened each year as nursing home costs increased. Their bill was on the *low end* of the national scale because their nursing home was located in a medium-sized town in central Texas. If they had lived in a similar home in the Northeast or on the West Coast, the cost would have been much higher.

There are more than 1.6 million Americans now living in nursing homes. According to the MetLife Mature Market Institute, in 2004 the average cost for a semiprivate room in a skilled nursing home was $61,685 a year, or $169 per day. In many metropolitan areas the cost is considerably higher than the national average.

Nursing Home Costs: 2004

Thirteen Most Expensive: Semiprivate Room, Daily Costs

1. Alaska: statewide	$435
2. New York, NY	$301
3. Stamford, CT	$297
4. Boston, MA	$266
5. Worcester, MA	$260
6. Hartford, CT	$254
7. Rochester, NY	$241
8. Washington, DC	$241
9. Syracuse, NY	$228
10. Bridgewater, NJ	$223
11. Cherry Hill, NJ	$220
12. Philadelphia, PA	$210
13. Vermont: statewide	$210

Twelve Least Expensive: Semiprivate Room, Daily Costs

1. Shreveport, LA	$87
2. Dallas/Fort Worth, TX	$109
3. Houston, TX	$109
4. Oklahoma City, OK	$114
5. Little Rock, AR	$114
6. Austin, TX	$118
7. Salt Lake City, UT	$119
8. Tulsa, OK	$121
9. Chicago, IL	$124
10. Indianapolis, IN	$125
11. Charleston, SC	$127
12. Wichita, KS	$127

The MetLife Market Survey of Nursing Home and Home Care Costs, 2004

Because I wrote the checks each month, I realized that within a few years my parents would go through all of their assets. Like most Americans, their savings would not last long with a negative cash flow of $4,000 a month. I needed sound advice on how to manage their dwindling resources. Several friends suggested that I see an elder lawyer—and they didn't mean an eighty-year-old attorney.

I'd never heard of elder law attorneys. The field is less than twenty years old and grew out of an American Bar Association meeting in the late 1980s during which a group of lawyers, sharing stories about their growing number of elder clients, asked themselves, "Why don't we make this a profession?"

The National Academy of Elder Law Attorneys was established in 1987 and now has around five thousand members, which is only a fraction of those who work in the field. To find an elder law attorney in your area, go to the website of the National Academy of Elder Law Attorneys at www.naela.org. Click on your state and city and you'll find a list of attorneys who specialize in elder law. The information will include names, addresses, phone numbers, and email addresses. You may also call your state bar association for a list of elder law attorneys in your town.

When you meet with an elder law attorney, the initial consultation may be free or at a nominal cost of a few hundred dollars. This is the time to ask the important questions and begin to develop a relationship with the attorney. Find out if the lawyer is prompt, professional, and experienced in elder law. How many seminars in elder law does she attend each year? Is the attorney active in NAELA and does she attend the group's annual conferences? You might also get references from friends who have worked with elder law attorneys and been pleased with the result.

Make certain you ask about legal fees in your initial conversation. The rates for attorneys vary greatly and you have a right to know what the full range of services will cost and if you can pay your bill in several installments. If you don't have good rapport with the first attorney you see, call another one. While price is an important consideration in planning your estate, it is not the most important one. It may be wise to invest more time and money with an attorney up front and save many thousands of dollars later.

While there is no rating service for attorneys, the National Elder Law Foundation awards a certification to elder law attorneys who have extensive experience in the field and have passed a day-long written examination. As of January 2006, there are only 350 Certified Elder Law attorneys in the entire country.

When I needed advice on my parents' financial affairs, I heard two names mentioned over and over. Friends said they were two of the best elder law attorneys in town. This made my job easy. I looked up their names in the phone book, made appointments, and was so impressed that I came back and interviewed them at length for this book. A few months later, I hired one of them to help me draft an estate plan for my parents. Once I began working

with an attorney who knew what I should do step by step, I could feel the pressure lift. When faced with fine print and legal lingo, I had an interpreter, advocate, guide, and friend.

H. Clyde Farrell served for ten years as an assistant district attorney for the State of Texas before opening an elder law practice in 1993. A graduate of the University of Texas School of Law, he is a certified financial planner and certified elder law attorney.

Marilyn G. Miller is a certified elder law attorney and a graduate of the University of Kansas Law School. She is a certified bankruptcy specialist and earned a master of law in taxation from the University of Missouri at Kansas City.

Lee Holmes, an elder law attorney in Oklahoma City, Oklahoma, was a founding member and former director of the National Association of Elder Law Attorneys.

Clifton Kruse, Jr., a former minister, is now an elder law attorney in Colorado Springs, Colorado. He has also served as president of the National Association of Elder Law Attorneys.

Why We Chose Elder Law

Marilyn: I was working for a bankruptcy court when my father sent me an article about elder law published by the Kansas State Bar Association. He scribbled in the margin: "This is the future." For once, I heeded Dad's advice, went to an elder law presentation, and knew immediately that was where I belonged.

Elder law provides a genuine emotional connection with families, and sometimes I'm as much of a counselor as a lawyer. Because there is tremendous stress on both parents and caregivers, it takes a certain temperament for lawyers who do this work. We may deal with deep-rooted family tensions, ancient quarrels, and hidden agendas.

Clyde: Most of my clients are over sixty-five, but many family members I meet with are much younger. Although my contact may be primarily with the younger generation, I make it clear that I represent the older person. They are my clients even if I never met them. I help families to plan for long-term care, understand their options, and make the best possible decisions about their estates. There are parents who want to stay in their own homes no matter what. They will resist any suggestion that they live in a care facility or even move in with a child. That may be possible if family members are willing and able to care for them or they have the financial resources to hire home health workers.

If there is no one to serve as a caregiver and the parents have a limited income, we may have to sell their home and move them into assisted living or a skilled nursing home. Since the average cost of a nursing home is more than $61,000 a year—and rising yearly—it may not take long for their savings to be depleted. Eventually they may have to apply for Medicaid benefits in order to get the care they need.

Getting Parents Qualified for Medicaid

Clyde: Elder law attorneys understand what's involved in qualifying for Medicaid. We help families keep assets to which they are rightfully entitled. There is tremendous confusion and misunderstanding about qualifying for Medicaid, and the rules and regulations vary from state to state and year to year. An elder attorney's job is to eliminate misinformation and help to guide families through the process.

Lee: Most people want to be able to leave an inheritance to their children. If they spend it all on nursing homes, they won't have that opportunity. We try to help families transfer some assets to their children or put them in trusts so they won't spend every penny on nursing homes and have nothing to leave to their sons and daughters.

The medical system is not even-handed. If you have a heart attack, stroke, or cancer, Medicare will pay tens of thousands of dollars for your care. But if you have dementia or Alzheimer's disease, they won't pay for a long-term-care facility or home care. Why should one disease be covered by the government and another not? That doesn't make sense. Elder law attorneys help families get Medicaid, which covers parents no matter what health problems they may have.

Long-term-care insurance is an excellent investment for those who can afford and qualify for it. Unfortunately, many of our clients don't have enough money to pay the premiums. Some who can afford it have health conditions and can't pass the physical exam. They will need Medicaid assistance if they have to go into a nursing home.

In addition, many people who buy long-term-care insurance don't buy enough to cover the cost of inflation. By the time they need to access their coverage, ten or twenty years after first purchasing it, prices are so high that the policy doesn't cover the costs unless they have an inflation rider. In New York State today, some nursing homes cost $100,000 a year. Even the best policies don't cover that price range. Who knows what skilled nursing care in that area will cost in ten years?

Do Your Best, but Know Your Limits

Marilyn: If I could give families one piece of advice it would be to open the lines of communication as early as possible. Explore options. Get all your brothers and sisters and their spouses involved and listen to each other.

I know a talented elder law attorney who could not get her own husband to take her advice about his mother. He bent over backward to make it possible for his mother to stay in her own home, and almost killed himself caring for her. He had a near-fatal heart attack before realizing that his mother needed to be in a care facility. He was living with an elder law expert, but he had to make that decision for himself.

In trying to help their parents, siblings should deal from their own strengths. The children with the strongest emotional connections to the parents may be the ones to take the lead in talking to them about making hard decisions. They may not be the most responsible day-to-day caregivers, but that doesn't matter. Think of them as star salespeople and involve them early and often.

A common myth is that the oldest child has some special right or responsibility. Age has nothing to do with caring, common sense, or the ability to persuade parents to act in their best interests. Seniority does not equal effectiveness.

Let me give you an example. A woman of seventy came to my office distraught about her ninety-two-year-old mother's terrible health and refusal to seek help. I told her to get her mom to a psychiatrist. She said, "I can't get her to go. She won't do that for me." Even though my client was seventy, she remained a child to her own mother.

Sometimes the family's best efforts are in vain. *Children are responsible for doing the best they can, not working miracles.* There is a limit to what we can do. Parent/child dynamics have deeply rooted boundaries. If children can't crack the invisible ceiling and convince their parents to make needed changes and take action, they must step back and not feel guilty about it.

Estate Planning

Marilyn: Gloria Steinem once said, "Rich people plan for three generations. Poor people plan for Saturday night." Most of us fall somewhere in between. People tend to think of estate planning as something for the wealthy, but that's a misconception.

Even families who plan for three generations sometimes find that they are not ready for the unexpected. If your mother has a stroke while caring for Dad, who is at home suffering from dementia, the best-laid estate plan may become strained. Suddenly $4,000 is going to the nursing home and $2,500 to home health care each month, plus regular household expenses. Most families will find that level of expense hard to sustain for an extended period of time.

Planning ahead can make a tremendous difference. In some states, parents can set up a special-needs trust in advance and place many of their assets into it. In most states, they can specify in their wills that their half of the estate goes into the trust for their spouse at the time of their death. Since one parent is likely to die before the other, it's important to have the same provision in both wills. If Dad dies first, his half of the money goes into the special-needs trust, not to the surviving spouse. Mother still has her portion of their estate until she dies.

The special-needs trust is extremely important when one parent is in a long-term care facility on Medicaid. Let's say a husband is in a nursing home on state assistance and his wife has named him the sole beneficiary in her will. If she dies first, her money will go to him. *That will disqualify him from receiving Medicaid.* Unless the money is willed to someone else or a special-needs trust has been set up, the entire estate may be spent on the nursing home care and not a penny will go to the children.

Procrastination Is an Avoidable Catastrophe

Marilyn: The number one mistake families make in planning their estates is waiting too long to begin getting the necessary documents together. They don't take action until there is an emergency; unfortunately, that may be too late to do what is best for all concerned. You can't wait until after a health crisis to ask the important questions.

Let's face it; most people are motivated by fear. They fear being incapacitated. They fear going into a nursing home. And they fear seeing a lawyer. Sometimes the anxiety about talking to an attorney outweighs all the other fears combined. As a result, people get their legal advice from friends, salespeople, or ads on the Internet. They make estate-planning decisions without professional counsel and risk making terrible mistakes.

Clyde: Some people manage to make several mistakes simultaneously. They buy an annuity and do nothing else. That's the worst of all possible worlds. The good news is that many mistakes can be corrected as long as the parents are alive and able to communicate clearly. If the children wait until their mother and father are no longer able to provide accurate information, their parents' wishes must be reconstructed from documents. Then lawyers get involved, and that can be time-consuming and costly.

Almost as bad as doing nothing is acting too quickly without benefit of good legal advice. Many couples make the mistake of transferring all of their assets to their children because they think this will help them qualify for Medicaid. I've seen cases where parents deed away their homes unnecessarily in order to get a Medicaid bed in a nursing home. They don't realize that a home, car, and burial plan are exempt assets in qualifying for Medicaid.

Marilyn: A common problem—especially for many older women—is when one person keeps the books and does not share financial details with the spouse. That's how people get to be seventy-five years old without knowing how to write a check. In our parents' generation, the uninformed mate was usually the woman. Husbands thought they were doing their wives a favor by protecting them from fiscal realities. Being financially illiterate is no favor, especially when in one instant the unprepared spouse may be dealing with an estate by herself. Fortunately, the younger generation is breaking this mold. In most families today, both parents work and women are as likely to be college graduates as men. In many families, the woman is the main breadwinner.

Often older couples, especially those who have cared for their own parents, hate the thought of burdening their children with their problems. As a result, they choose not to discuss their financial or medical situation and hope for the best. It's important for children to let parents know they want to help and be a part of the caregiving process. Too many children fail to communicate their love for their parents. We may assume that our parents understand that we care about them, but it never hurts to say that out loud. It's like hearing someone say "I love you." We may know it already, but we like to hear the words.

Many of the Problems We See Are Not Legal Issues

Clyde: It's essential for the older generation to get access to professional services. I'm not just talking about legal services, but medical assistance as well. Finding a good geriatric psychiatrist may be the first step. Until your parent has been thoroughly tested by a competent professional, you really don't know if the problem is a chemical imbalance, emotional distress, or the early onset of Alzheimer's.

I see so many people not getting the help they need. If parents are clinically depressed, they need treatment for depression. If one of them has an unusual amount of anxiety, he may need to see a specialist. Don't rely solely on your family doctor. He or she may be a great friend of your parents, but not up on the latest treatments. If your parents are in an HMO, they may be required to go through their primary care doctor to get a referral to a specialist. If a parent is denied access, appeal the decision. If you lose the appeal, pay for a specialist. If they aren't eating right, call Meals on Wheels or other service organizations that provide hot meals delivered to the home. Call the local Area Agency on Aging to get free information about senior care services where you live.

Caregivers Must Also Care for Themselves

Clyde: Forty- to sixty-five-year-olds may find themselves dealing with parents, children, and grandchildren simultaneously while also trying to work a high-stress job and pay the mortgage. It may be important for caregivers to get counseling, to ask for help from family members, or to join a support group.

Amy Matta, formerly with the Austin Alzheimer's Association, says, "The caregivers' biggest problem is finding time to nurture themselves. They need to make sure that they give themselves a regular break."

Marilyn: I couldn't agree more. Caregivers are under a lot of pressure. On the stress scale, dealing with aging parents is right up there with death, divorce, and home renovation. The caregiver may be the one who has a breakdown, heart attack, or ends up in the hospital. The stress is often most severe where there is great love.

Caregiving can open up old rifts and expose jealousies that have been simmering for years. It may exacerbate tensions and tear families apart, or heal wounds and bring families together. Parents and children need to have an opportunity to say what's on their minds, express their love, and forgive each other for mistakes and shortcomings.

Clyde: I see many families treat each other with dignity, grace, and compassion. On the other hand, some scream, yell, and fall apart at the seams. Each case is different. I believe families who communicate openly and prepare in advance get through the process more easily than those who remain in denial.

Elder Law Is a Calling

Clifton: If one of my clients has to be in a nursing home, I visit them as soon as possible so I can check on the quality of the home. Recently I got a call from a man in Canada whose sister was here in Colorado Springs and had moved the day before into a local nursing home. He asked if I would see how his sister was doing and tell him what I thought about the facility.

As soon as we hung up, I went to the nursing home and walked into the sister's room. It was a small space about five feet wide by ten feet long and she was sharing it with someone else. My client's sister was lying on a cot and I could see that the top of her head had been rammed into a board above her. It looked as if someone had stuffed her into that tiny space. In the process, her head had been cut and I could see blood on the wall.

I went to the nurses' station and asked, "Who's in charge here?" When I found the charge nurse, I told her I was astonished that any nursing home would treat a helpless woman with such carelessness.

"I'm getting her out of this place and I'm getting her out now. If you don't like it, then come after me." I reported that nursing home immediately because I had a moral obligation to tell the state authorities what I'd seen.

Then I called her brother and told him, "How soon can you get down here from Canada?" By the time he arrived, I had his sister in a fine nursing home a few miles away. I went to see her an hour after she checked in and found her in bed, smiling and happy.

Unfortunately, some lawyers are only interested in the bottom line. They ask themselves, "How much money can I make from a client?" *However, that is not the attitude of most elder law attorneys.* It's not how I run my practice. My job is not to make a lot of money, but to take care of my clients. The lawyer in me is less important than what can I do to make people's lives better.

Comer's Commandments

- Get professional assistance before you make major or minor legal decisions.

- Find an elder law attorney who deals with senior issues regularly.

- Negotiate your fees up front. If you wouldn't buy a used car from the attorney, don't entrust your parents' future to her.

- Make certain that your parents have up-to-date wills.

- Do not wait until an emergency arises to get powers of attorney and advance directives.

- Don't believe that estate planning is only for the rich. Talk to an elder law attorney about how to plan wisely for your family.

- Open lines of communication as early as possible and get your parents and all of your siblings involved.

- It may take years to get your parents to execute wills and sign powers of attorney. Don't give up just because they say no the first time or the twentieth. Keep bringing up the subject until they agree to get the documents signed.

- Remember that you do not have supernatural powers. If your parents absolutely refuse to do anything about their estate, you may have to accept that fact.

Anne Haynie Comer (age 18) and John Smith Comer (age 20)

32

Documents Every Family Needs

Wills: Where there's a will, there's a way.
Where there's no will, there will be hell to pay.

Only three out of every ten Americans have a will. *Ten out of ten are going to die*. Some people avoid getting a will because they are in denial. After all, a Last Will and Testament is legal proof of our mortality. Others mistakenly believe that getting a will is an expensive, complicated, and depressing process. What's depressing is having a parent who never bothered to write one. It is tragic to see an inheritance tied up in probate and frittered away on lawyers' fees. The presumptive heirs may spend years in probate purgatory.

If you don't believe that many bright people neglect to spend an hour to dictate their will, remember the words "John Denver." Despite his talent, charm, and intelligence the singer-songwriter died without a will. His estate was estimated at seven million dollars. Some attorneys got rich. Some deserving family members did not.

You're not hiring a lawyer simply to prepare documents. You go to an attorney to get their experience and advice, as well as the documents that accompany them. My cousin, Randy Stump, does a good basic will for around $500. He will charge considerably more if his client has complicated issues and needs more time spent on his estate. The job of a competent attorney is

ize each will to each client. One size does not fit all. If you're in
wn, Texas, you can find Randy at Stump & Stump, off the court-
house square.

To prepare an estate that meets the needs of your family $500 may be
appropriate or $2,000 may not be enough. It depends on the complexity of
your estate. Cheapest is not always wisest. Do you pick doctors because they
charge the least or because they have the experience, training, and ability to
do the job? The key to getting a good will is to find an attorney you trust,
establish a relationship with that person, and make sure that your will is cus-
tomized to your family's needs.

A will is the most important legal document that you and your parents
need, but not the only one. You must have forms that allow you to make medical and legal decisions on their behalf. Without these documents, you may
find yourselves unable to follow your parents' wishes or act in their best
interests. No matter how healthy your parents are today, that could change
in a few seconds. The question is: will you be ready when the time comes?

A *Durable Power of Attorney* is almost as important as the will because it
provides you the authority to act in your parents' best interest and to make
financial and legal decisions for them if they become mentally or physically
incapacitated. You will need it to obtain bank records, investment, or insurance information. You may need to amend a trust or make gifts. There are a
number of options that may be included in the Power of Attorney documents.
Many parents only have one child's name as power of attorney. It might be a
good idea to consider putting all of the children on this form so that they all
share in the responsibilities and none has too much power.

A *Medical Power of Attorney* names the persons who will make medical
decisions for your parents in the event they cannot make these decisions for
themselves. This form has nothing to do with finances, only health care decisions. Usually one person is given this responsibility; however, all of the children can be on the form. It does not have to be limited to one individual.
There does not need to be a family dictator over medical decisions.

If there is no Medical Power of Attorney, and a parent is in a hospital or
nursing home, state law will determine which family member becomes the
medical decision maker—and the state has no idea which siblings are
responsible and who is dysfunctional or greedy. Another reason to have all of
your children on this form is that something may happen while you are out
of town visiting a child and are hundreds of miles away from the rest of the
family. If each child's name is on the Medical Power of Attorney, any of them
can act on your behalf immediately.

If Parents Won't Cooperate

According to Lee Holmes, an elder law attorney who has dra dreds of wills and powers of attorney, persistence is essential. Keep bringing up the subject over and over again until your parents agree to see a lawyer, have a will drawn up, and sign it. Then pull out the powers of attorney and get them signed. If you have to badger your parents to make this happen, badger away. If you need to bring in a minister, rabbi, doctor, or best friend to influence them, bring them in. Use whatever means of influence you have, including the sibling that no one except for your mother can stand. He or she may be the one to get the will signed.

Holmes tells about a couple: The wife wanted to get their will and powers of attorney completed, but the husband wouldn't sign the forms. So Holmes drew up the papers for the wife and had the husband come along so he could explain them to him. By the time he'd gotten half way through the explanation, the husband said, "All right, you've convinced me. Let's do my documents, too."

Timing is also important. A good time to bring up subjects like wills, powers of attorney, and directives to physicians is when your parents are already thinking about these issues. Maybe they have a friend who is struggling with a terminal illness or the death of a spouse. That might be the perfect moment to ask if they've thought about what they'd want in a similar situation.

If they have friends who are having trouble caring for themselves or living alone, ask how they plan to handle that situation if it happens to them. If they know someone who had difficulty qualifying for Medicaid benefits, ask them if they have thought about getting long-term-care insurance.

Mental Health Directives address the one area that the Medical Power of Attorney does not include: mental health decisions. This might include psychotropic medications, admission to a mental health facility, or electroshock therapy. You can name your decision maker separately on this document.

A *Living Will (Directive to Physicians)* covers situations where your parent's condition is terminal and/or irreversible. The choice is between: "Yes, I would want life support continued" or "No, I would want life support discontinued." Life support includes putting a loved one on feeding tubes and forced nutrition. Keep this document on hand at the hospital because many physicians feel bound and determined to keep a patient alive no matter what—even when there is no quality of life.

There is one Directive to Physicians for "in hospital" situations and another for "out of hospital" emergencies. Both forms should be signed. If an emergency medical rescue team becomes involved and the patient is off hospital grounds, EMR is required by law to do everything possible to save the patient's life, unless there is a specific "out of hospital" directive.

The *Directive to Control Disposition of Remains* form can be filled out in advance without an attorney or notary, simply stating your wishes about burial, cremation, funeral services, or other matters of personal preference. These forms can be obtained from an attorney, state medical association, or at the Texas Human Rights Foundation website at www.thrf.org.

Organ Donor Cards are so important. Hundreds of thousands of Americans are on lists waiting to receive organs that will save their lives or make them better. Many of them will die because the organ they need is in short supply and does not get to them in time. I can think of no greater legacy than donating an organ so that another person might live, see, or get off dialysis. But the family can't donate an organ—even if they want to—unless the deceased has an organ donor card filled out prior to his or her death.

The family can't make the decision after the fact. The card must be filled out in advance. These cards make it possible to donate organs such as corneas, bone, skin, and heart valves after cardiac death. In the event of brain death, the family must agree to organ donation, including heart, lungs, and kidneys. Organ donor cards do not have to be notarized and can be obtained from the state medical association or online from www.organdonor.gov.

Know Where These Documents Are Kept

Finding these forms should not be a treasure hunt. Make sure that all siblings know where they are kept, whether it's in a lock box, a safe, or in the files with the family lawyer. If they are under lock and key, make sure you have a copy of the key. It is also a good idea to have duplicate copies kept in several locations in case of fire, flood, or an unreliable attorney.

After all those legal terms, it's time for a story that will bring a smile. Barbara Anne Stephens of San Antonio, Texas, one of my closest college friends, shared this reminiscence about her father.

Barbara Anne: I wish I had known that my father's world was shrinking so rapidly. Once he was my provider, comforter, and worthiest advisor. Now he only knows I'm his daughter because I call him Daddy.

I wish we had discussed financial and legal issues when Daddy was at the top of his game. I could have learned from a master. He survived the depression and World War II, saved money, and planned for the future. By the time I had the courage to say, "Where is your will?" he was already deep into Alzheimer's and could only respond, "I don't have a will." Fortunately, he was mistaken. He executed a will in 1976 and signed forms giving me durable and medical powers of attorney, as well as signing authority on his bank accounts. Of course, he never told me about it.

I wish I'd insisted on a full accounting of his financial holdings ten years ago. Tracking them down and dealing with financial institutions designed to protect him has been painful. Even though I have the necessary documents, I am often viewed as an opportunist.

I wish I had known that my father's second wife was going to lob a scud missile into my life. One morning when I went to see him she handed me his suitcase and said, "You take your father. I can't take care of him anymore." And I did. I often reflect on the wisdom of Daddy's doctor, who told me, "I never cease to be amazed at the coping ability of some people and the inability of others in the same situation."

When I moved my father into a care facility, he was greeted by a welcoming committee of women who could spot a good-looking man a corridor away. Miss Laura glommed onto Daddy as she must have with her late husband, a West Point graduate. One day I took my aunt and uncle to visit Daddy. When we went into his room, I invited Miss Laura to join us. Within a few minutes, a staff member knocked at the door and said, "Miss Laura, what are you doing in Mr. Marx's room?" I told her that I had invited Laura to come in.

The conscientious employee pulled me near and whispered, "We found a pair of Miss Laura's panties in your father's room last week." This news did not shock me and has become a real source of inspiration to my husband.

33

Long-Term-Care Insurance

My parents were nothing if not insured. They owned five life insurance policies, home insurance, car insurance, and supplemental Medicare insurance. They even insured me when I turned sixteen. They had policies for everything *except an extended stay in a long-term-care facility*. Today my mother is in her sixth year at a nursing home. Already they have spent more than $250,000 from their savings and shrinking investments.

I wish I could give a firsthand report about my parents' long-term-care policy and how it delivered on its promises. By the time they needed coverage, one of them was ninety and the other eighty-eight. Mother had Alzheimer's, Dad had suffered a stroke, and both had broken their hips. They were an underwriter's nightmare. Like my parents, most people don't think about long-term-care insurance until they have serious health problems. After a heart attack, they might call their insurance agent. That's like applying for car insurance after you've had a head-on collision.

Even though Americans are living longer than ever before, fewer than 10 percent of those over sixty-five have long-term-care policies. In all age groups, only four million Americans have long-term-care insurance policies. The median cost of a yearly long-term-care premium in 2005 was approximately $2,000, although that cost varies greatly depending on the age and health of the insured.

Most people don't consider long-term-care policies until they reach their sixties or seventies. While taking action then is better than taking no action at all, it's much like visiting a career counselor at the senior center. It makes better sense to start earlier, when we are healthy and more likely to qualify for a comprehensive policy at a reasonable rate.

Unfortunately, people under fifty generally don't want to spend money on a policy they may "never need." Most of us first consider long-term-care insurance for ourselves when we become involved in caring for our parents. As we observe their health decline, it dawns on us that someday we may face the same situation. That comes as a painful surprise to those of us who heretofore considered ourselves immortal. Suddenly we see the wisdom in having a plan to provide for our own security and take the pressure off children or other family members.

The catch is that long-term-care insurance is not for everybody. For many families, it is not a practical option. The question is not what plan is right for you, but whether you—or your parents—are good candidates for *any* plan. You can qualify yourselves by answering a few basic questions.

- Do you have assets of at least $50,000? (To qualify the answer should be *yes*.)

- Is your only source of income a social security benefit or Supplemental Security Income? (*No*)

- Are you already having a hard time paying your monthly bills? (*No*)

- Can you afford long-term-care insurance premiums? (*Yes*)

- Will you be able to afford the premium if the price rises substantially? (*Yes* or *I hope so:* This is the toughest question for most people.)

If you have few assets and are already stretched to your limit financially, long-term-care insurance may not be a wise investment. If your assets are above $50,000 and you have enough disposable income to pay the monthly premiums—or plan to build substantial assets by the time you retire—long-term-care insurance may be a prudent choice.

Choosing the Right Company and the Right Plan

Caveat emptor. If you know only one phrase from Latin, that's a good one to remember: Let the buyer beware. That warning applies whether you are purchasing a used car or a long-term-care policy.

Nationally, there is a wide selection of companies offering long-term-care policies; however, every year some companies enter and others leave the field. In addition, policies vary greatly in scope and cost. Some plans include the whole continuum of care: assisted living, nursing home, Alzheimer's units, home care, and adult day care. Others pay for care facilities only and some cover home care only.

The long-term-care insurance industry is about thirty years old. In many ways it is going through its adolescence, growing and adapting to the realities of the marketplace. Like teenagers, some companies make big mistakes. They may go out of business and leave their policy holders in the lurch.

When it comes to making important decisions, selecting a long-term-care plan is right up there with choosing a spouse or buying a house. The key to making an informed decision is to take your time and do your homework. When Donald Trump buys a company, his staff investigates every aspect of the firm's history, operations, and financials. That's called due diligence. You need to perform the same type of investigation on the company you pick.

If you have determined that long-term-care insurance is a good option for you or your parents, consider these factors in selecting an insurance company:

- How long has the company been in the long-term-care business? Just because a firm has been successful in other areas of insurance does not mean it will succeed in long-term care. Many experts, including nationally known financial planner Suze Orman, believe that a company should be in the long-term-care business for at least ten years.

- How much insurance does the company currently have in force? A large number is a good sign. We're talking billions, not millions.

- Has the company ever increased its premiums? If so, how much was the price increase and how often has the company increased rates?

- In the last three years, how many complaints have been filed against the company in your state? If it has a history of substantial rate increases, that's a red flag. If you've already bought a policy and your insurer raises rates exorbitantly, check with your state department of insurance to make sure the company has a right to demand such an increase.

- Will the company take people with pre-existing conditions, such as stroke or diabetes?

- Does the company have a proven track record? This is a good sign that it intends to stay in the long-term-care business. Of course, there is no way to guarantee a company's future. Enron had a reputation as one of America's fastest-growing, best-managed companies and it collapsed in months. Capitalism, like the legislative process, is not always pretty.

- What are the company's ratings from respected independent insurance analysts? You can find out these ratings by calling the companies or going to their websites.

A.M. Best Company
908-439-2200
www.ambest.com

Weiss Research, Inc.
800-289-9222
www.weissratings.com

Moody's Investor Service, Inc.
212-553-0377
www.moodys.com

Standard & Poor's Insurance Rating Service
212-438-2400
www.standardandpoors.com

An excellent source of information is *A Shopper's Guide to Long-Term Care Insurance,* published by the National Association of Insurance Commissioners (NAIC). In forty readable pages, it provides an overview of the long-term-care industry and consumers' options. NAIC is a non-profit group with no axe to grind or product to sell. Get your copy by writing, calling, or faxing them at:

NAIC
2301 McGee Street, Suite 800
Kansas City, MO 64108-2662
816-842-3600
Fax: 816-783-8175
www.naic.org

Another reliable source of information is your state department of insurance. In the resource section at the back of this book—pages 255 to 304—there is a list of state insurance offices with addresses, phone numbers, and website addresses. These agencies can give you up-to-date information about long-term-care insurance in your state, including two important facts:

1. the number of complaints filed against each company operating within its borders; and

2. how often companies have raised their rates in the last five years and the size of the rate increases.

As public agencies, state departments of insurance cannot recommend a plan, but they can provide important insights to help you make that choice. Before you make a decision, it would be wise to talk with one of their consumer specialists.

It's important to choose a company that has sound *underwriting standards*. These are the guidelines insurers use to accept or reject potential policyholders. Having strict qualifications means the company will likely have healthier policyholders and pay fewer claims, which safeguards its financial solidity. At the same time, tough underwriting standards may lead to higher rates and limit the number of people who qualify for coverage. This, of course, may be *you*.

Underwriting is a balancing act for both insurance companies and their policyholders. Loose standards allow companies to sell more policies but create a higher-risk group of policyholders who are likely to file a larger number of claims. If the company is not prudent about its underwriting standards, it may end up having to raise its premiums or go out of business. Some insurers caught in this squeeze have been known to increase rates between 100 and 500 percent in one year, forcing policyholders who live on a fixed income to drop their policies.

When an insurance company goes out of business, states offer policyholders protection from unscrupulous or badly managed companies. If your insurance company goes out of business or is liquidated by the courts, contact the state life and health guaranty association. You can find their telephone number by calling the state department of insurance.

Get Help Choosing a Long-Term-Care Insurance Plan

Even if you spend the time required to research companies and compare prices and benefits, insurance is a complex business and policies are full of complex, mind-numbing industry jargon. Most policies include terminology that is alien to English as we know it. Small print can contain big exclusions. That's why it's important to have a knowledgeable, reputable advocate who is looking out for your best interests. That person is your insurance agent.

To evaluate a policy requires a trained eye, years of experience, and the ability to match your needs to an appropriate, affordable policy. A good insurance agent provides that kind of service; however, like lawyers and politicians, insurance agents vary from caring to callous. Some may talk a good game but disappear once you sign the policy. I recommend finding an insurance agent who specializes in long-term care. You may want to use an agent who represents a large company with a proven track record or consider an independent agent who offers plans from many companies and is not bound financially to one provider.

How do you find a knowledgeable, ethical long-term-care insurance agent?

• Get a referral from a person you trust, preferably someone with a family member who is now collecting on a policy.

• Call your state department of insurance.

• Contact the Independent Insurance Agents Association in your state.

• Call your local Area Agency on Aging or the state Alzheimer's Association.

• All of the above.

When you talk to an agent, ask how many long-term-care policies he or she has written in the last twelve months. If the number isn't substantial, this person is not an expert in the field. There are four main variables in the price of a long-term-care policy:

• *Benefits:* This refers to what you want the policy to cover. This includes how much it pays per day, what facilities are covered, and the length of the elimination period, which is the gap between the date you activate the policy and when it starts paying benefits. A typical elimination period is one to three months. Shorter is better.

• *Your age:* This refers to your age when you take out the policy, not when you begin to use it.

• *Where you live:* Care facilities in small towns, the South, and Midwest tend to be less expensive than those in cities, the Northeast, or West.

• *The quality of your health when you take out the policy:* Do you have pre-existing medical conditions such as diabetes?

If you take out a policy when you are relatively young and in good health, you will have a lower monthly premium. If you wait until you are sixty-five or older and have one or two pre-existing conditions, the policy will ‿ more expensive.

Let me use myself as an example. I'm sixty-one years old, single, and living in Austin, Texas. Here's what I want in a long-term-care policy:

- *Flexibility*. I want it to cover home health care, assisted living, and nursing home care.

- *Full benefits*. I want benefits of at least $140 a day that are adjusted annually for inflation.

- *Reliability*. I want a company that has been in the business for at least fifteen years and that has a good financial reputation.

- *No elimination period*. I want benefits to start immediately when I need them.

- *Affordability*. I want to be able to eat Häagen-Dazs and watch cable TV after paying my premium.

Obviously, I want a lot. The question is how to find it. Fortunately, I know an agent who has a reputation for treating clients like family members.

Lynn Shank is an independent insurance agent who, along with her husband Harry Shank, runs Texas Assurance Care, Inc. Senior Plans. They have been in the long-term-care business for more than ten years and have sold hundreds of policies from more than thirty insurance companies. In 2005, Lynn was honored by the Society of Certified Senior Advisors with their first Service to Seniors Samaritan Award.

Lynn: There are six key factors to remember when you begin shopping for a long-term-care insurance policy.

1. *Analyst ratings. They are important, but they are not everything.* While companies with an A+ financial rating may be desirable, they may be too expensive for many people. I have placed clients with companies that have B+ ratings and found them to provide excellent service. The difference in ratings may have nothing to do with the quality of the insurance but whether the parent company is financially diversified. For instance, if an insurance carrier doesn't have

241

a strong life insurance business, the company may receive a lower rating from analysts because life insurance tends to be so profitable.

There are many ways to judge a company's performance apart from its rating from A.M. Best or Moody's. As an independent agent, I talk regularly with care facilities to find out whether a company is paying its claims promptly. I also check with the state department of insurance to see how many complaints an insurer has had filed against it. In addition, I ask my current clients about the quality of customer service from their insurers.

2. *When you fill out the application, tell the truth, the whole truth, and nothing but the truth.* If your parent has dementia, say so. Don't pretend Mama is just a touch forgetful. Having "a little dementia" is a contradiction in terms. Like a pregnancy, it will grow. You can't hide that fact forever. Most companies require a physical exam up front while others rely on paper. Either way, if you fail to disclose a pre-existing condition in your application and turn in a claim six months later, the insurance company will conduct a comprehensive medical exam and discover the truth. Insurers have two years to contest a claim. Misrepresentation on an application can void the policy. If you have not made full disclosure, they will not pay the claim and will cheerfully cancel your policy.

I knew a woman who was sixty-seven and had experienced some memory loss but had not been diagnosed with dementia. There was no red flag in her medical record so she looked good on paper. An insurance company accepted her application, but didn't give her the medical exam for six months. When she went in for her physical, the dementia was apparent. She didn't meet the stated medical requirements and her policy was canceled immediately.

3. *Don't assume that a pre-existing health condition will keep you from getting coverage.* Many people are self-underwriting. Because they fear being turned down, they never seek long-term-care coverage. Don't make that assumption and count yourself out. People who have suffered heart attacks or have recovered from some forms of cancer have nothing to lose by applying for a policy. Some excellent companies will insure people with health issues if they are willing to pay a higher price. The monthly cost may be steep, but would you rather pay $2,000 to 4,000 a year now or $60,000 a year in the future?

Individuals who suffer from Parkinson's, multiple sclerosis, osteoporosis, dementia, hepatitis C, or HIV are unlikely to qualify for a regular long-term insurance policy. They should consult a financial planning professional about the possibility of investment vehicles that have a rider providing for long-term-care benefits.

4. *If your parents can't afford a policy but have good health, the children might want to take out policies for them.* This not only provides security for the parents, but it also takes a potential burden off of the children. As long as the parents sign the

forms and meet the underwriting requirements, the company does n̲ẉ̲
who pays the premiums. If the children have the resources, taking out a policy
for their parents may be a good solution for the entire family.

5. *Choose a long-term-care insurance agent who will be there to help you when it's time to access your benefits.* You want an agent who is not only eager to sell you a policy and collect a commission, but who will also be there to walk you through the process and run interference when it's time to use the policy. A good agent is not just a commission-generator but a consultant, troubleshooter, and friend.

Because long-term-care insurance is changing so quickly, there may be hybrid plans that are worth investigating. There are life insurance policies with accelerated death benefits that can be used for long-term care if a person is terminally ill and has to go to a nursing home. There are also financial vehicles such as annuities that may offer long-term care tied to the principal. The key to finding the right plan is to have an agent who knows what you need and will look out for new products and benefits that fit your situation.

6. *When you buy a long-term-care policy, make sure that you discuss the following terms with your agent and fully understand them and how they apply to your policy:*

• Daily Benefit Level: How much does your policy pay per day?

• Benefit Term: How long is the maximum length of your policy?

• Types of Care Covered: Does it cover home health care and assisted living, skilled nursing, and Alzheimer's facilities?

• Elimination Period: Does your policy take effect immediately, or is there a waiting period before it begins?

• Inflation Protection: Is your policy compounded annually to protect against inflation?

• Tax qualified vs. Non-Tax Qualified: Do you want to deduct your premium from your income tax?

• Indemnity vs. Reimbursement: Does your policy pay all at once, or is it paid monthly?

Larry Thomas, Chief Marketing Officer for Equitable Life and Casualty of Salt Lake City, Utah, gave me a candid perspective on the long-term-care insurance business. He has worked in the insurance industry for thirty-five years. Equitable is a respected provider of long-term-care insurance that Lynn Shank has described as "affordable and effective."

Larry: Equitable was one of the first companies in America to offer long-term-care policies. We've been writing policies since 1974, which makes us a pioneer in the field. Although long-term-care insurance has grown steadily, in the last few years growth has been flat for the entire industry.

Two things could change the climate overnight. First, Congress could make long-term-care insurance premiums an above-the-line tax deduction available to everyone. Those who use Schedule A and itemize their returns already receive a tax deduction; however, most seniors don't itemize their deductions and therefore don't qualify for the tax break. A deduction taken directly off adjusted gross income, like an IRA, would encourage consumers to invest in long-term-care insurance. Over time, the tax deduction would pay for itself because it would save the federal government billions of dollars in Medicaid costs.

Second, Americans may come to realize that Medicaid is not meant to care for everyone and does not have the resources to do so. Medicaid is not an entitlement program like Medicare, but rather a safety net for low-income Americans who can not afford long-term care. Over the last thirty years, millions of middle-class Americans have transferred assets to their children, artificially impoverishing themselves, and then used Medicaid to pay for nursing home care. This unintended result of the Medicaid program has drained state governments, lowered the quality of care, and made the system less able to serve those who really need it.

Steven A. Moses, president of the Center for Long-Term Care Reform, a private think tank working to ensure quality long-term care to all Americans, has stated the problem succinctly: "If the baby boom is the Titanic, long-term care is the iceberg." He feels that the coming crisis in long-term care is just beginning to emerge and that people need to take responsibility for planning for their own long-term-care needs.

Individuals who buy long-term-care insurance will have more choices, a higher quality of care, and a wide variety of long-term-care options. Those who opt for Medicaid will have to take what's available and, as resources become more strained, it may not be the high quality they expect. As tens of millions of baby boomers begin to need care, those who lack long-term-care insurance may find their choices severely limited.

One myth of long-term-care insurance is that you can wait around until you need it and then apply. That would be like applying for fire insurance after the house is on fire. Long-term-care insurance companies get calls from fifty-year-olds who suddenly realize there is a major health problem with Mom or Dad and that in six months one or both of them may have to be in a long-term-care facility. When the family applies for coverage, they are shocked that no one wants to underwrite their parent(s).

Another misconception is that you can't get long-term-care insurance when you are older. That is not true. The average long-term-care applicant at Equitable is sixty-nine years old, and the company writes many policies for people in their seventies who are in relatively good health. Of course, the younger people are when they take out a policy, the less expensive it is likely to be.

The most difficult applicants to insure are those who have a triple threat: they are overweight, have high blood pressure, and suffer from diabetes. They are almost impossible to insure because they have multiple problems that can cause them to become impaired and unable to continue the activities of daily living. If they are just overweight, companies can underwrite them. If they have high blood pressure alone, they can get a policy, as can those who just suffer from diabetes. But people who have all three conditions are almost uninsurable. The same is true with someone who suffers from severe osteoporosis.

People need to understand that insurance is about sharing risk. Every insurance company is splitting the risk with the policyholder. Consumers want a company that they can count on to stay in business and pay their claims when the time comes. To do that, insurance companies must enroll the healthiest people so they can invest their money wisely, hold it long enough to pay their expenses, make a fair profit, and be able to pay claims when they time comes. If they insure large numbers of unhealthy, high-risk people, the company won't be able to stay in business. Many companies that have taken on too many high-risk policyholders are no longer in business.

When consumers consider buying a long-term-care policy, they should consider a number of factors. These three are among the most important:

• Look for a company that has been in the business consistently for a number of years and has a stable track record.

• Don't buy more insurance than you can afford or less than you'll need in your area. Unlike hospitalization, long-term-care insurance pays a fixed dollar amount for each day. If you take out a policy that is $125 a day, that's what you'll receive whether you live in a high-cost or low-cost area. That rate might work well in Shreveport, Louisiana, but be inadequate in Hartford, Connecticut.

• Choose a long-term-care insurance agent with the same care you employ in selecting an insurance company. The company and the agent will work together to provide you the quality care you expect and deserve.

Comer's Commandments

- Before you consider which plan is best for you, find out if you are a good candidate for any plan. Long-term-care insurance is not for everyone.

- Take your time in choosing a long-term-care plan and do your homework on the insurance companies.

- Call your state department of insurance for up-to-date information on long-term-insurance companies in your state.

- Work with a reputable, caring insurance agent.

- Compare prices, benefits, and options.

- Don't assume that having a pre-existing condition means that you are uninsurable.

- If you're a good candidate for long-term-care insurance, do not wait until you have a major health problem to apply.

- Don't assume that Medicaid will always have the resources to provide for your long-term-care needs.

34

Funeral Planning: Get It in Writing

Because I'm the only surviving child, no one questioned my decisions about Dad's burial plan, casket, funeral service, or what to do with his few remaining possessions. His will was not contested and his estate was probated in a few months. There was no controversy and no squabbling.

This is not the case in many families. There are often great differences among siblings about burial plans, funeral arrangements, and who gets which possessions. Long-simmering resentments may suddenly surface. That's why having a will, as well as burial and funeral plans in writing, is so important.

Max Jones has run a funeral home in Smithville, Texas, for more than fifty years. Now in his late seventies, he has worked with thousands of bereaved families. I asked Max what he considered the most important element in planning a funeral. He didn't pause for a second before answering, "Pre-need burial plans, without a doubt. If a family hasn't picked out a casket ahead of time, they are likely to make a decision based solely on emotion. Funeral home operators know that. When a family walks through the display room, they take them by the most expensive caskets first. When people are grieving, they are vulnerable. Once they have seen the high-priced caskets, it's hard to choose something less elegant. That's why many families buy an expensive casket even when they can't afford it."

Since Max has spent more than half a century in the funeral business, I wanted to know what he'd found to be the most common dispute among family members.

"Money! By the time they get to the funeral home, some families are already fighting about who's going to get what or if someone will be cheated. I've seen sisters and brothers sit in the same visitation room and stare daggers at each other.

"When I first got into the funeral business, I dealt with a family where there was obvious tension in the air. After they'd chosen the casket, a large man with an air of authority came up to me and said, 'Sir, you don't know these people. Don't let them out of this building until they've paid for that casket because they won't come back.' Then he drew a gun and said, 'You in-laws get out of here because only the kids are going to stay. Get going or I'll shoot your guts out.' The room cleared quickly and I got paid for the casket."

While most families may not go for the gun, the death of a parent brings out the best and worst in the survivors.

My friend Rev. Ann Rosewall is an ordained Presbyterian minister who is currently finishing her Ph.D. in Pastoral Theology at Garrett-Evangelical Theological Seminary in Evanston, Illinois. She has spent fifteen years as a chaplain in large metropolitan hospitals. She has counseled and consoled hundreds of dying people and their families and has conducted scores of funerals.

I asked Ann some of the most basic questions people need to know when dealing with a dying parent or planning a funeral service for someone they love.

Ann: The two biggest mistakes families make in dealing with death are not having brought up difficult subjects ahead of time and not writing down what they want done. Those who are most prepared have experienced the death of a spouse or have someone they love who is dealing with illness, especially chronic pain. Usually they have made choices about what they want or don't want and have written them down. These choices include:

• Cremation or burial

• Visitation

• Open or closed casket

• Funeral or memorial service

• Who will speak at the service, as well as choices about readings and music

Despite the simplicity of these decisions, psychological barriers keep many families from discussing them ahead of time.

Some families are less prepared than others. Individuals under fifty-five, especially those with no connection to a church, seem to have the most difficulty. When it comes time to plan the funeral they want someone leading the service, but they may not know where to turn or what readings and music to use.

Most families from small towns usually have a burial plot. Those from urban or highly mobile families often do not. There is a growing trend toward cremation, and many people have a place in mind where they would like their ashes scattered. Unfortunately, having it "in mind" carries no weight legally. *Only what is written down counts. And it doesn't hurt to have it notarized.*

When there is a sudden death, the difficulty comes primarily from shock. Families just try to get through each day. Planning a funeral immediately after an unexpected death can be emotionally taxing and prolong healing from the loss. Having a written burial plan in place makes things much easier on everyone.

When a death is expected, there are different kinds of problems. Simple decisions may become complicated by too many people trying to exert power in settling the estate. Petty concerns can become magnified a hundredfold. I've seen it happen over and over again. A seemingly minor conversation about who gets certain photographs or place settings can become as emotionally volatile as a disagreement about stocks or child custody.

What Is the Single Most Important Thing Families Can Do to Prepare for End-of-Life Decisions?

Ann: *Talk to each other!* That sounds so easy and obvious, but many families never do it. Because of our reluctance to discuss death, people have a hard time bringing up the subject. Sometimes they need a springboard for the conversation such as the loss of a friend or attending another person's funeral. That's a natural time to talk to your parents about what they want and don't want when they die. It's important to ask one another, "What would you want done? What music, scripture, and order of worship do you want?"

Write down your preferences. I can't overemphasize the importance of getting things in writing. When I hear people say, "Oh, I hope my daughter doesn't do that when I'm gone," I respond, "Get out a pen."

When relatives are standing in a hospital room and are called on to make life-and-death decisions without written guidance, such as advance directives, they face a real dilemma. They may say to themselves, "I wish we had talked to Uncle Bob about life support and artificial nutrition, but it's too late."

Why Is It So Difficult to Know What to Say to Those Who Have Lost a Loved One?

Ann: "I love you" is what people need to hear. All we have to do at a visitation or funeral is to be there, give a hug, and express our love. Don't try to say the right thing because there is no right thing to say. Clichés, unsolicited advice, and retelling your own experiences of loss are not helpful. The bereaved are not expecting you to provide answers. They are expecting you to listen. Just be there and be real.

How Do Families Plan a Funeral Service That Brings Comfort to Those Who Attend?

Ann: It's important for a minister and key participants in the funeral to talk about the deceased in a real and honest way. I believe it's good to have a moment of levity somewhere in the service that reminds them of their loved one's lighter side. It is also moving to be able to address family members individually, even if briefly. It's good to hear someone say, "Molly, your love for your brother will always keep you connected to each other."

I presided at a funeral for a forty-eight-year-old man who had only one living relative; however, there were dozens of his co-workers at his service. I visited with his relative prior to the service to learn about his character, important relationships, and the impact he made on those around him. I was able to incorporate those specific details into my remarks and it made a real difference to his friends and associates. One of them came up to me after the service and said, "You must have known him well." I replied, "I wish I had."

❧

Practicing What I Preach

Choosing my parents' burial plans got me thinking about my own preferences. Although I trust these instructions won't be implemented for decades, Ann will be pleased to know that, finally, I have them down in writing.

Jim Comer's Earthly Departure Instructions

1. I want my body cremated and the ashes placed in an inexpensive but tasteful urn that will be purchased in advance.

2. I want the ashes scattered from a rowboat in the Colorado River across from Austin's new arts center.

3. I prefer a small, private service for family and a few close friends. I will have the scripture readings and music picked out in advance.

4. I want this epitaph engraved on a simple flat stone marker next to my parents' markers. My cousins can bury the urn privately whenever they want, but I don't want any of me next to I-35.

James Balmore Comer

1944–

Relaxed at Last

5. The scattering service will be in the morning. In the afternoon, I want a memorial service at my church with music, singing, readings, and eulogies that stretch the truth, but do not break it. I'd like friends to share stories about my life, especially funny ones.

6. After the service, I want a joyful reception with good food and lively music. The reception will be catered and paid for by me in advance. I don't want my friends to cook, clean, or bring casseroles but just enjoy themselves.

7. I will write my own obituary in advance and supply a flattering photograph.

8. I will have prepared an up-to-date list of friends and relatives to be contacted about the memorial service, along with their phone numbers and email addresses.

9. I will leave all these instructions with the executor of my estate and several close friends who will suffer a devastating curse if they fail to heed my wishes.

Obituaries Are Our Chance to Write History

While the funeral home will do this chore for you, it's a good idea for a family member to write a parent's obituary so it will reflect the family's taste and feelings. Make sure you circulate it among other members of the family before sending it to the newspaper so you don't leave out a relative, misspell a name, or get an important fact wrong. Write down the key moments of your parents' life well ahead of time so that, when the time comes, composing the obituary is a relatively simple task.

Obituaries vary from three or four paragraphs to twenty or more. They include a list of the survivors, a biographical sketch of the person's life that includes achievements and honors, and details about the funeral service. Most obituaries include a picture of the deceased. The photograph can be current or from an earlier time of life. Some families choose to run two photos: one contemporary and the other from younger days.

Comer's Commandments

- Don't be afraid to bring up the subject of death. The passing of a friend or relative may be the right time to ask your parents what they want when the time comes.

- Get your parents' preferences down in writing. Don't let their last act be written by someone else. While you're at it, write down your own preferences as well.

- If your family doesn't have a pre-need burial plan, consider buying one. Otherwise the family's burial decisions may be dictated by the emotion of the moment.

- Shop around for the most reasonable burial plan. Prices vary greatly and there is no reason to spend money on an expensive casket or showy funeral unless the family wants to make that investment.

- Write down your funeral preferences and have them with your papers. Make sure the executor of your estate and close relatives have a copy of your wishes.

- Don't let someone else write your history. Either write your own obituary or make sure that someone knows what you want in it.

Resources: Finding the Help You Need

35

Geriatric Care Managers

One of the most difficult issues for millions of children with aging parents is the one I faced for thirty years: distance. I lived in New York or Los Angeles and my parents lived on Spring Branch Drive in Dallas. For the many years that their health was good, we had no problem. When Mother's memory began to fail and Dad did not choose to acknowledge that fact, our lack of geographic proximity became a major issue.

In today's mobile society, many children live too far away to provide regular supervision and support for parents who need it. The length of the distance is not the main issue: the separation can be one hundred, five hundred, or five thousand miles. The problem is the inability to check on parents easily, to see how they are doing, and to quickly respond to problems or changes.

I wish I'd known that geriatric care managers existed back in the early nineties. I would have hired one to work with my folks and we might have avoided Dad's stroke. For children who live far from their parents, it's a tremendous advantage to have trained professionals who can be neutral observers and serve as your eyes and ears. Today there are thousands of professional geriatric care managers in metropolitan areas, although few are yet found in small towns and rural areas.

I interviewed Byron Cordes of San Antonio, Texas, who has a B.S. from Oklahoma State University and a master's in social work from Our Lady of the Lake University. His company, Sage Care Management, employs nurses

and social workers. Byron will explain how he works with families to create a plan, follow up regularly, and manage the seemingly unmanageable.

Byron: I realize that most people have never heard of a geriatric care manger. We are like family, only with years of training and experience. We do the things that a family would want to do for an aging parent if they knew what to do.

Eighty-five to 90 percent of the families who hire me do not live in the same town as their parents. One of my clients is a physician who lives in California; his sister lives in Seattle. They want their mother to live near them, but she won't leave San Antonio and move to the West Coast. My job is to serve as a surrogate sibling.

The first thing a geriatric case manager should do is a complete assessment of the senior. This should include medical history, financial resources, social support systems, religious preferences, and the legal documents that are—or need to be—in place. The assessment should always include an extensive personal interview. After analyzing the data, the geriatric care manager should write a comprehensive report and a plan of care that will make the environment safer and daily life better. It should also provide a sense of security for their families, near or far away.

It takes me four to six hours to create an individual plan that offers a variety of options. The average price for this assessment is $85–125 per hour. Agencies with large offices and high overhead are likely to charge more. Those of us who work out of our homes are able to charge less. For $400–600, a family should receive an accurate, up-to-the minute, comprehensive snapshot of their parent's condition and needs. They should expect to find out how he is doing, what problems he has, and a specific plan with options to meet those needs. Some Employee Assistance Programs and long-term-care insurance companies will pay for the assessment.

The first eight pages of my assessment will include what the senior has told me, as well as what I have observed when I visited the home or facility where she is living. I have been trained, like a detective, not to miss anything. I want to know where her nearest friends live, where the spare key is kept, whether the water heater is set too high, and if the bathroom needs any modifications. I also look for any potential safety hazards, such as loose rugs.

Sometimes little things tell me a lot. I go through the refrigerator to see what's in it—and what's not. Has food gone bad? Is the milk fresh? What's the temperature of the refrigerator? I check the medications to see if the senior has been taking them regularly. Finally, I make a list of everything I've observed and outline all the things we can do to improve safety and lower risks in the home. Rugs can be removed or taped to the floor. Night lights can be placed in the bedroom and bath. An emergency response system can be installed. A plumber can fix the water heater if the temperature is too high. A yard man can be hired to mow the grass.

Once I've given my assessment, the job could be over, or it could be just beginning. The family may ask me to stay on and provide additional support and periodic updates.

The second part of my job is to carry out the plan. If the family decides that Mother should stay at home, but needs help in making her life safer, I will find the right people to make that happen. If necessary, I will recommend a highly qualified agency to provide home health care workers, interview them, and let the family know about costs. Geriatric care managers understand the vast differences among home health care agencies. We are aware which agencies have high standards and hire qualified workers and which do not. All home health care agencies are not created equal.

For example, in San Antonio there are around seventy home health care agencies. I would not recommend three-quarters of them. In fact, I only work with the top five. I'm sorry to say that too many people are in the home health care business only for the money, and they often hire people who have little experience or training. The agencies I use provide extensive background checks on their employees and don't have problems with stealing. Just as most people wouldn't go to a doctor, dentist, or mechanic without a referral, they shouldn't bring a home health care worker into their parent's home without putting the agency and worker through a careful screening process.

If the family wants follow-up service, my staff or I will visit the senior regularly to reassess the situation. We see many clients on a monthly or weekly basis to make sure there have been no sudden changes in their condition. For example, if a parent has been missing medications, my nurse will set up med boxes with all the pills sorted, labeled, and ready to be taken. Of course, someone with dementia isn't going to tell us if she is taking medications correctly, but the med box works well for many clients.

There are new devices that will actually dispense medications in the home. One of these is the MD2 Medication Dispenser and Reminder, which costs around $800 a month. Medication instructions are programmed into the system; when it's time to take a certain pill a recorded voice says, "Mrs. Smith, it's time to take your medication." The system can also give specific reminders such as "take with food." If Mrs. Smith doesn't take the pill, the system can contact the caregivers by phone. It can also send a weekly or monthly report stating how often she's missed her medications. This additional monitoring costs about $30 a month.

An essential part of my job is keeping peace in the family. Diplomatic skills are essential for a geriatric care manager. Sometimes there are bad feelings between siblings. Those who live far away are concerned that a brother or sister who lives nearby is not doing a good job in caring for the parent. I become a neutral party that all family members can trust. Often my most important job is to tell the brother in Boise, Idaho, "Your sister is doing a good job with your mother." He believes me, but he might not believe her.

If I conclude that it is no longer safe for the parent to live at home and that she should move to an assisted-living facility, I will give the family my candid opinion. I'm not being paid to tell them what they want to hear but what they need to hear.

I can't tell you how many times I've heard a son or daughter say, "My mother is living alone and shouldn't be, but she won't go into assisted living. Do you have any strategies that might help us to persuade her?"

Yes, I do, but there is no one strategy that works every time. Because I'm *not* a member of the family, my opinion may carry a lot of weight with some parents. For those whose minds are clear, a logical approach may be effective.

I'll say to the parent, "Here at home you have a lot of expenses, but you aren't able to get out much or see other people. You spend most of your time watching television. On top of that, you aren't eating well. At an assisted-living residence you won't have to worry about cooking or cleaning. There will be transportation provided for you. You'll have social activities and entertainment if you want them. You'll meet some wonderful people and make new friends. And if you have a problem, you'll have help a few feet away."

Often I'll negotiate with assisted-living residences and ask them to give my client two weeks' stay, free of charge, to see if they like being there. Unlike the average person who walks in off the street, a geriatric care manager should be able to negotiate a tryout period. Then I've got to convince my client. I say, "Just try it for two weeks and then we'll bring you home and you can think about where you liked living more."

To be honest, this approach is a crapshoot. After the two weeks, about one-half the parents will say, "I really liked that place. They drove me everywhere I needed to go. The food was good. I met some nice people. They had sing-alongs and an exercise class. I hate to admit it, but everything I thought about assisted living was wrong." That's the response I love to hear and I get it a lot.

The other half will announce, "Assisted living was exactly like I thought it would be. The shower was too small. The food was bad. I didn't like the people at my table. Everyone was old. I'd rather die tomorrow than live there." I hear that as well.

Still, one out of two is not bad odds. Half of my most resistant clients change their minds after trying assisted living and agree to move in. Until they spend time there, most seniors think assisted living is like a nursing home from the 1960s. No wonder they don't want to go. Once they've experienced life in a well-run assisted-living residence, many of them have a totally different opinion.

Sometimes doctors don't like to confront patients about moving out of their homes. They beat around the bush on the subject. With luck, a geriatric care manager can do some powerful persuading. When I work with doctors, I give them the report I've done on the client. Then we set up a meeting with the family, even if it has to be a conference call.

I've had doctors say, "I thought she needed to be in an assisted-living facility and I've mentioned it to her." Of course, mentioning is not the same as prescribing or insisting! I'm not shy with physicians. I'll ask the doctor, "What's the prognosis if she continues living in her own home and keeps falling down?"

"If she breaks a hip, she'll have to go to a nursing home. Assisted living won't even take her." When the doctor says that, the family is often shocked and becomes willing to take action.

I remember taking one elderly client to her doctor. I'd given him a copy of my assessment to read ahead of time. He looked the eighty-five-year-old in the eye and said, "I believe it's time for you to be in an assisted-living facility. My own mother lives in one and she loves it." My client said, "Which one is she in? I'll go look at it today." That was the best of all possible responses.

Sometimes the patient misunderstands what the doctor has said. That's why it's so important to have a family member—or a geriatric care manager—go with the parent to see the physician. The parent may tell the kids on the phone, "He told me I had to go to a nursing home," when what the doctor really said was "I think you need to be in assisted living."

Most of our placement is in assisted living. We rarely move clients from their home into a nursing home; in fact, that's what we're trying to avoid by intervening early. Nursing homes are for people with serious medical problems, and they are much more expensive than assisted-living facilities.

I've had one or two families hire me when their parent is eligible for a Medicaid bed in a nursing home, but they don't know how to apply for Medicaid or what nursing home to choose. I walk them through the process and make recommendations on homes. Unfortunately, when people are

Medicaid eligible, they may not need a geriatric care manager because their options are limited. I work closely with several elder law attorneys and recommend that the family see one of them for Medicaid planning.

A few geriatric care managers have gone into the business of providing caregivers in the home. That's not something I want to do. Most of my peers stay away from the caregiving side of the business so we can remain neutral and avoid a potential conflict of interest. For instance, if your mom is living at home and a geriatric care manager who is also providing caregivers at $16 an hour comes to reassess her, he may be less likely to tell the family that it's time to move Mom to assisted living.

Unfortunately, today most geriatric caregivers are located in metropolitan areas. Small towns and rural areas are largely underserved. However, as the need for our services continues to increase—as it will in the coming years—there will be many more people entering the field and greater geographic diversification.

Geriatric care managers have been around for twenty-five years, but the field has grown tremendously since the mid-1990s. Our professional association is NAPGCM, the National Association of Professional Geriatric Care Managers. Our two thousand members are made up primarily of nurses and social workers. We have an excellent website at www.caremanager.org that allows families to do a search across the county and find a care manager within twenty-five miles of their zip code. I just tried it out and it took less than thirty seconds to enter my zip code and get information on seven geriatric care managers in my local area.

In choosing a geriatric care manager, I strongly suggest interviewing several people because personal chemistry and trust are key elements in the relationship. I'd also ask for references and check them out. In addition, I'd want to know the geriatric care manager's educational background. Most of us have a master's degree in the geriatric field. There are also four nationally recognized professional certifications. Two are from the National Association of Social Workers: the Care Manager Certified (CMC) and the Certified Case Manager (CCM). Starting in 2007 members must have one of those certifications to belong to our national organization.

My friend Thom Singer told me this story about his dad and I said it had to go into the book. Please feel free to borrow his family's brilliant Home-Grown Emergency Response System.

Thom: My father's name is Al Singer. He's ninety-one but looks like he's in his late seventies. He's outlived the roof on his house, his oven, and his

Cadillac. He had to break down and buy a brand-new car last summer. He just keeps going.

He lives in Arcadia, a suburb of Los Angeles, California, in the same home where my brothers and I grew up. He's been widowed for twenty-one years and none of his four sons live nearby; two are in the San Francisco area, one is in New York, and I'm in Austin. But my dad doesn't live his life through us. He is in fantastic health and drives, bowls, goes golfing, and dancing; has dinner with his friends; goes to the club; and has four girlfriends.

We were worried that none of us lived close by so we asked him to order the *Los Angeles Times* because it's a daily paper. He only wanted to take it on Sunday because his schedule was so busy that he didn't have time to read it. My brother told him that he had to order it seven days a week whether he reads it or not because we have an agreement with the neighbor across the street. He makes sure there is never more than one paper in the driveway. That way we'd know within twenty-four hours if something happened to Dad in the house or outside the house and we'd be alerted. All the neighbor has to do is monitor whether the paper has been picked up.

We've been doing this for eight years and it's worked great. Dad's only missed getting the paper one day in all that time and the system worked beautifully. His neighbor came over and pounded on his door and looked through the window and called my brother, who then called my father. It turned out that nothing was wrong. Dad just forgot to pick up paper that day. He was too busy. Because everybody got so concerned, he's never missed a day since.

We have one more trick to tell how Dad is doing. It works especially well now that he has a new car because before older people have major car accidents, they usually have minor ones. Now that Dad has a brand-new vehicle, it's like a clean slate. Every time my brothers go down to L.A., they walk all the way around the car and look it over to see if there are any scrapes or scratches. Without Dad knowing it, they do a 360-degree inspection. Dad's had the car for just six months and has already put nine thousand miles on it without a scratch. He's still a good driver.

Dad has something on his calendar to do every day, whether it's bowling or having dinner with a friend or seeing his brother and sister-in-law, who are both ninety. There's an event on his date book 365 days a year, so there's never a day when he's sitting home alone. His attitude is that as long as he can keep going and take care of himself, that's just what he's going to do. I'm glad I have his genes.

36

Area Agencies on Aging

Area Agencies on Aging are designed to help people sixty years or older maintain their independence and get information on health care, transportation, housing, caregiver issues, senior centers, and wellness programs—many of the most important issues they may face. The agencies also provide services for caregivers and work as advocates for families to help them get the services to which they are entitled.

There is no charge to use the services of Area Agencies on Aging, and they are not limited to lower-income families. Many seniors have assumed, "This can't be for me. I still have an ability to pay." That's not true. Anyone sixty or older can come into an area agency—or call one of its hundreds of offices across the country—to receive a wide range of services. The organization's goal is to help seniors save time and energy, and learn to navigate bureaucratic systems. Even Bill Gates could get help, as soon as he turns sixty!

Area Agencies on Aging were established following the Older Americans Act of 1965. They are a nationwide organization that covers every county in every state in the nation. Like McDonald's and Wal-Mart, they are everywhere. Unfortunately, they don't have the same advertising budget!

Patricia Bordie, Program Manager at the Area Agency on Aging in Austin, Texas says, "One of our greatest challenges is helping people find out that we exist. We are one of the best-kept secrets in America and that needs to change. We are working hard to get the word out about our services. We speak to church groups and civic organizations, attend health fairs, and place

...ɔes in local papers and senior guides. But we need more television exposure or a celebrity spokesperson. Maybe Oprah would do a show about us!"

Although offices are funded under different departments in each state, your local office can be found in the phone book under Area Agency on Aging. Another easy way to locate the Area Agency on Aging in your area is through the Eldercare Locator. It has a toll-free phone number—1-800-677-1116. Its lines are open on Monday–Friday from 8:00 A.M. to 9:00 P.M. Eastern Standard Time. The operator will answer your questions and refer you to the nearest Area Agency on Aging. For example, you can call the toll-free number and say, "My mom is in St. Paul, Minnesota, and she needs help in finding a home health care agency." They will give you the number of the Area Agency on Aging in her area and that local agency will help you find a list of home health care agencies in St. Paul.

The Elder Locator also has an easy-to-use website at www.eldercare.gov. Even if you are not Internet savvy, you should be able to navigate it with no trouble. If you have any problems, call the toll-free number and ask for assistance.

Area Agency on Aging programs include:

- In-home care: If your parent has a health crisis and comes out of the hospital and needs help in getting back on her feet, the Area Agency on Aging will provide non-medical assistance. This includes help in doing chores, running errands, and installing emergency response systems and medical equipment. The agency can provide personal assistants who do custodial care, bathing, grooming, toileting, and homemaking. They can also remind seniors to take their medications; however, only a registered nurse may administer medication.

- Benefits counseling: This program provides information about Medicare, Medicaid, social security, and community programs for which seniors might be eligible. It also helps families to fill out forms, which are often long and complicated, and better understand how the system works.

- Meals: It's important that seniors who have been assessed as being at nutritional risk get at least one hot, nutritious meal per day. One of the most widely used services provides meals for people over sixty. These meals might be served at a senior center or delivered to the home. For example, in central Texas the Capital Area Agency on Aging serves more than ten thousand meals a month. That's more than three hundred hot lunches every day.

- Transportation: The Area Agency on Aging helps to fund senior transportation, especially rides to and from senior centers where meals are served.

- Personal Emergency Response System: This is a bracelet or necklace with a button that seniors can press if they fall or have an emergency. The device connects with a center that contacts the family. If family members are not available, local emergency responders will be called.

- The Ombudsman Program: This program provides up-to-date information on the quality of local nursing home care based on visits from paid staff members and a large group of volunteers. They visit the nursing homes weekly and turn in written reports, providing more current information than annual state inspections.

    For example, a caregiver living in Boston who needs to put a parent in a nursing home in Phoenix can call the agency there and ask for information on choosing a nursing home. The agency can't specifically recommend a nursing home, but it can point the person to the regulatory agency that does the surveys of homes in that area. In addition, they can share the findings of their ombudsmen and volunteers.

    Similarly, an agency can't recommend a home health care agency, but can say, "In our experience we haven't had many complaints on this agency. The workers show up on time and are honest."

The Area Agency on Aging provides information to help people make wise choices and aims them in the right directions. For example, there aren't many nursing homes that offer specialized care for people with Alzheimer's. They may admit Alzheimer's patients and say they have "memory care" or "special care" units. This doesn't mean that they have an actual program to care for Alzheimer's patients.

If someone calls an Area Agency on Aging asking for a local nursing home with an Alzheimer's program, the staff can tell them which twenty-five homes won't even look at anybody with Alzheimer's. That may save a family twenty-five phone calls. The staff can also tell them which facilities do provide Alzheimer's care. It's all about educating the consumer, which can be done without making specific recommendations. There's a fine line between the two.

Caregiver Support

When the government reauthorized the Older Americans Act in 2000, they added a new program, the National Family Caregivers Program, with the goal of helping families care for older relatives at home. The program provides caregiver education and training, support groups, services to the caregiver, and respite care. The client is really the caregiver, usually a spouse or adult child, or even a neighbor or friend.

Many caregivers think that their situation is unique, which keeps them from asking for help. Too often agency staff members hear comments such as, "I can't handle this so I must be weak. Something must be wrong with me. I must not be a good child." The fact is that all caregivers struggle. Nobody can do it day after day, all day, forever.

Sometimes all the care falls on one person. It doesn't matter if they have six brothers or sisters; there's no guarantee that any of them can or will help. There are "serial caregivers" who take on that role over and over again. They tell agency staff members, "I took care of my mother and then she died and I took care of my father for five years. Then I took care of my aunt."

Many in the older generation think caregiving is expected of them, no matter what it does to their health or the quality of their lives. Many younger adult children understand that they can't do it all. There are also some differences between most men and women in their approach to caregiving. Many adult sons pick up the phone and call an agency and ask for help, whereas too many daughters still think that they have to figure everything out on their own.

Services for Caregivers

Respite Care

This program offers relief for the caregiver: someone to take care of the senior while the regular caregiver takes care of business or gets a much-needed break. In rural counties, if there is no agency available, caregivers can choose a family member, friend, or neighbor to provide respite care and the agency will pay that person.

Education and Training

Agencies offer basic caregiving programs, such as how to transfer a person from bed to chair. Learning how to do that correctly, without injuring yourself or your loved one, takes time and training.

Emotional Support

It's essential to know how to take care of yourself during the process of caring for your parents. These services include seminars, ongoing classes, and regular support groups.

Home Modification

The program installs equipment such as wheelchair ramps that will help the caregiver better care for their loved one.

Advocacy in the Community

This program works to help caregivers and care receivers get what they are entitled to under Medicare, while paying for some services that Medicare does not cover. Home health care is funded primarily through Medicare from a physician's diagnosis; however, home health care agencies will only provide services ordered by a physician and deemed "medically necessary." The Area Agency on Aging staff can educate the family about the services their loved one(s) may be entitled to under Medicare, including personal care and bathing.

The number of Area Agencies on Aging in each state is determined by population, not by geographic area. California, with thirty-six million people, has at least sixty area agencies on aging. Wyoming, with only five hundred thousand people, handles these services through the aging division of the Wyoming Department of Health. In large western states with smaller populations, individual agencies must cover a much larger service area.

Let me put the program in three short sentences. Area Agencies on Aging should be your first call for help. They will point you in the right direction. They will save you time and energy.

A Few Words about Bureaucracies

The word that best describes most bureaucracies would give this book an undeserved "X" rating so it will not be used, but it is the one going through your head. When approaching a federal, state, or local bureaucracy, it's important to remember these key strategies:

- Bureaucracies grow like trees, and sometimes have dead wood among the healthy branches. What was once a healthy, functioning branch of an organization may now be a hollow shell. Think FEMA and Hurricane Katrina.

- Bureaucracies are always more complicated than is necessary. There is a reason for this: chaos creates jobs.

- Bureaucracies require patience. Bring along a good book. In fact, bring two.

- Smile at the clerks, keep calm, and treat the workers like fellow human beings. This is not only right, but it's also smart.

- When talking to a clerk on the phone, do not raise your voice or employ a tone you'd use with a magazine salesman.

- Do not expect bureaucratic forms to make sense. Just fill them out as completely as possible and keep the scowl off your face.

- Ask questions when you must, but ask politely.

- Navigating a bureaucracy is like working your way up the tributaries of the Amazon River. It's a jungle out there. Don't wander into it alone.

- The bureaucracy is more interested in forms than in content. Once you accept that sobering fact, you realize that your job is to do the paperwork correctly. Don't question it: answer the questions.

- Bring all the supporting paperwork required even if it fills a wheelbarrow.

- It is best to have professional help in dealing with a bureaucracy, or bring along a good friend who's been through the process before. Remember: the more vulnerable you are the more help you need.

37

Medicare and Medicaid Planning

If you live long enough, eventually you will become a Medicare recipient. Today that age is sixty-five. Given the current actuarial tables for the U.S. population, most people reading this sentence will get their Medicare card.

The Centers for Medicare and Medicaid Services (CMS) is the federal agency that oversees Medicare, the federal health care program for:

- Those over sixty-five years of age

- Disabled persons, regardless of age

- Those over sixty-five who paid into social security for ten years or those who are eligible for railroad retirement

- Federal workers employed before January 1, 1983

- Those over sixty-five who have been married more than one year to a person who has applied for social security benefits

- A widow or widower—who is still single—from a marriage of more than nine months to a social security beneficiary

- A person who is divorced and still single following a marriage of at least ten years to a spouse who is eligible and applied for either retirement or disability social security benefits

At this point the federal government does not recognize domestic partnerships. You cannot be eligible for Medicare benefits based on the work history of a domestic partner.

You'll know that you are eligible for benefits because a Medicare enrollment package is mailed to those about to join the club three months prior to their sixty-fifth birthday. In this package will be the booklet, "Medicare and You." It's had more copies printed than *The Da Vinci Code,* but not because it's readable. It is free, forty pages long, and full of jargon. However, it is a place to start if you are looking for information concerning Medicare. The booklet is available at federal offices or online at the CMS website at www.medicare.gov. In addition, you may call Medicare at 800-MEDICARE (800-633-4227) and ask them to send you a copy.

Medicare is a universal entitlement program available to all Americans who meet one of the requirements listed above. *Medicare benefits are not based on income.*

Medicare has three parts:

1. **Part A** covers hospitalization and is automatic when a person turns sixty-five.

2. **Part B** covers non-hospital medical care, but it must be applied for specifically. There is a premium of $88.50 per month for this coverage that is taken out of the social security check. Many people don't even realize they are paying these premiums. If the Medicare recipient continues to work, the premium can be deducted or paid directly to Medicare.

   Delaying the application for Part B coverage will increase the monthly premium by 10 percent per year after the first eligible year, except in special cases. In addition to the monthly premium, there is a yearly deductible of $124.00 (as of 2006).

   Federal Medicare law provides a minimum set of rights for people with Medicare anywhere in the country. A state can choose to offer its residents more protections and rights than the federal minimum. In such cases, state law supersedes federal law. For example, federal law does not require insurance companies to sell Medigap policies to people under the age of sixty-five but some states do. In addition, some states offer special assistance programs for people with Medicare, such as covering the deductible for Medicare Part B.

   The difference between the going rate for some medical services and the amount Medicare pays for those services is growing wider, so it's

When

important to find out whether or not a provider will acc
patients. Providers who accept Medicare patients agree to
directly and accept Medicare payment amounts. Those who
this process—a growing number—can charge Medicare be............. up
to 115 percent of the Medicare rate, and expect payment when services
are rendered. The patient then submits a claim to Medicare for reimbursement.

3. **Part D** covers prescription drugs. On January 1, 2006, Medicare began a
new prescription drug benefit which is designed to help millions of
Americans save on drug costs. No, it's not a perfect plan and, yes, it did
have some serious start-up problems—as you would expect from a new
program that affects forty million people. Nevertheless, I believe it is a
move in the right direction.

Medicare drug coverage is much like insurance. Private companies
provide the coverage and Medicare beneficiaries choose a plan that they
feel best meets their needs. Of course, that is the hard part because there
are so many competing plans and it's difficult for many people to tell what
plan is best for them. That's why it's essential to ask for help from someone you trust. I went to the benefits coordinator at my parents' nursing
home and got her opinion on which plan my mother should choose. Even
though she's on Medicaid, she must choose a plan. The benefits coordinator couldn't tell me what to do, but she did show me a chart compar-
ing the plans' benefits, and then the choice was not difficult. To select
Dad's plan, I called his former employer and talked to their retiree benefit manager. She told me in no uncertain terms, "Absolutely do not sign
up for a Medicare Part D plan. Your dad will lose his medical coverage
through his retirement plan, as well as the drug coverage we supply."

You might also talk to your doctor, an elder law attorney, or one of the
senior advocacy agencies in your town. You can call AARP, the Consumer's
Union, or the local Area Agency on Aging for advice. Do *not* choose a plan
unless you are sure it meets your needs and does not invalidate better coverage you are already getting from a former employer or other insurance plan.

Everyone with Medicare must make a decision about the coverage.
Sometimes the best decision is not to sign up for it. If you already have good
prescription drug coverage with an employer, union, Medicare supplement
policy, Medicare Advantage Plan, or some other source, you can choose to
keep that coverage. In fact, if you sign up for Medicare coverage without

understanding all the facts, you may lose some important insurance benefits from your current plan. Be sure to check with your current insurance plan before you make this decision.

In 2006, most Medicare drug plans will have a premium of about $32 a month. You will pay the first $250 in drug costs each year—called a deductible—and the plan pays 75 percent of the next $2,000. That saves you $1,500. Once you have paid a total of $3,600 out of pocket, the standard plan will cover 95 percent of the remaining costs.

By the time you read this, the initial sign-up period of May 15, 2006, will have passed. Congress is likely to make changes or adjustments to this program, so it's important to keep up to date with changes or improvements in the program. You can call Medicare, AARP, or your local Area Agency on Aging for information regarding possible changes.

Applying for Medicaid

This process takes patience, lots of paperwork, finding the necessary documents, facts, and figures—and a little help from your friends. But you can get through it successfully. I know because I completed the application for my mother and lived to tell the tale.

What Is Medicaid and Why Do You Need to Know About It?

First of all, Medicaid is not a universal entitlement program like Medicare. Medicaid is designed to cover the medical needs of low-income Americans, the disabled, children, pregnant women, and elderly Americans with limited financial resources. You may not have limited financial resources today, or at seventy or eighty, but if you spend a few years in a nursing home and did not invest in Wal-Mart stock, you may eventually rely on this program.

Originally, Medicaid was a small piece of the landmark 1965 Medicare legislation, but in forty years its scope and importance have expanded greatly. Today approximately fifty million Americans receive medical care through Medicaid. However, nowhere has the program grown faster than in providing nursing home care. Today approximately 80 percent of U.S. nursing home residents are covered by Medicaid, and the percentage continues to rise each year.

Medicaid is funded jointly by the federal and state governments, though it is administered by the individual states. Rules, regulations, benefits, and the amount paid for patient care vary widely from state to state. Some states are generous; others are stingy. The daily rate paid by Texas and New York to nursing homes or home health care agencies is vastly different. I'll let you guess which state appropriates more funds to care for its elderly citizens.

As the number of Americans needing basic care, and especially nursing home care, has increased, costs have skyrocketed for both federal and state governments. In 2006, the federal government cut thirty billion dollars in Medicaid funding at a time when an increasing number of seniors require Medicaid for nursing home care. States will have to make up that difference or cut back on services. Funding Medicaid will be a major issue for years to come. Obviously, we can't solve that ongoing crisis in this chapter, but we can help you get qualified if you meet the criteria and need this assistance.

Getting through the Paperwork Jungle

Although the application process is rigorous, Medicaid benefits are substantial.

Benefits

Before we discuss forms and bureaucracies, let's consider what Medicaid provides. Federal law requires states to provide:

- Nursing home coverage

- In-patient and out-patient hospital services

- Home health care

- Physician and certified nurse practitioner's visits

- Laboratory tests and x-rays

- Some states even cover Medicare deductible costs and other additional benefits

As you help your parents fill out that long form, keep remembering all that they will receive when it is approved.

Because this is such an important benefit for your parents, I suggest that you do as I did and seek professional help as you go through this process. Before attempting to enroll your parent in the Medicaid program, I highly recommend investing in the services of an elder law attorney. Depending on the attorney you choose and the complexity of your parent's estate, an investment of $1,500–2,500 may save you tens or even hundreds of thousands of dollars and untold grief in the long run. *The more complicated their estate and the more assets they have, the more important it is to get top-notch legal advice.* I hired an elder law attorney when I did my mother's application and it went through in six weeks without a hitch. I do not begrudge one of the 200,000 pennies ($2,000) I spent.

Whether you hire an elder law attorney, seek legal aid, visit an Area Agency on Aging, or ask for help from a relative or friend who is good at filling out complicated forms, **do not apply for Medicaid without assistance.** I feel so strongly on that point that I just broke my rule about not using bold-face type. Professional assistance is best, but anyone who has negotiated this complex process successfully might be a helpful advocate.

One way to find someone to help you fill out your application is to go to the Department of Health and Human Services "Eldercare Locator" site at www.eldercare.gov/Eldercare/Public/Home.asp. They will list agencies and elder law specialists in your area who can guide you through the application process, as well as point you toward other helpful local resources. Another option is to contact the National Association of Agencies on Aging (call 202-872-0888 or go to www.n4a.org/default.cfm). A third resource is to check the website of the National Council on Aging at www.n4a.org/default.cfm for locations of their regional offices.

If you choose to deal with the government directly, which I'm sorry to say I do not recommend, you can go to the Medicare website at www.medicare.gov. It is difficult to navigate, full of jargon, and includes more information than the average mortal can absorb. I stay away from it if possible.

What You Will Need When You Apply

No matter who advises you, be prepared to answer detailed questions about your parents'

• background

• assets

• income

• medical condition

• insurance coverage

If their assets are in trusts, there will be additional questions regarding asset transfers going back five years.

To qualify for Medicaid, a person must fall within the income and resource guidelines of their state. *Typically that is $2,000 in total assets and income of approximately $1,700 a month.* The actual figure will vary from state to state, but this is a basic indicator of income qualifications.

Income includes social security payments, pensions, interest or dividends from investments, and other sources of income.

Assets

If your parents have assets (money in the bank, savings, stocks, bonds, rental property) and are over fifty-five years of age, these assets will figure heavily in the state's decision to accept or reject their Medicaid application. Assets include anything a person may own, *excluding their home or automobile.* In some states, high medical bills will qualify a person who has an income above the standard Medicaid limits for eligibility.

The more assets your parent has, the more important it is to have an experienced elder law attorney to counsel you on how to transfer assets legally to avoid penalties. One resource for finding an experienced attorney is through the AARP Legal Services Network. It offers reduced rates to AARP members and a screened list of providers.

A home or car is not considered an asset when determining benefits eligibility. You do not have to sell your parents' home or car in order for them to qualify. They are more likely to qualify for benefits with low cash assets and a valuable home than if they have no home but a lot of money in the bank.

Lookback Period

Your parents cannot artificially impoverish themselves by transferring their assets to children, relatives, or charities and then immediately apply for Medicaid. There is a five-year lookback period in which the state will check to see if they have transferred their assets. *In early 2006, the lookback period was raised from three years to five years in order to discourage people from transferring assets prior to applying for Medicaid.*

States can "look back" to find transfers of assets for sixty months prior to the date your parent applies for Medicaid. If a transfer of assets is found, the state will withhold payment for nursing facility care for a prescribed penalty period.

The length of the penalty period is determined by dividing the value of the transferred asset by the average monthly private-pay cost of nursing facility care in the state. For example, if your parent transferred an asset worth $80,000 and the cost of nursing home care was $4,000 a month, divide $4,000 into $80,000 for a twenty-month penalty period. That means they could not begin collecting Medicaid for twenty months and there is no limit to the length of the penalty period. Avoiding such penalties is why it is so important to have an elder law attorney help you plan for any transfers of assets.

Applying for Medicaid in California, Florida, New York, and Texas

These states have a combined population of around ninety million people, almost one-third of all Americans. The procedures used to apply for Medicaid in these states are likely to be similar to those in most other states.

In every state you'll need to fill out an application that will include:

- Proof of identity (birth certificate, passport)

- Proof of state residency (rent or utility receipt, wage statement)

- Documentation of income (income tax return, bank statements, pay stub, pension award letters)

- Medicare benefit card

In most states, it takes at least eight weeks to be approved, and often longer depending on the state and its caseload.

California

In California, Medicaid (Medi-Cal) is directly operated by Medical Care Services, a division of the California Department of Health Services. To apply, first fill out the four-page application and take it or mail it to your local welfare office. The application is available in eleven languages (Armenian, Chinese, English, Farsi, Hmong, Khmer, Korean, Lao, Russian, Spanish, and Vietnamese). You can get the application online or at a local county welfare office, where you can also get help in filling out the form.

The office will acknowledge receipt of the application within ten days, and give you the name of the person you will contact about your application. Depending on how completely you have filled out the application, they may request more information. Eligibility is decided within forty-five days. Disability applications may take up to ninety days.

If your parents are entering a nursing home and applying for Medi-Cal, immediately contact your local welfare office for a copy of the notice regarding standards for Medi-Cal eligibility (form DHS 7077). This form will explain exempt resources, protections against spousal impoverishment, and some circumstances under which an interest in a home may be transferred without affecting eligibility.

Florida

Medicaid assistance for persons who are over sixty-five or disabled is administered through supplemental security income (SSI), which is under the state's Agency for Healthcare Administration (www.fdhc.state.fl.us). In Florida, Medicaid eligibility is handled by the Department of Children and Families' Office of Self-Sufficiency. Call toll-free at 866-762-2237. You can apply online at www.dcf.state.fl.us/ess/index.html (Access Florida). Elderly or disabled persons already on SSI assistance will have their eligibility determined by SSI. Contact your local Social Security Administration office or go to www.ssa.gov for more information.

New York

In New York, Medicaid is available to persons who are eligible for public assistance or supplemental security income (SSI). In addition, the Medicaid Surplus Income Program is available for persons over sixty-five or who are blind or disabled and whose incomes are too high to qualify for public assistance or SSI, but who spend down any excess income on medical costs until they reach the Medicaid income level.

Once this eligibility threshold is met, Medicaid covers all medical care including hospital care, doctor bills, nursing home coverage, home care, and prescriptions. If the person is already on Medicare, then Medicaid covers the Medicare deductibles and many of the services not provided by Medicare.

All Medicaid applications are issued through the local department of social services. A list of these offices can be found online at www.health.state.ny.us/health_care/medicaid/ldss.htm. You must call or write to make an interview appointment. Housebound applicants can make arrangements through the local social services department.

New York does not currently offer an online application. When you go for your interview, have the following information:

- In New York City, contact the Human Resources Administration at 718-557-1399. Residents of the five boroughs of New York City may call toll-free at 877-472-8411.

- Determination of eligibility for benefits is generally by the local district, usually within forty-five days of the application. If a disability must be evaluated, it may take up to ninety days to determine eligibility. If you are dissatisfied with the decision made by the local social services district, you may request a conference with the agency. You may also appeal to the New York State Office of Temporary and Disability Assistance and request a Fair Hearing by calling the New York State Office of Temporary and Disability Assistance Fair Hearing Office at 800-342-3334.

- For the answers to frequently asked questions, go to www.health.state. ny.us/health_care/medicaid.

Texas

Medicaid is administered through the Health and Human Services Commission (HHSC). Those who are on supplemental security income (SSI) are automatically on Medicaid. Everyone else should apply directly through their local Health and Human Services Commission office. Information on location of these offices is available at 888-834-7406 or, for the hearing impaired, at 888-425-6889 (TDD number). You should assemble the same material as recommended for other states. Up-to-date information on what you'll need for your application can be found at www.hhsc.state.tx.us/medicaid/index.html.

As of November 1, 2005, Texas measures its lookback penalty by day, not month. For example, a transfer of $34,848 divided by $117.08 (the daily rate paid by the state to the nursing homes) totals 297 days if measured from the first of the month. As of February 2006, transfers don't run from the date of the transfer, but from the date that the applicant would be eligible except for the transfer penalty. That means if Mom transfers the $34,848 and the five-year lookback period hasn't passed, the 297-day penalty doesn't start until she's spent down all her assets, nursing home care is necessary, and her income falls below the limit. Someone, most likely her children, will have to pay for those 297 days before she can get Medicaid. If the children were the ones who originally received the $34,848, they'll be paying it back or taking care of Mom at home.

Estate Recovery

If your parents receive medical services paid for by Medicaid on or after their fifty-fifth birthday, or when permanently residing in a medical institution, Medicaid may recover the amount of the cost of these services from the estate upon death. States can—and will—pursue recompense for Medicaid benefits awarded from the estate of the beneficiary after death, including assets such as a home that are not considered originally for Medicaid eligibility.

38

Veterans Benefits

Veterans benefits are available to honorably discharged members of all branches of the military service, as well as to commissioned officers of the Public Health Service and the Environmental Science Services Administration. Both male and female veterans are eligible for the same benefits. If you have any question about a parent's eligibility, check with your local Department of Veterans Affairs office or call the VA Health Benefits Service Center toll-free at 877-222-8387.

The process begins with getting VA Form 10-10EZ, the Application for Health Benefits. Further:

- You can find Form 10-10EZ online in the forms section of the VA website. Go to www.va.gov/vaforms and click on the 10-10EZ link.

- The form is also available at any VA health care facility or regional benefits office, where you can also find assistance in filling out the form.

- The form can be submitted by mail or directly to the local VA facility. All submissions must be submitted locally, not through the national Department of Veterans Affairs.

- If the applicant cannot come to the facility personally, his designated representative will need a power of attorney to apply for him.

- For more information on the application process, call 877-222-8387.

Before you visit your local VA facility, it's wise to call ahead and find out what documents you should bring with you. The documents may vary depending on the service for which you are applying. You can also request that the VA send you a copy of "Federal Benefits for Veterans and Dependents 2005." This booklet indicates the information needed to complete the application. Before making the trip to the VA facility, give yourself plenty of time to gather the documents you need. Be warned: A fire in the veterans archives in the 1970s destroyed a large number of service records, so don't depend on the government to retrieve service records or discharge papers. It is extremely helpful to know the veteran's service number, and it is a great advantage to have a copy of his or her discharge papers.

The VA website, like other government websites, can be frustrating to negotiate. Remain patient and you will find what you need. If you have trouble negotiating the site, call the office and ask for help. You may also find veterans information through the AARP website at www.aarp.org by entering "veterans" in the site's search field.

Service-Related Disability Benefits

Disability pensions are available to:

• Honorably discharged veterans who were partially or totally disabled by disease or injury incurred or aggravated during active military service (this pension varies with the degree of disability, and is paid monthly)

• Some veterans with non-service-related disability, if the veteran falls below specific income levels

• Former prisoners of war (POWs) who suffer a disability from their POW experience

• Long-term POWs who suffer additional disabilities related to the stress of their captivity

Other special disability groups include:

• Agent Orange and other herbicide exposure during the Vietnam War

• Exposure to radiation

• Gulf War Syndrome

Veterans with service-connected disabilities are also eligible for grants to build, buy, or adapt a home to meet disability-related requirements. Automobile adaptation benefits are also available.

VA Hospital Services

Historically, VA hospitals have come under criticism for poor record keeping, inconsistent medical care, lax patient safety, and sometimes even unsanitary conditions. However, in the last ten years the situation has improved dramatically.

Gilbert M. Gaul, writing in the *Washington Post* in August of 2005, said, "Some experts point to the VA makeover as a lesson in how the nation's troubled health care system might be able to heal itself."

The quality of a VA hospital, like that of a nursing home, can vary tremendously depending on the character and commitment of top administrators. Before admitting your parent to a specific hospital, you may want to visit the hospital or seek references from those who have relatives there.

Community Services

The availability of veteran services varies greatly depending on where you live. Most metropolitan areas have a wide range of services available, including health care systems, medical centers, outpatient clinics, community-based outpatient clinics, and financial services centers. To find services, call the VA facility number in your area or go to www1.va.gov/directory/guide/home.asp?isFlash=1 for a services locator guide.

Armed Forces Retirement Home

Some veterans are eligible to live in the Armed Forces Retirement Home in Washington, DC. (The Armed Forces Retirement Home in Gulfport, Mississipi, was severely damaged by Hurricane Katrina and is not in operation. Repair may take several years to complete.) At the time of admission, applicants must be capable of living independently. The Armed Forces Retirement Home is an independent federal agency. For information, call 800-332-3527 or 800-422-9988, or visit their website at www.afrh.gov.

Telephone Numbers for Veterans Service

VA Benefits: 800-827-1000
Life Insurance: 800-669-8477
Education (GI Bill): 888-442-4551
Health Care Benefits: 877-222-8387
Income Verification and Means Testing: 800-929-8387
Mammography Helpline: 888-492-7844
Gulf War/Agent Orange Helpline: 800-749-8387

Status of Headstones and Markers: 800-697-6947

Telecommunications Device for the Deaf (TDD): 800-829-4833

Internet Resources for Veterans Service

Main VA Internet home page: www.va.gov/

VA online forms for downloading: www.va.gov/vaforms/

AARP: www.aarp.org

VA services locator by area:

www1.va.gov/directory/guide/home.asp?isFlash=1.

39

National Agencies

I have selected some of the most important national agencies that can help you deal with parental care issues. In this chapter you will find their addresses, phone and fax numbers, and websites. In some cases there is no national 800 number, so I have provided Internet references only. The websites will lead you to the most current information about resources in your area.

The goal is to get you connected to the people who can answer your questions and provide solutions as quickly as possible. There is no need to spend hours on the telephone working your way through a bureaucracy one receptionist at a time. An organization's website is more likely to direct you to the number you need in your area. Internet sites are updated more frequently than internal phone directories.

AARP (formerly the American Association of Retired Persons) was founded in 1958 and is the best-known group advocating the interests of senior citizens. In addition, it offers members information on issues affecting seniors, educational programs, and special travel packages and benefits. Membership is available to anyone over the age of fifty for $12.50 per year.

601 E. Street NW
Washington, DC 20049
800-424-3410 (M–F 8:00 A.M. to 8:00 P.M. EST)
www.aarp.org

American Association of Homes and Services for the Aging is an industry-supported informational website.

> 2519 Connecticut Avenue NW
> Washington, DC 20008-1520
> 202-783-2242
> 202-783-2255 (fax)
> info@aahsa.org
> www2.aahsa.org

Department of Housing and Urban Development (HUD) has a senior housing assistance program. For regional phone numbers and information about local programs, go to their website at www.hud.gov/groups/seniors.cfm.

FirstGov for Seniors is a portal website created by the U.S. General Services Administration with links to the portions of U.S. government agency websites that deal with senior citizens' issues. It is great timesaver when you're trying to figure out where to plug in to the bewildering labyrinth of federal government programs. Go to www.seniors.gov/about.html.

Gray Panthers is extremely active in political issues affecting the lives of senior citizens, especially issues surrounding health care. They are a valuable source of information on current legislation and offer an opportunity to become politically involved.

> 733 15th Street NW, Suite 437
> Washington, DC 20005
> 800-280-5362 or 202-737-6637
> 202-737-1160 (fax)
> info@graypanthers.org
> www.graypanthers.org

National Citizens' Coalition for Nursing Home Reform (NCC-NHR) was formed because of public concern about substandard care in nursing homes. Its membership base is made up of local citizen action groups, state and local long-term-care ombudsmen, legal services programs, religious organizations, professional groups, nursing home employees' unions, concerned providers, national organizations, and growing numbers of family and resident councils. Their resources include fact sheets and advocacy.

> 1424 16th Street NW, Suite 202
> Washington, DC 20036
> 202-332-2276
> 202-332-2949 (fax)
> www.nccnhr.org

National Senior Citizens Law Center advocates nationwide to promote the independence and well-being of low-income elderly individuals and persons with disabilities. As a national support center, NSCLC works through litigation, legislative and agency representation, and assistance to attorneys and paralegals in field programs.

> Washington, DC office:
> 1101 14th Street NW, Suite 400
> Washington, DC 20005
> 202-289-6976
> 202-289-7224 (fax)

> Los Angeles, CA office:
> 3435 Wilshire Blvd., Suite 2860
> Los Angeles, CA 90010-1938
> 213-639-0930
> 213-639-0934 (fax)
> www.nsclc.org/index.html

Mother and Dad at her ninetieth birthday party, September 15, 2002

40

Local Resources: State Insurance Departments and Agencies on Aging

Insurance Departments, Agencies on Aging, and State Health Insurance Assistance Programs

Alabama

*Alabama Department
of Senior Services*
770 Washington Avenue
RSA Plaza, Suite 470
Montgomery, AL 36130
334-242-5743
334-242 5594 (fax)
877-425-2243 (toll free)
www.adss.state.al.us or www.age-
line.net

Alabama Insurance Department
201 Monroe St., Suite 1700
PO Box 303351
Montgomery, AL 36104
334-269-3550
334-241-4192 (fax)

insdept@insurance.state.al.us
www.aldoi.org

Alaska

Alaska Commission on Aging
Division of Senior Services
Department of Administration
Juneau, AK 99811-0209
907-465-3250
907-465-4716 (fax)
acoa@admin.state.ak.us
www.alaskaaging.org

Alaska Insurance Departments
Division of Insurance
Department of Commerce, Com-
munity, and Economic Development
Robert B. Atwood Building

550 W. 7th Avenue, Suite 1560
Anchorage, AK 99501-3567
907-269-7900

Division of Insurance
Department of Commerce,
Community and Economic
Development
PO Box 110805
Juneau, AK 99811-0805
907-465-2515
907-465-5437 (TDD/TTY)
907-465-3422 (fax)
www.commerce.state.ak.us/insurance

American Samoa

Territorial Administration on Aging
Government of American Samoa
Pago Pago, American Samoa 96799
011-684-633-2207
011-684-633-2533 or
011-684-633-7723 (fax)

Arizona

Arizona Aging and
Adult Administration
Department of Economic Security
1789 W. Jefferson #950A
Phoenix, AZ 95007
602-542-4446
602-542-6575 (fax)
www.de.state.az.us/aaa

Arizona Insurance Department
Department of Insurance
2910 North 44th St., Suite 210
Phoenix, AZ 85018-7256
800-325-2548 (toll free AZ)
602-912-8444
602-954-7008 (fax complaints)
consumers@id.state.az.us
www.id.state.az.us

Arkansas

Arkansas Department
of Human Services
PO Box 1437, Slot 1412
1417 Donaghey Plaza South
Little Rock, AR 72203-1437
501-682-2441
501-682-8155 (fax)
www.state.ar.us/dhs/aging

Arkansas Department of Insurance
1200 West 3rd St.
Little Rock, AR 72201-1904
800-282-9134 (toll free AR)
800-852-5494 (toll free all else)
501-371-2600
501-371-2640 (consumer services)
501-371-2618 (fax)
www.arkansas.gov/insurance

California

California Department of Aging
1600 K Street
Sacramento, CA 95814
916-322-5290
916-324-1903 (fax)
www.aging.ca.gov

California Department of Insurance
300 Capitol Mall, Suite 1500
Sacramento, CA 95814
800-927-4357 (toll free CA)
916-492-3500
415-538-4010 (San Francisco)
213-897-8921 (Los Angeles)
916-445-5280 (fax)
www.insurance.ca.gov

Colorado

Division of Aging and Adult Services
1575 Sherman St., 10th floor
Denver, CO 80203
303-866-2800

303-866-2696(fax)
www.cdhs.state.co.us

Division of Insurance
1560 Broadway, Suite 850
Denver, CO 80202
800-930-3745 (toll free CO)
303-894-7490 or 303-894-7499
303-894-7880 (TDD/TTY)
303-894-7455 (fax)
www.dora.state.co.us/insurance

State Health Insurance Assistance
Colorado only:
888-696-7213

Connecticut
Division of Elderly Services
25 Sigourney St., 10th Floor
Hartford, CT 06106-5033
860-424-5277
860-424-4966 (fax)
adultserv.dss@po.state.ct.us
www.dss.state.ct.us

Department of Insurance
Consumer Affairs Dept.
PO Box 816
Hartford, CT 06142-0816
800-203-3447 (toll free)
860-297-3900
860-297-3872 (fax)
www.state.ct.us/cid

State Health Insurance Assistance
800-994-9422 (toll free CT)
860-424-5297 or 860-24-5232
860-424-4966 (fax)

Delaware
Department of Insurance
841 Silver Lake Blvd.
Dover, DE 19904
800-282-8611 (toll free DE)

302-739-4251
302-739-6278 (fax)
consumer@deins.state.de.us
www.state.de.us/inscom

*Division of Services for Aging and
Adults with Physical Disabilities*
Department of Health and Social
Services
1901 North DuPont Highway
New Castle, DE 19720
302-577-4791
302-577-4793 (fax)
www.dsaapd.com

State Health Insurance Assistance
302-739-6266
302-739-5280 (fax)

District of Columbia
*Department of Insurance,
Securities, and Banking*
810 First St. NE, Suite 701
Washington, DC 20002
202-727-8000
202-535-1196 (fax)
info.disb@dcgov.org
www.disb.dc.gov

District of Columbia Office on Aging
One Judiciary Square—9th Floor
441 Fourth St. NW
Washington, DC 20001
202-724-5622
202-724-4979 (fax)
www.dcoa.dc.gov

State Health Insurance Assistance
202-496-6240
202-293-4043 (fax)

Florida
Department of Elder Affairs
Building B, Suite 152
4040 Esplanade Way
Tallahassee, FL 32399-7000
904-414-2000
904-414-2004 (fax)
information@elderaffairs.org
www.elderaffairs.state.fl.us

Elder Help
800-963-5337 or 800-955-8770
(toll free)
800-955-8771 (toll free TDD/TTY)
850-414-2002 (fax)

Office of Insurance Regulation
Department of Financial Services
200 East Gaines St.
Tallahassee, FL 32399-0300
800-342-2762 (toll free FL)
850-413-3100
850-410-9700 (TDD/TTY)
850-488-2349 (fax)
www.fldfs.com

State Health Insurance Assistance
850-414-0000

Georgia
Division of Aging Services
Department of Human Resources
2 Peachtree Street NE, 36th Floor
Atlanta, GA 30303-3176
404-657-5258
404-657-5285 (fax)
dhrconstituentservices@dhr.state.ga.us
www.state.ga.us/Departments/DHR/
aging

Insurance and Fire Safety
Two Martin Luther King, Jr. Dr.
Atlanta, GA 30334
800-656-2298 (toll free GA)

404-656-2070
404-656-4031 (TDD/TTY)
404-657-8542 (fax)
www.inscomm.state.ga.us

State Health Insurance Assistance
800-669-8387 (toll free)
404-657-5347
404-657-5285 (fax)

Hawaii
Executive Office on Aging
250 South Hotel St., Suite 109
Honolulu, HI 96813-2831
808-586-0100
808-586-0185 (fax)
www.hawaii.gov/eoa

Insurance Division
Department of Commerce and
Consumer Affairs
PO Box 3614
Honolulu, HI 96811-3614
808-586-2790
808-586-2799
808-586-2806 (fax)
insurance@dcca.hawaii.gov
www.hawaii.gov/dcca/ins

State Health Insurance Assistance
808-586-7300
808-586-0185 (fax)

Idaho
Commission on Aging
PO Box 83720
Boise, ID 83706
208-334-3833
208-334-3033 (fax)
senglesby@aging.idaho.gov
www.idahoaging.com

Department of Insurance
700 West State St.

PO Box 83720
Boise, ID 83720-0043
800-721-3272 (toll free ID)
208-334-4250
208-334-4398 (fax)
www.doi.state.id.us

State Health Insurance Assistance
800-488-5713 (toll free central ID)
800-488-5725 (toll free north ID)
800-488-5764 (toll free southeast ID)
800-247-4422 (toll free southwest ID)
208-334-4350
208-334-4389 (fax)

Illinois
Department on Aging
421 East Capitol Ave., Suite 100
Springfield, IL 62701-1789
217-785-2870
312-814-2916 (Chicago)
217-785-4477 (fax)

Divisions of Insurance
Department of Financial and
Professional Regulation
100 West Randolph St., Suite 5–570
Chicago, IL 60601-3395
312-814-2420
312-814-2603 (TDD/TTY)
312-814-5435 (fax)
director@ins.state.il.us
www.state.il.us/us

*Department of Financial and
Professional Regulation*
320 West Washington St.
Springfield, IL 62767
877-527-9431 (toll free; Office of
Consumer Health Insurance)
217-782-4515
217-524-4872 (TDD/TTY)

217-782-5020 (fax)
director@ins.state.il.us
www.idfpr.com

State Health Insurance Assistance
800-548-9034 (toll free IL)
212-785-9021
217-782-4105 (fax)

Indiana
*Bureau of Aging
and In-Home Services*
Division of Disability, Aging, and
Rehabilitative Services
Family and Social Services
Administration
402 West Washington St., #W454
PO Box 7083
Indianapolis, IN 46207-7083
317-232-7020
317-232-7867 (fax)

Department of Insurance
311 W. Washington St., Suite 300
Indianapolis, IN 46204-2787
800-622-4461 (toll free IN)
317-232-2385
800-452-4800 (toll free; in-state
senior health insurance information)
317-232-5251 (fax)
www.state.in.us/idoi

State Health Insurance Assistance
800-452-4800 (toll free)
317-233-2551
317-232-5251 (fax)

Iowa
Department of Elder Affairs
Clemens Building, 3rd Floor
200 Tenth Street
Des Moines, IA 50309-3609
515-281-4646
515-281-4036 (fax)
www.state.ia.us/elderaffairs

Division of Insurance
330 Maple St.
Des Moines, IA 50319
515-281-5705
515-281-3059 (fax)
www.iid.state.ia.us

State Health Insurance Assistance
800-351-4664 (toll free)
515-281-6867
515-281-3059 (fax)

Kansas
Department on Aging
New England Building
503 South Kansas Avenue
Topeka, KS 66603-3404
785-296-4986
785-296-0256 (fax)
mail@aging.state.ks.us
www.agingkansas.org/index.htm

Insurance Division
420 SW 9th St.
Topeka, KS 66612-1678
800-432-2484 (toll free KS)
785-296-7801
877-235-3151 (toll free TDD/TTY)
785-296-2283 (fax)
commissioner@ksinsurance.org
www.ksinsurance.org

State Health Insurance Assistance
Senior Health Information
Counseling Line (messages only)
800-860-5260 (toll free)
316-337-7386
316-337-6018 (fax)

Kentucky
Office of Aging Services
Cabinet for Commonwealth of
Kentucky
275 East Main St.

Frankfort, KY 40621
502-564-6930
502-564-4595 (fax)
www.chs.state.ky.us/aging

Office of Insurance
215 West Main St.
Frankfort, KY 40601
800-595-6053 (toll free)
502-564-3630
502-564-1650 (fax)
www.doi.ppr.ky.gov

State Health Insurance Assistance
502-564-7372
502-564-4595 (fax)

Louisiana
Department of Insurance
1702 N. Third St.
Baton Rouge, LA 70802
800-259-5300 or 800-259-5301
(toll free)
225-342-0895 or 225-342-5900
225-342-3078 (fax)
www.ldi.state.la.us

Governor's Office of Elderly Affairs
PO Box 80374
Baton Rouge, LA 70898-0374
504-342-7100
504-342-7133 (fax)
www.gov.state.la.us/depts.htm

State Health Insurance Assistance
225-342-5301
225-342-5711 (fax)

Maine
Bureau of Elder and Adult Services
Department of Human Services
35 Anthony Avenue
State House – Station #11
Augusta, ME 04333

207-624-5335
207-624-5361 (fax)
www.maine.gov/dhs/beas

Bureau of Insurance
34 State House Station
Augusta, ME 04333
800-300-5000 (toll free ME)
207-624-8475
207-624-8563 (TDD/TTY)
207-624-8599 (fax)
www.maineinsurancereg.org

State Health Insurance Assistance
800-262-2232 (toll free)
207-287-9200
207-287-9229 (fax)

Maryland
Insurance Administration
525 St. Paul Place
Baltimore, MD 21202-2272
800-492-6116 (toll free)
410-468-2000
800-735-2258 (toll free TDD/TTY)
410-468-2020 (fax)
www.mdinsurance.state.md.us

Office on Aging
State Office Building, Room 1007
301 West Preston St.
Baltimore, MD 21201-2374
410-767-1100
410-333-7943 (fax)
www.mdoa.state.md.us

State Health Insurance Assistance
800-243-3425 (toll free MD)
410-767-1109
410-333-7943 (fax)

Massachusetts
Division of Insurance
Consumer Service Section

One South Station, 5th Floor
Boston, MA 02110
617-521-7777
617-521-7490 (TDD/TTY)
617-521-7575 (fax)
www.state.ma.us/doi

Executive Office of Elder Affairs
One Ashburton Place, 5th Floor
Boston, MA 02108
617-727-7750
617-727-9368 (fax)
elder.affairs@state.ma.us

State Health Insurance Assistance
800-882-2003 (toll free)
617-222-7435
617-727-9368 (fax)

Michigan
*Office of Financial and
Insurance Services*
611 West Ottawa St., 3rd Floor
PO Box 30220
Lansing, MI 48933
877-999-6442 (toll free)
517-373-0220
517-335-4978 (fax)
www.michigan.gov/ofis

Office of Services to the Aging
611 West Ottawa, North – Ottawa
Tower, 3rd Floor
PO Box 30676
Lansing, MI 48909
517-373-8230
517-373-4092 (fax)
www.miseniors.net

State Health Insurance Assistance
800-803-7174 (toll free)
517-886-0889
517-886-1305 (fax)

Minnesota
Board on Aging
444 Lafayette Road
St. Paul, MN 55155-3843
612-297-7855
mba@state.mn.us
www.mnaging.org

Department of Commerce
Market Assurance Division
85 7th Place East
St. Paul, MN 55101
800-657-3602 (toll free MN)
651-296-2488
651-296-4328 (fax)
www.commerce.state.mn.us

State Health Insurance Assistance
800-333-2433 (toll free)

Mississippi
Department of Insurance
PO Box 79
Jackson, MS 39205
800-562-2957 (toll free MS)
601-359-3569
601-359-1077 (fax)
consumer@mid.state.ms.us
www.doi.state.ms.us

Division of Aging and Adult Services
750 North State St.
Jackson, MS 39202
601-359-4925
601-359-4370 (fax)
www.mdhs.state.ms.us/aas.html

State Health Insurance Assistance
800-948-3090 (toll free)
601-359-4929
601-359-9664 (fax)

Missouri
Division on Aging
Department of Social Services
PO Box 1337
615 Howerton Court
Jefferson City, MO 65102-1337
573-751-3082
573-751-8687 (fax)
www.dhss.state.mo.us/Senior
Services/index

Department of Insurance
PO Box 690
301 West High St., Room 530
Jefferson City, MO 65102-0690
800-726-7390 (toll free MO)
573-751-4126
573-526-4536 (TDD/TTY)
573-751-1165 (fax)
www.insurance.state.mo.us

State Health Insurance Assistance
800-390-3330 (toll free)

Montana
Department of Insurance
840 Helena Ave.
Helena, MT 59601
800-332-6148 (toll free MT)
406-444-2040
406-444-3497 (fax)
www.state.mt.us/sao

Senior and Long Term Care Division
Department of Public Health &
Human Services
PO Box 4210
111 Sanders, Room 211
Helena, MT 59620
406-444-7788
406-444-7743 (fax)
www.dphhs.state.mt.us/slte

State Health Insurance Assistance
800-332-2272 (toll free MT)
800-624-3958 (toll free general)
406-442-1837

Nebraska
Department of Health and Human Services
Division on Aging
PO Box 95044
1343 M Street
Lincoln, NE 68509-5044
402-471-2307
402-471-4619 (fax)
www.hhs.state.ne.us/ags/agsindex.htm

Department of Insurance
Terminal Building
941 "O" St., Suite 400
Lincoln, NE 68508-3639
877-564-7323 (toll free NE)
402-471-2201
800-833-7351 (toll free TDD/TTY)
402-471-6559 (fax)
www.nol.org/home/NDOI

State Health Insurance Assistance
800-234-7119 (toll free)
402-471-6559 (fax)

Nevada
Division for Aging Services
Department of Human Resources
State Mail Room Complex
340 North 11th St., Suite 203
Las Vegas, NV 89101
702-486-3545
702-486-3572 (fax)
dasvegas@aging.state.nv.us
www.nvaging.net

Divisions of Insurance
Department of Business and Industry
788 Fairview Dr., Suite 300

Carson City, NV 89701
775-687-7650
775-687-3937 (fax)
insinfo@doi.state.nv.us
www.doi.state.nv.us

Department of Business and Industry
Division of Insurance
2501 East Sahara Ave., Suite 302
Las Vegas, NV 89104
702-486-4009
702-486-4007 (fax)
www.doi.state.nv.us

State Health Insurance Assistance
702-486-3545 or 702-486-9500
702-486-3572 (fax)

New Hampshire
Department of Insurance
21 South Fruit St., Suite 14
Concord, NH 03301-2430
800-852-3416 (toll free NH)
603-271-2261
800-735-2964 (toll free NH, TDD/TTY)
603-271-0248 (fax)
requests@ins.state.nh.us
www.nh.gov/insurance

Division of Elderly and Adult Services
State Office Park South
129 Pleasant St., Brown Bldg. #1
Concord, NH 03301
603-271-4680
603-271-4643 (fax)
www.dhhs.state.nh.us/ddh/dhhs_site/default

State Health Insurance Assistance
603-271-1110
603-271-4643 (fax)

New Jersey
Department of Banking and Insurance
20 West State St.
PO Box 325
Trenton, NJ 08625
609-633-7667
609-292-5571 (fax)
www.njdobi.org

Department of Health and Senior Services
New Jersey Division of Senior Affairs
PO Box 807
Trenton, NJ 08625-0807
800-792-8820 (toll free)
609-588-3141
609-588-3601 (fax)

State Health Insurance Assistance
800-792-8820 (toll free NJ)
609-943-3378
609-943-3379 (fax)

New Mexico
Department of Insurance
PO Box 1269
Santa Fe, NM 87504-1269
800-947-4722 (toll free NM)
505-827-4601
505-827-4734 (fax)
www.nmprc.state.nm.us

State Agency on Aging
La Villa Rivera Building
228 East Palace Ave., Ground Floor
Santa Fe, NM 87501
505-827-7640
505-827-7649 (fax)
nmaoa@state.nm.us
www.nmaging.state.nm.us

State Health Insurance Assistance
800-432-2080 (toll free NM)

505-827-7640
505-476-4836 (fax)

New York
Consumer Services Bureaus
Insurance Department
One Commerce Plaza
Albany, NY 12257
800-342-3736 (toll free)
518-474-6600
518-474-6630 (fax)
www.ins.state.ny.us

Insurance Department
65 Court St. #7
Buffalo, NY 14202
800-342-3736 (toll free NY)
716-847-7618
716-847-7925 (fax)
www.ins.state.ny.us

New York State Office for the Aging
2 Empire State Plaza
Albany, NY 12223-1251
800-342-9871 (toll free)
518-474-5731
518-474-0608 (fax)
nysofa@ofa.state.ny.us
www.aging.state.ny.us/index.htm

State Health Insurance Assistance
800-333-4114 (toll free NY)
518-473-5108
518-486-2225 (fax)

North Carolina
Department of Insurance
430 North Salisbury St., Dobbs Bldg.
1201 Mail Service Center
Raleigh, NC 27699-1201
800-546-5664 (toll free NC)
800-662-7777 (toll free general)
919-733-7349

919-733-0085 (fax)
consumer@ncdoi.net
www.ncdoi.com

North Carolina Division of Aging
CB 29531
693 Palmer Drive
Raleigh, NC 27626-0531
919-733-3983
919-733-0443 (fax)
www.dhhs.state.nc.us/aging

State Health Insurance Assistance
800-443-9354 (toll free NC)
919-733-0111
919-733-3682 (fax)

North Dakota

Department of Human Services
Aging Services Division
600 South 2nd St., Suite 1C
Bismarck, ND 58504
701-328-8910
701-328-8989 (fax)
www.state.nd.us/humanservices/servi
ces/adultsaging

Insurance Department
600 East Boulevard Ave., 5th Floor
Bismarck, ND 58505
800-247-0560 (toll free ND)
701-328-2440
800-366-6888 (toll free TDD/TTY)
701-328-4880 (fax)
insurance@state.nd.us
www.state.nd.us/ndins

State Health Insurance Assistance
701-328-4880 (fax)

Ohio

Department of Aging
50 West Broad St., 9th Floor
Columbus, OH 43215-5928

614-466-5500
614-466-5741 (fax)
www.goldenbuckeye.com

Office of Consumer Services
Department of Insurance
2100 Stella Court
Columbus, OH 43215-1067
800-686-1526 (toll free consumer hotline)
800-686-1527 (toll free fraud hotline)
800-686-1578 (toll free senior hotline)
614-644-3378
614-644-3745 (TDD/TTY)
614-387-1302 (fax)
nancy.colley@ins.state.oh.us
www.ohioinsurance.gov

State Health Insurance Assistance
800-686-1578 (toll free)
614-644-3399
614-752-0740 (fax)

Oklahoma

Aging Services Division
Department of Human Services
PO Box 25352
312 NE 28th Street
Oklahoma City, OK 73125
405-521-2281 or 405-521-2327
405-521-2086 (fax)
www.okdhs.orglaging

Insurance Department
2401 NW 23rd St., Suite 28
PO Box 53408
Oklahoma City, OK 73152-3408
800-522-0071 (toll free OK)
405-521-2828
405-521-6635 (fax)
okinsdpt@telepath.com
www.oid.state.ok.us

State Health Insurance Assistance
800-763-2828 (toll free OK)

Oregon
Insurance Division
350 Winter St. NE, Room 440-2
PO Box 14480
Salem, OR 97310-3883
888-877-4894 (toll free OR)
503-947-7984
503-378-4351 (fax)
dcbs.insmail@state.or.us
www.insurance.oregon.gov

Senior and Disabled Services Division
500 Summer Street NE, 2nd Floor
Salem, OR 97310-1015
503-945-5811
503-373-7823 (fax)
dhs.info@state.or.us
www.dhs.state.or.us/seniors

State Health Insurance Assistance
800-722-4134 (toll free)
503-947-7984

Pennsylvania
Bureau of Consumer Service
Insurance Department
1321 Strawberry Square, 13th Floor
Harrisburg, PA 17120
877-881-6388 (toll free)
717-787-2317
717-787-8585 (fax)
www.insurance.state.pa.us

Pennsylvania Department of Aging
Commonwealth of Pennsylvania
555 Walnut St., 5th floor
Harrisburg, PA 17101-1919
717-783-1550
717-772-3382 (fax)
aging@state.pa.us
www.aging.state.pa.us

State Health Insurance Assistance
800-783-7067 (toll free)
717-783-8975
717-772-2730 (fax)

Puerto Rico
Governor's Office of Elderly Affairs
Commonwealth of Puerto Rico
Call Box 50063
Old San Juan Station, PR 00902
787-721-5710 or 787-721-4560 or
787-721-6121
787-721-6510 (fax)

*Office of the Commissioner
of Insurance*
Call Box 8330
Fernandez Juncos Station
Santurce, PR 00910-8330
787-722-8686 or 787-721-5848
787-722-4402 (fax)
www.ocs.gobierno.pr

Rhode Island
Department of Elderly Affairs
160 Pine St.
Providence, RI 02903-3708
401-277-2858
401-277-2130 (fax)
www.dea.state.ri.us

Insurance Division
Department of Business Regulation
233 Richmond St., Suite 233
Providence, RI 02903-4233
401-222-2223
401-222-2999 (TDD/TTY)
401-222-5475 (fax)
www.dbr.state.ri.us

State Health Insurance Assistance
401-462-0508
401-462-0586 (fax)

South Carolina
Consumer Services
Department of Insurance
300 Arbor Lake Dr., Suite 1200
PO Box 100105
Columbia, SC 29202
800-768-3467 (toll free SC)
803-737-6180
803-737-6231 (fax)
cnsmMail@doi.state.sc.us
www.doi.stae.sc.us

*Office of Senior and
Long Term Care Services*
Department of Health and Human
Services
PO Box 8206
Columbia, SC 29202-8206
803-898-2501
803-898-4515 (fax)
www.dhs.state.sc.us

State Health Insurance Assistance
800-868-9095 (toll free)
803-255-8202 (fax)

South Dakota
Division of Insurance
Department of Revenue and
Regulation
445 E. Capital
Pierre, SD 57501
605-773-3563
605-773-5369 (fax)
www.state.sd.us/drr

Office of Adult Services and Aging
Richard F. Kneip Building
700 Governors Drive
Pierre, SD 57501-2291
605-773-3656
605-773-6834 (fax)
ASA@state.sd.us
www.state.sd.us/social/ASA/index.htm

State Health Insurance Assistance
605-773-3656
605-773-6834 (fax)

Tennessee
Commission on Aging
Andrew Jackson Bldg., 9th floor
500 Deaderick Street
Nashville, Tennessee 37243-0860
615-741-2056
615-741-3309 (fax)
www.state.tn.us/comaging

*Department of Commerce
and Insurance*
500 James Robertson Pkwy., 5th
Floor
Nashville, TN 37243-0565
800-342-4029 (toll free TN)
615-741-2241
615-532-6934 (fax)
www.state.tn.us/commerce

State Health Insurance Assistance
800-525-2816 (toll free)
615-741-4955

Texas
Department of Insurance
333 Guadalupe St.
PO Box 149104
Austin, TX 78614-9104
800-252-3439 (toll free TX consumer help line)
512-463-6169
512-475-2005 (fax)
rbordelon@opic.state.tx.us
www.tdi.state.tx.us

Department of Aging
and Disability Services
701 W. 51st St.
Austin, TX 78751
512-438-3011
512-424-6890 (fax)
mail@dads.state.tx.us
www.dads.state.tx.us

State Health Insurance Assistance
800-252-9240 (toll free)
512-305-7463 (fax)

Utah
Department of Insurance
State Office Bldg., Room 3110
Salt Lake City, UT 84114-6901
800-439-3805 (toll free UT)
801-538-3805
801-538-3826 (TDD/TTY)
801-538-3829 (fax)
www.insurance.state.ut.us

Division of Aging & Adult Services
Box 45500
120 N. 200 West
Salt Lake City, UT 84145-0500
801-538-3910
801-538-4395 (fax)
www.hsdaas.utah.gov

State Health Insurance Assistance
800-541-7735 (toll free UT)
801-538-3910 (toll free general)
801-538-4395 (fax)

Vermont
Department of Aging and Disabilities
Waterbury Complex
103 S. Main St.
Waterbury, VT 05671-2301
802-241-2400
802-241-2325 (fax)
www.dad.state.vt.us

Department of Banking,
Insurance, Securities, and
Health Care Administration
89 Main St., Drawer 20
Montpelier, VT 05620-3101
802-828-3302
800-964-1784 (toll free VT)
800-631-7788 (toll free VT: health
insurance)
802-828-3306 (fax)
www.bishca.state.vt.us

State Health Insurance Assistance
800-250-8427 (toll free VT)
802-241-2325 (fax)

Virgin Islands
Division of Banking and Insurance
Kongen's Gade #18
St. Thomas, VI 00802
340-774-7166
340-774-9458 (fax)
vidoi001@aol.com

Senior Citizen Affairs
Virgin Islands Department
of Human Services
Knud Hansen Complex, Bldg. A
1303 Hospital Ground
Charlotte Amalie, VI 00802

340-774-0930
340-774-3466 (fax)

Virginia
Bureau of Insurance
State Corporation Commission
PO Box 1157
Richmond, VA 23218
800-552-7945 (toll free VA)
804-371-9206 (TDD/TTY)
www.state.va.us/scc

Department for the Aging
1600 Forest Avenue, Suite 102
Richmond, VA 23229
804-662-9333
804-662-9354 (fax)
aging@vda.virginia.gov
www.aging.state.va.us

State Health Insurance Assistance
800-552-3402 (toll free)
804-662-9354 (fax)

Washington
*Aging and Adult Services
Administration*
Department of Social
& Health Services
PO Box 45050
Olympia, WA 98504-5050
360-493-2500
360-438-8633 (fax)
www.aasa.dshs.wa.gov

*Office of the Commissioner of
Insurance*
Insurance 5000 Building
PO Box 40255
Olympia, WA 98504-0255
800-562-6900 (toll free WA)
360-725-7103
360-586-0241 (TDD/TTY)
360-586-3109 (fax)

mikek@olc.wa.gov
www.insurance.wa.gov

State Health Insurance Assistance
800-397-4422 (toll free)

West Virginia
Bureau of Senior Services
Holly Grove, Bldg. 10
1900 Kanawha Blvd. East
Charleston, WV 25305
304-558-3317
304-558-0004 (fax)
info@boss.state.wv.us
www.state.wv.us/seniorservices

*Offices of the Insurance
Commissioner*
P.O. Box 50540
Charleston, WV 25305-0540
888-879-9842 (toll free WV)
304-558-3386
304-558-4965 (fax)
wvins@wvinsurance.gov
www.wvinsurance.gov

*West Virginia Bureau of Senior
Services*
304-558-3317
304-558-5609 (fax)
www.state.wv.us/seniorservices

Wisconsin
*Bureau of Aging and
Long-Term Care Resources*
Department of Health and Family
Services
PO Box 7851
Madison, WI 53707
608-266-2536
608-267-3203 (fax)
www.dhfs.state.wi.us/Aging

Office of the Commissioner
of Insurance
125 S. Webster St.
Madison, WI 53702
800-236-8517 (toll free WI)
608-266-3586
608-266-9935 (fax)
information@oci.state.wi.us
www.oci.wi.gov

State Health Insurance Assistance
800-242-1060 (toll free)
608-266-3585

Wyoming

Department of Insurance
Herschler Bldg.
122 West 25th St., 3rd Floor East
Cheyenne, WY 82002-0440
800-438-5768 (toll free WY)
307-777-7401
307-777-5895 (fax)
wyinsdep@state.wy.us
www.insurance.state.wy.us

Office on Aging
Department of Health
117 Hathaway Bldg., Room 139
Cheyenne, WY 82002-0710
307-777-7986
307-777-5340 (fax)
wyaging@state.wy.us
www.wdhfs.state.wy.us/aging/index.htm

State Health Insurance Assistance
800-856-4398 (toll free)
307-856-6880
307-856-4466 (fax)

Acknowledgments

Ramsey Wiggins provided research and editing expertise and a comprehensive knowledge of the publishing process. His assistance was invaluable. Barbara Langham pushed me to turn an idea into an outline, and her expert editing gave shape to the manuscript.

I am indebted to all those I interviewed: Chris Spence, Chris McCormick, Neil Chur, Sr., Jim Santarsiero, Todd Hyde, Lynn Watkins, Tim Stuteville, Vanessa Grall, Lois Brown-Mosley, David and Cindy Bragg, H. Clyde Farrell, Marilyn Miller, Lee Holmes, Clifton Kruse, Jr., Lynn and Harry Shank, Larry Thomas, Max Jones, Rev. Ann Rosewall, Richard and Elizabeth Hess, Michael Turner, Jamison Gosselin, Byron Cordes, Patricia Bordie, Barbara Anne Stephens, Maryanne Longenecker, Norma Almanza, Thom Singer, Doug Hall, and Ed and Barbara Dickinson.

Liz Schechter provided encouragement and incisive comments; Dacia Osborne is a virtual assistant par excellence; Lee Moczygemba serves as agent, speech coach, and proofreader. Greg Godek provided publishing perspective and marketable ideas. Margaret Thomas's photographs make me look almost as good on film as I do in my mind. Roxie Mast gave me an invitation to speak and a deadline for the first edition. Lucy Cordell, Betsy Tyson, and Margaret Fletcher employed their superior editing skills.

Many thanks to the proofreaders who provided feedback, caught errors, and made the book better for their efforts: Lorri Allen, Peg Armstrong, Anne Black, Nancy Brenner, Liz Carpenter, Joan Fodor, Doris Hamrick, Richard Hess, Wade Huie, Ed McCann, Emily McIntosh, Kathi Miller, Craig Rhea, Gretchen Ricker, Tom and Beth Robb, Annie Robinson, Bob and Linda Smith, Janie Stone, Eloise Sutherland, and Linda Swindling.

I am grateful to our family friends: Peg and Harry Furr, Mary and Grant Hammond, Gean and Edith Smith, Tom and Betsy Gowan, Jane and Jerry Clements, Lisa Huff, Jerry and Lucy Ray, John and Margaret Cantrell, and Tina Young.

The residents and staff of the Wesleyan have a special place in my heart. They have cared for my parents lovingly and lift my spirits every time I visit.

I would not have gotten through the last ten years without the love and support of my central Texas family: my cousins Randy and Donna Stump and their children, Wren, John Michael and Luke; my cousins Bill and Dr. Bonnie Stump and their children, Dr. Kimberly Stump, David and Jeffrey; and my aunt, Mary Beth Comer.

Index

About the Author

Jim Comer is a speaker, author, speech coach, and communications consultant. He has worked with the CEOs, politicians, sales managers, and top executives of numerous Fortune 500 companies.

Jim's articles have been published in *Reader's Digest* and on the op-ed pages of the *New York Times, Washington Post, Los Angeles Times,* and *Austin American-Statesman*. His book *How to Survive a Roommate* landed him on the *Today Show* with Jane Pauley. His play *Behind Every Good Woman, There's Another One!* was produced in Los Angeles.

An inspiring and dynamic speaker, Jim has entertained audiences from Los Angeles to Halifax, Nova Scotia. His presentations include: "The Message is You," "How Not to Speak Like a Geek," "If I Can Make It There, You Can Make It Anywhere," and "Parenting Your Parents."

After an absence of thirty years, Jim moved back to Texas and lives in Austin. If you have questions, comments, or stories about your parental care experiences—or would like to book Jim to speak at an event—contact him at jimcomer@earthlink.net.

Hampton Roads Publishing Company

. . . for the evolving human spirit

HAMPTON ROADS PUBLISHING COMPANY publishes books on a variety of subjects, including metaphysics, spirituality, health, visionary fiction, and other related topics.

For a copy of our latest trade catalog, call toll-free, 800-766-8009, or send your name and address to:

HAMPTON ROADS PUBLISHING COMPANY, INC.
1125 STONEY RIDGE ROAD • CHARLOTTESVILLE, VA 22902
e-mail: hrpc@hrpub.com • www.hrpub.com